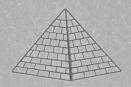

WoEB

What on Earth Books, The Black Barn, Wickhurst Farm, Tonbridge,
Kent TN11 8PS, United Kingdom

First published in the United Kingdom in 2018

Text copyright © 2018 Christopher Lloyd
Illustrations by Andy Forshaw copyright © What on Earth Books
Illustrations on pages 25, 33, 60, 61 and 63 by Will Exley copyright
    © What on Earth Books
Cover illustrations by Justin Poulter copyright © 2018 Justin Poulter
Designed by Assunção Sampayo

Staff for this book: Ali Glossop, Project Editor; Nancy Feresten, Text Editor;
Andy Forshaw, Art Director; Assunção Sampayo, Designer; Felicity Page,
Photo Editor

A CIP catalogue record for this book is available from the British Library

ISBN: 978-1-9998028-2-0

Printed in Ukraine

2 4 6 8 10 9 7 5 3 1

whatonearthbooks.com

ABSOLUTELY EVERYTHING!

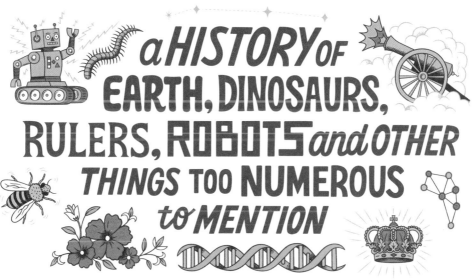

a HISTORY of EARTH, DINOSAURS, RULERS, ROBOTS and OTHER THINGS TOO NUMEROUS to MENTION

CHRISTOPHER LLOYD

What on Earth Books

Contents

Foreword

· 6 ·

1. NOTHING TO SOMETHING

13.8 billion–450 million years ago
The beginning of the universe,
life and everything

· 10 ·

2. LAND AHOY!

470 mya–252 mya
Creatures wriggle out of the seas
and forests cover the land

· 32 ·

3. DINOSAURS

252 mya–5 mya
Terrible lizards and what
comes after

· 50 ·

4. HANDS FREE

5 mya–65,000 years ago
Some apes walk
on two feet

· 72 ·

5. YOU AND ME

200,000 years ago–5000 BCE
How a single species of humans,
Homo sapiens, became the last on Earth

· 88 ·

6. CIVILISATION BEGINS

5000–1500 BCE
Writing kicks off
a new era

· 104 ·

7. MEANWHILE, IN ASIA

3000–200 BCE
More powerful
civilisations thrive

· 130 ·

8. RISE AND FALL

1400 BCE–476 CE
Classical empires
come and go

· 152 ·

9. MEANWHILE, IN THE AMERICAS

1500 BCE–1530 CE
More empires
rise and fall

· 176 ·

10. INVENTION CONNECTION

570–1279 CE
Powerful ideas emerge in the
Muslim world and East Asia

· 198 ·

11. MEDIEVAL MISERY

476–1526 CE
Christian Europe struggles following
the collapse of the Roman Empire

· 224 ·

12. GOING GLOBAL

1415–1621
European explorers race
to conquer a 'New World'

· 248 ·

13. REVOLUTIONS ALL AROUND

1543–1905
Science, freedom
and robots

· 270 ·

14. WORLD AT WAR

1845–1945
When everyone started
fighting everyone else

· 294 ·

15. TO BE CONTINUED...

1945–Present
The shaping of the world we
know and what might come next

· 314 ·

Afterword

· 338 ·

References

· 340 ·

Glossary

· 344 ·

Index

· 348 ·

Foreword

Have you ever been on a camping trip? Camping is one of the best things my family and I have ever done – we had such a lot of fun!

If you have ever camped, you'll know there are quite a few different jobs that need doing when you visit a campsite. As well as a few other chores, it was always my job to wash the dirty dishes.

It was OK. Actually, I started to enjoy washing up. As soon as I checked in at the washing-up station, I could ask people what the place was like, where we should visit or, just as importantly, where we should *not* visit. So whenever I washed up my mind was always bursting with questions.

And then one day, just after we had arrived at a new campsite, I went to wash the dishes and, although there were loads of cars, tents and camper vans, there was absolutely no one else there washing up. It was just me. All on my own.

I was gutted.

"Honestly," I thought. "How on earth am I supposed to do my research when there is no one here to talk to?"

And then I heard a tweeting noise coming from somewhere behind me. It was a beautiful day and, as with all the best campsites, the washing-up station was open-air.

About fifty metres behind me I saw a bird high up in a tree. And then a thought struck me that I will never forget.

"If only I could speak Bird!"

That creature, with its amazing wings, must have such a wonderful view of all that is worth seeing in the area. The only thing stopping me from finding out everything I want to know is a communication barrier. How frustrating to think that, despite us sharing the same air, the same sunshine and time of day, that bird and I could never talk.

Another thought then wriggled its way into my brain. Not only can I not speak "Bird" but I have no idea what kind of bird this is, twittering high up in that untouchable world of leafy green.

Small and brown, sure, but what species? How ignorant of me not to know!

Things got worse.

I looked at the tree. I had no idea what kind of tree it was.

I looked down at the ground.

I realised I didn't even have a clue as to how old the planet Earth is.

I was shocked and ashamed!

There I stood, a history graduate and newspaper writer, yet I didn't seem to know the answers to questions about the everyday things I was looking at! How much more information was missing from my mind? How could I find out what other things I didn't know?

Now my head was spinning. I needed a book, something simple enough to understand but sweeping enough to connect together the dots of the past. My brain felt like it was a pane of shattered glass. I knew lots of bits of information, but if I were to take a step back, there was no big picture to make sense of it all.

After the camping trip I searched many bookshops, trying to find that simple guide to the history of everything.

The bookshop managers I quizzed said they had all the information, but it was spread out among many different books.

"But I want it all in just one book that connects it together…"

"Sorry sir, I can't help you there…"

So that was it. I decided then and there to write this book.

Absolutely Everything: A History of Earth, Dinosaurs, Rulers, Robots and Other Things Too Numerous to Mention will take you on an epic journey from the beginning of the universe, about 13.8 billion years ago, all the way to the modern world we live in today.

I hope it will answer all kinds of questions you have. Some things you will already know and other things you will not. That's how it was for me when I did all the research and writing.

How old is the universe? What happened to the dinosaurs? When did humans first discover how to make fire? Why does climate change affect us all?

Of course, this book doesn't really include *absolutely* everything everyone knows. That would be impossible. Instead the book is meant to be a gateway to all the knowledge in the world. For every question it answers, it sparks more questions, which I hope will lead you into a lifelong love of questioning and finding answers.

So if you're the sort of person who loves to ask questions as much as you like to find answers, this story is the one for you. And *hold on tight* because there is one other fascinating thing I have found out along the way – the real world is far more amazing than anything you can make up!

Christopher Lloyd
June 2018

Oh, and by the way, since I came back from that camping trip I always wash up the dirty dishes at home, because, well, I have learned that you never really know what's going to happen next.

Chapter 1

NOTHING TO SOMETHING

13.8 billion–450 million years ago
The beginning of the universe,
life and everything

Timeline

○ **13.8 billion years ago**
The Big Bang

○ **13.6 billion years ago**
The Milky Way forms.

○ **4.6 billion years ago**
The solar system forms.

○ **4.5 billion years ago**
Earth and Theia collide,
forming the Moon.

4 billion years ago
Early microscopic life appears in the seas.

3.2 billion years ago
Plate tectonics begin shuffling continents around the planet.

2.5 billion years ago
Cyanobacteria are making oxygen, changing the Earth's atmosphere.

540 million years ago
The Cambrian Explosion

Take a good look around. Put everything you can see inside an imaginary but super-powerful crushing machine. Plants, animals, buildings, your entire house, your home town, even the country where you live. See it all get mashed into a tiny ball. Now put the rest of the world in there too. Add the other planets in our solar system, and the Sun.

Now put in our galaxy, the Milky Way, which includes between 100 and 400 billion other suns. Finally, add all the other galaxies in the universe. See all this stuff squeezed together to the size of a tennis ball. See it crushed even smaller than the dot on top of this letter i, until you can't see it at all. All those stars, moons and planets in a speck of nothing. That was it.

The universe began as a dot too small to see. This dot was so hot and under such pressure from all the energy trapped inside it that something big was bound to happen. About 13.8 billion years ago it did. It burst.

You've probably heard of the Big Bang – the theory that tries to explain the beginning of the universe. But hang on a minute – the beginning? That's what's so hard to

An artist's impression of how everything in the universe came from the Big Bang. Although it happened over billions of years, the picture shows it all together.

understand. If the universe had a beginning, what happened before the beginning? No one really knows. As you'll see, there are plenty of mysteries that even modern science hasn't solved yet.

An unimaginably big blast of energy was released when the Big Bang happened. Next came the basic forces of the universe. Gravity is one of those forces. It is one of the most important because it makes all the stuff in the universe pull together. Next came countless too-tiny-to-see building bricks called subatomic particles. Think of them as miniature bits of Lego ready to build a whole wide universe. It's amazing to think that everything in the world is made out of billions of these subatomic particles created by the Big Bang. And that includes the furniture in your home and the hair on your head.

> DURING THIS TIME [THE DARK AGES], THE UNIVERSE QUIETLY WAITED FOR CLOUDS OF HYDROGEN TO OBEY THE INFLUENCE OF GRAVITY AND COLLAPSE INTO THE VERY FIRST STARS AND GALAXIES.

Aaron Parsons, astrophysicist

About 380,000 years after the Big Bang, the universe had cooled down enough so that the subatomic particles stuck together to make larger (but still too-tiny-to-see) structures that we call atoms. First, there was only one kind of atom – hydrogen – gathered into giant clouds of very hot dust. Then, after a long pause known as the Dark Ages, the hydrogen atoms crushed together and lit up as the first stars. That's what stars are. They are fiery balls full of atoms and energy left over from the Big Bang.

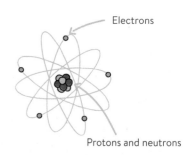

Electrons

Protons and neutrons

An atom is made up of subatomic particles called electrons (which zip around the centre, or nucleus, of the atom) and protons and neutrons (which make up the nucleus).

Stars gathered together into galaxies of many shapes and sizes. Stars were born and stars died. More stars were born. More stars died. Then, about 4.6 billion years ago, about two-thirds of the way through the history of the universe, the leftover gas and dust cloud from an old burned-out star crushed together and lit up to form a new star. We care about this one the most. It's the one closest to our home: the Sun. And our planet, along with several others, was formed at about the same time as the Sun, from a mixture of leftover dust and rock. This was our solar system.

Our solar system is part of the great assembly of stars called the Milky Way. We are in one of the Milky Way galaxy's arms, spinning around the centre of the galaxy at about 800,000 kilometres per hour. You can't feel how fast you're going because our whole solar system is travelling with us at the same speed.

The early solar system was totally unsuited to life. You couldn't have survived there for an instant. An invisible rain of deadly particles poured out of the Sun like a storm of razor-sharp daggers.

As for the planet Earth, a thick, melty crust of boiling hot, sticky lava oozed across its surface. To begin with, there was no solid ground and definitely no life. The early Earth spun so fast on its axis that each day was only about four hours long.

The Sun's solar flares are deadly to all living organisms, but the Earth is protected by its atmosphere and an electro-magnetic shield.

The Earth and
Theia colliding

What happened next was a total freak. Experts
believe that two young planets were on the same orbit
around the Sun but moving at different speeds. One
was the Earth. The other was a smaller planet known
as Theia. You can guess what happened next.
Incredible as it sounds, about 4.5 billion
years ago, so 100 million years after
the Earth was formed, these two
newborn planets smashed into
each other.

Just think of the force of
two planets crashing together.
Theia's outer layers instantly broke
up into billions of tiny particles.
They covered the Earth with a thick
blanket of hot dust and rock. Volcanoes
erupted over all the Earth. Countless
tonnes of gas that had been trapped
inside the Earth's core blew out into the
sky, making our planet's early atmosphere.

Actually, it's just as well for life on Earth that this
great collision happened. Remember those tiny
deadly particles that poured out of our Sun? Well, the storm has
never stopped. Even today about 20 billion tonnes spew out of the
sun in just twenty-four hours. This scary stuff is known as the solar

wind. It can even go through the toughest space suits and hardest helmets worn by astronauts.

But the solar wind doesn't hurt us on Earth. When Theia and the Earth smashed into each other, the huge shockwave fused the two planets' cores into one hot metallic ball. Ever since, this core has produced a magnetic shield that keeps the lethal solar wind away from our planet's surface. The shield also keeps the world from losing its precious supplies of water, which otherwise would have been blown into space. No liquid, no life. It's as simple as that.

Today there is no visible evidence on Earth of this dramatic collision. There is no crater because the force of the impact made all the outer material vaporise into space as dust. That dust wrapped itself around the Earth in a great cloud, which eventually stuck together again thanks to gravity.

> " THEIA WAS THOROUGHLY MIXED INTO BOTH THE EARTH AND THE MOON, AND EVENLY DISPERSED BETWEEN THEM… "
>
> Edward Young, cosmochemist

Can you guess what this enormous cloud of dust turned into? Of course! It became our beautiful luminous companion – the Moon. The Moon has no metallic core, which means it's not protected from the solar wind. So there's no liquid there. It also has no atmosphere, which means no sound can be heard on the Moon and the sky is always black and speckled with stars.

Scientists are still unsure about lots of things to do with the early history of our planet Earth. That's because the Earth has changed so much over time that there's nothing much left of that early time for us to study. But they can look at how the world works today and come up with some good guesses.

Of all the planets in our solar system, Earth is the only one with such a large amount of liquid water. Why does our world contain so much water? Where did it all come from? Without water, life as we know it could not have developed, so these questions are important.

Some experts think water came from deep inside the early Earth. Others have a much more other-worldly idea. They think that more than half of the world's water may have arrived on a giant storm of icy comets or asteroids about 4 billion years ago.

Just imagine thousands of giant objects, some more than 160 kilometres wide, smashing into the early Earth. As they scorched through the atmosphere, the ice on them melted, producing vast amounts of water. All that water still exists today. It's mostly in our giant global oceans. That's something to think about next time you take a bath. More than half the water in your tub possibly came from outer space.

How and where did life begin? This is another question that scientists don't quite agree on. Some experts think the stuff needed by the first living things may have arrived on those comets or asteroids from outer space. Most of them think that life started somewhere deep down at the bottom of the seas. Even today underwater volcanoes provide chemical food and warmth for teeny-tiny living things. Back at the beginning of life on Earth, each of these life forms was just one cell. That's one tiny bundle of material that could eat, grow, and – most importantly – split to

These structures in Shark Bay, Australia, are stromatolites. They are made up of cyanobacteria, the earliest form of life to give off oxygen.

become two teeny-tiny living things. That's one thing that makes life special. The ability to reproduce.

As time passed, some single-celled life forms called cyanobacteria found a way to survive nearer the ocean's surface. They grouped together in shallow waters to make bumpy formations called stromatolites. They also used photosynthesis. This is the same process plants use today, to turn sunshine, nutrients and water into the energy they need to survive. And like all living things, the cyanobacteria gave off waste. But this waste was special. Cyanobacteria filled the air and the seas with oxygen, completely changing the story of life on Earth.

The technical term for living things developing and changing and adapting to new environments is evolution, and we're about to see a lot of it.

Cyanobacteria enlarged

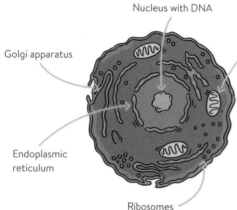

Nucleus with DNA

Mitochondria

Golgi apparatus

Endoplasmic reticulum

Ribosomes

Eukaryotic cells have a nucleus containing genetic information called DNA. They also contain organelles responsible for different functions such as producing energy (mitochondria), producing proteins (ribosomes and endoplasmic reticulum) and transporting protein (Golgi apparatus).

All this world-changing took a long time. Let's leap forward to about 2.5 billion years ago. A new type of life form called eukaryotes is now emerging. Eukaryotes use a process called respiration. Respiration takes in oxygen to use as an ingredient to make energy. This marks another big change in the story of life on Earth. All plants, fungi and animals are eukaryotes. As you might have guessed, we humans are too.

Imagine the Earth's history on a twenty-four-hour clock. The Earth formed right at midnight. The first signs of life emerged at about 3:00 in the morning. But already we have travelled to just gone 1:00 in the afternoon. Amazingly, all the life on Earth that existed until this point were these life forms in the seas that were too small to see. That leaves only eleven hours (less than half the day) for all the rest of life as we know it to emerge.

Remember how the Earth travels with the solar system around the Milky Way unbelievably fast, far faster than any racing car? Well, we are moving in other ways, too. The Earth is travelling around the Sun, and it is spinning on its axis. And there's yet another kind of movement. You are sitting on a crust of rock that is *very slowly* drifting, like a giant raft, on an underground sea of

North America Plate

Cocos Plate

Pacific Plate

Nazca Plate

boiling-hot magma, the same stuff that is called lava when it comes out on to the Earth's surface. With all this travelling and spinning and floating, nobody ever really sits still!

The Earth's surface is divided into moving pieces. The pieces are constantly drifting apart or bashing into one another, like slow-motion bumper cars at a funfair. It's a process called plate tectonics, and the pieces are called tectonic plates. When continents riding on these plates collide, they form mountain ranges soaring high up into the sky. When they drift apart, they form huge oceans or deep

As you read this, you are sitting on a crust that is floating like a giant raft on an underground sea of boiling-hot magma. Here is how the Earth's tectonic plates are arranged today.

Eurasian Plate

Caribbean Plate

Pacific Plate

Arabian Plate

Philippine Sea Plate

Indian Plate

African Plate

South America Plate

Australian Plate

Scotia Plate

Antarctic Plate

valleys. This gradual movement of the Earth's plates is so powerful that it creates earthquakes and volcanoes, geysers and tsunamis.

There is an important positive side to this violent process, too. The amount of salt in the seas has to be just right for life to survive. If the sea gets too salty, living things die. Thanks to the constant movement of the Earth's plates, salt gets buried deep beneath mountain ranges. This process removes salt from the ocean, leaving the saltiness low enough so it's safe for life.

These moving plates also change the climate. Some scientists think that about 700 million years ago, moving plates plunged the Earth into a super-cold ice age. This period is known as Snowball Earth. Ice gripped the globe almost all the way from pole to pole. When the weather eventually warmed up again and the ice retreated, the story of life took a new turn. There were still plenty of microscopic life forms. But now larger creatures made of many cells began to join them in the seas.

This leads us into one of the most amazing moments in our story. It is 540 million years ago. A quick check on our twenty-four-hour clock shows it's now just after 9:00pm. There are still no plants, no flowers, no birds or animals or humans. But finally, finally the first of the kind of life forms that will one day bring us into the familiar world around us are starting to appear.

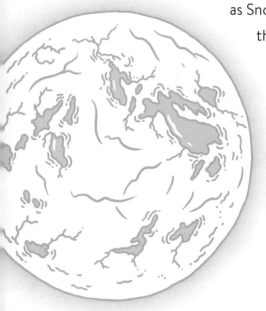

The average global temperature during the Snowball Earth period was about -27°C.

This fossil of a spiky animal called *Wiwaxia* is one of thousands found in a place in Canada known as the Burgess Shale.

Fossils are the preserved remains of long-lost creatures or the impressions they leave behind. When creatures die, usually their bodies rot or dissolve. Sometimes, though, minerals in the ground near a bone replace the living cells in that bone, turning it into a fossil. The same thing can happen to shells or teeth. Fossils are wonderful for helping scientists understand what kinds of creatures once lived on the Earth. Expert fossil hunters are called palaeontologists.

Charles Doolittle Walcott was a palaeontologist. He was born in the United States of America in 1850. As a young boy he found school quite boring. It wasn't that he had no interest in things, rather the opposite. He was so curious that he wanted to get outside and explore the world for himself – in particular, he liked to look for minerals, rocks, birds' eggs and fossils.

Anomalocaris

One day in 1909 a freak accident changed the rest of Walcott's life. According to some people, he was walking high up in a remote part of the Canadian Rockies, and his horse slipped and lost a shoe. As the creature stumbled, its foot turned over a glistening rock. Walcott picked it up and saw a row of remarkable silvery fossils. These showed the perfectly preserved shapes of creatures dating back to a time known as the Cambrian Period.

Remember how the land is always moving and changing? Well, it turned out that the mountainside Walcott was standing on had been on the sea floor 505 million years before. Way back then, something – maybe a mudslide – had killed these creatures and preserved them like a time capsule. Walcott's fossils are some of the oldest ever found. The place where he found them is known as the Burgess Shale, named after nearby Mount Burgess. Walcott returned to the site many times and eventually wrote a shelf of books about his finds.

And what a bizarre range of creatures they were! There was the strange-looking *Anomalocaris*. Possibly the biggest hunter of its day, it could grow up to a metre long. It used a pair of grasping arms to capture and hold its prey.

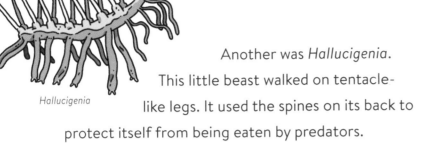
Hallucigenia

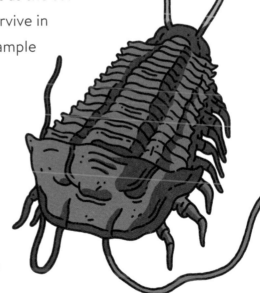
Opabinia

Another was *Hallucigenia*. This little beast walked on tentacle-like legs. It used the spines on its back to protect itself from being eaten by predators.

But nothing can prepare you for *Opabinia*. This oceanic oddbod had five eyes, a fan-like tail for swimming and a long nose with a mouth on the end. There's nothing remotely like it alive today.

One of the Cambrian Period's most common forms of animal life was a group of sea creatures called trilobites. Their fossils range from the size of your thumb to three-quarters of a metre long and have been found all over the world. One very important thing about them is that they were possibly the first creatures ever to have fully developed eyes.

Some experts think that trilobite eyes triggered a new race for survival in the ancient seas. They could choose what they wanted for dinner by looking around. Of course, creatures that were easy to see were the ones most likely to be dinner. Hiding underground or being the same colours as the sea floor would have been good ways to survive in this brave new world. This is a great example of how nature works, how new better adapted creatures replace old ones over time.

The Burgess Shale creatures give us a glimpse into the very beginning of a time called the Palaeozoic Era.

Trilobite

Timeline of Earth's history

Era	Period		Species	Evolutionary stage	Twenty-four-hour clock
4,600 HADEAN				No life on Earth; volcanoes; rain cools the surface; oceans form	00:00
4,000 ARCHAEAN				Methanogens (prokaryotes); cyanobacteria; stromatolites; oxygen in air	03:08
2,500 PROTEROZOIC				Eukaryotes	13:04
850	Cryogenian			Snowball Earth	
635	Ediacaran			Multi-cellular creatures	
541 PALAEOZOIC	Cambrian			Shells, bones and teeth	21:11
485	Ordovician			Vertebrates	
444	Silurian			Primitive land plants; worms	
419	Devonian			Bony fish; tetrapods	
359	Carboniferous			Amphibians; reptiles; forests	
299	Permian			Mammal-like reptiles; Pangaea	
252 MESOZOIC	Triassic			First dinosaurs; small mammals; ichthyosaurs	22:41
201	Jurassic			Dinosaurs dominate land; pterodactyls in the air	
145	Cretaceous			Last dinosaurs; social insects; flowers; birds	

Era	Period	Epoch	Species	Evolutionary stage	Twenty-four-hour clock
66 CENOZOIC	Tertiary	Palaeocene		Mammals grow larger	23:40
56		Eocene		Whales return to the oceans	
34		Oligocene		Horses evolve in the Americas	
23		Miocene		Monkey migrations	
5.3		Pliocene		First bipeds and humans	
2.6 HISTORIC	Quaternary	Pleistocene		Megafauna extinctions	23:59
0.01		Holocene		Farming; first human civilisations	
today		Anthropocene		Globalisation; rise in CO_2 levels	24:00

Era start date in millions of years ago

Over time, many living things developed and later died out. Looking at fossils and the rocks they're embedded in helps scientists figure out when each one lived. Here's a chart showing time from the formation of the Earth to the present day.

There have been lots of fossils found from this time, which saw an incredible explosion of life in the seas.

Let's go on an imaginary dive to check out some creatures which lived in the first part of the Palaeozoic Era, during periods called Cambrian, Ordovician, Silurian and Devonian. Before we start, another quick time check on our twenty-four-hour clock of Earth history shows that this time lasts from 9:11 to 10:08pm.

Sponges were among the simplest of all animals living in the ancient Cambrian seas. They are still alive today. About 5,000 different species of sponge have been discovered so far. For a long time people thought sponges were plants, but actually sponges are animals. In fact, you and I are much more closely related to a sponge than to, say, a daffodil.

Coral reefs are built over hundreds of thousands of years by tiny sea creatures. The corals grow on top of the skeletons of their dead ancestors. With their bodies, they create a rich habitat for other creatures. Today up to 9,000 different species camp out

Coral reef

Jellyfish like this one, a sea nettle (*Chrysaora fuscescens*), have been in the ocean for more than 500 million years. If a jellyfish is cut into two, it can regenerate and turn into two new jellyfish.

in the Earth's biggest coral reef – the Great Barrier Reef off the coast of Australia. It's made up of almost 3,000 indivdual reefs and stretches for more than 2,300 kilometres. The ancestors of today's corals first appeared in the Cambrian Period.

Jellyfish are related to corals but are nowhere near as friendly. They swim using a pumping action of their bell-like heads. Jellyfish have a very simple nervous system and only one opening – a combined mouth and bottom. Some can pack a nasty punch. They sting using an array of poison-tipped harpoons hidden in cells along their tentacles. Jellyfish were very common in the Cambrian seas.

The ancestors of ammonites appeared during the Devonian Period. Ammonites went extinct 65 million years ago, at the same time as most dinosaurs. They looked like giant snails, but their closest living cousins are octopus and squid. Ammonites had spiral shells to protect them against attack. We know those shells came in handy. Their fossils have been found all over the world with teeth marks and scars.

Ammonite

Sea squirts

At first glance, sea squirts seem similar to sponges. But sea squirts have babies that swim about like tadpoles. They push themselves through the water with a special tail containing an early kind of backbone called a notochord. These creatures are still around today, but they first appeared in the Cambrian Period. Sea squirts are thought to be distant ancestors of vertebrates – animals with backbones. Vertebrates include fish, amphibians, reptiles, birds and mammals. Since humans are mammals, baby sea squirts are super important. Some experts think they should go down in prehistory as our great-great-great ... grandparents!

Among the most fearsome creatures of the Silurian and Devonian seas was the now-extinct placoderm. It was a giant fish that had jaws and teeth. Heavy armour plating covered its head and throat. Its body had thick scales, and some placoderms had

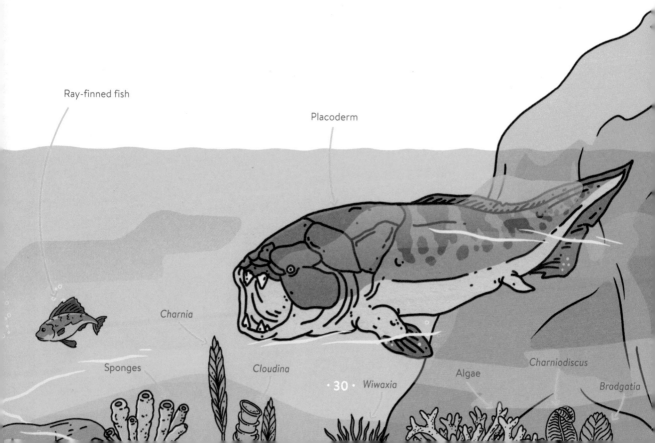

Ray-finned fish

Placoderm

Charnia

Sponges

Cloudina

Charniodiscus

Algae

Bradgatia

Wiwaxia

fins covered in armour-plated tubes. These were nature's first war machines, built like tanks. A placoderm could grow up to ten metres long and weigh over four tonnes. If it were alive today, it could easily snap a shark in two with a single bite.

You wouldn't want to bump into a sea scorpion, either. It had a long, spiked tail that may have been equipped with a deadly venomous sting. This creature could grow to more than two metres long. Sea scorpions appeared during the Ordovician Period and died out along with many other species in what's called the Permian Mass Extinction, 252 million years ago.

The Earth was formed 4.6 billion years ago. Life first appeared about 4 billion years ago. Now, it is 470 million years ago. The ocean is a busy place, home to our swimming and swaying, hunting and hiding ancestors. The land, not so much. Mostly it is raining.

Sea scorpion

Orthoceras

Vauxia

Chapter 2

LAND AHOY!

470 million–252 million years ago
Creatures wriggle out of the seas
and forests cover the land

○ **470 million years ago**
Primitive plants live on
land by the water's edge.

○ **420 million years ago**
Millipede-like creatures
wriggle out of the seas.

○ **400 million years ago**
Fungi help plants live
further away from
water.

○ **375 million years ago**
Vertebrates adapt
to life on land.

○ **360 million years ago**
Plants develop seeds.

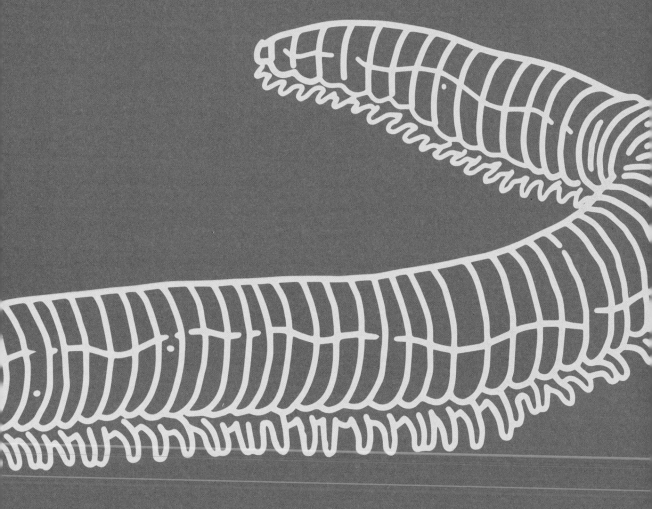

○ **360 million years ago**
The Earth's land
is covered with trees.

○ **350 million years ago**
Oxygen levels rise
as some insects take
to the skies.

○ **312 million years ago**
Reptiles develop eggs
with waterproof shells.

○ **280 million years ago**
Some animals are able
to control their body
temperature.

○ **252 million years ago**
Life suffers its worst-
ever brush with death.

It was raining. It had rained the day before, and the day before that, too. For millions of years, life swarmed in the seas and rain hammered the land. There was nothing to see except lifeless rock and mud.

Then, about 470 million years ago, a little bit of green appeared. The first land plants were growing near the water's edge. These were squidgy liverworts and mosses. They had evolved from green algae, a water plant still around today. Like all plants, these used photosynthesis to make the energy they needed.

Next came a new type of plant that could grow much taller. They had a system of tubes to carry food and water from the ground to the tops of their bodies, sort of like the way we transport blood around our body in our blood vessels. We call these plants vascular plants.

The first vascular plants were just a few centimetres high, with thick stems. We know about them from an accidental discovery made in 1912 by William Mackie, a Scottish doctor, when he was out and about near the village of Rhynie. Quite by chance he spotted some curious-looking fossils in an old stone wall. You see, it turns out that about 400 million years ago Rhynie was a steaming cauldron. There were boiling-hot pools of bubbling mud. Every so often a giant geyser would spout out a huge fountain of scorching water on to nearby plants. When the water landed on the plants, minerals in it cooled and turned them into stone. When this happens it is called petrification. That's where the word petrified comes from.

An artist's impression of early vascular plants (*Rhynia*) and giant fungi (*Prototaxites*) growing around 420 to 395 million years ago. The *Rhynia* plants were up to 20cm tall, and the *Prototaxites*' trunks rose as high as 8m.

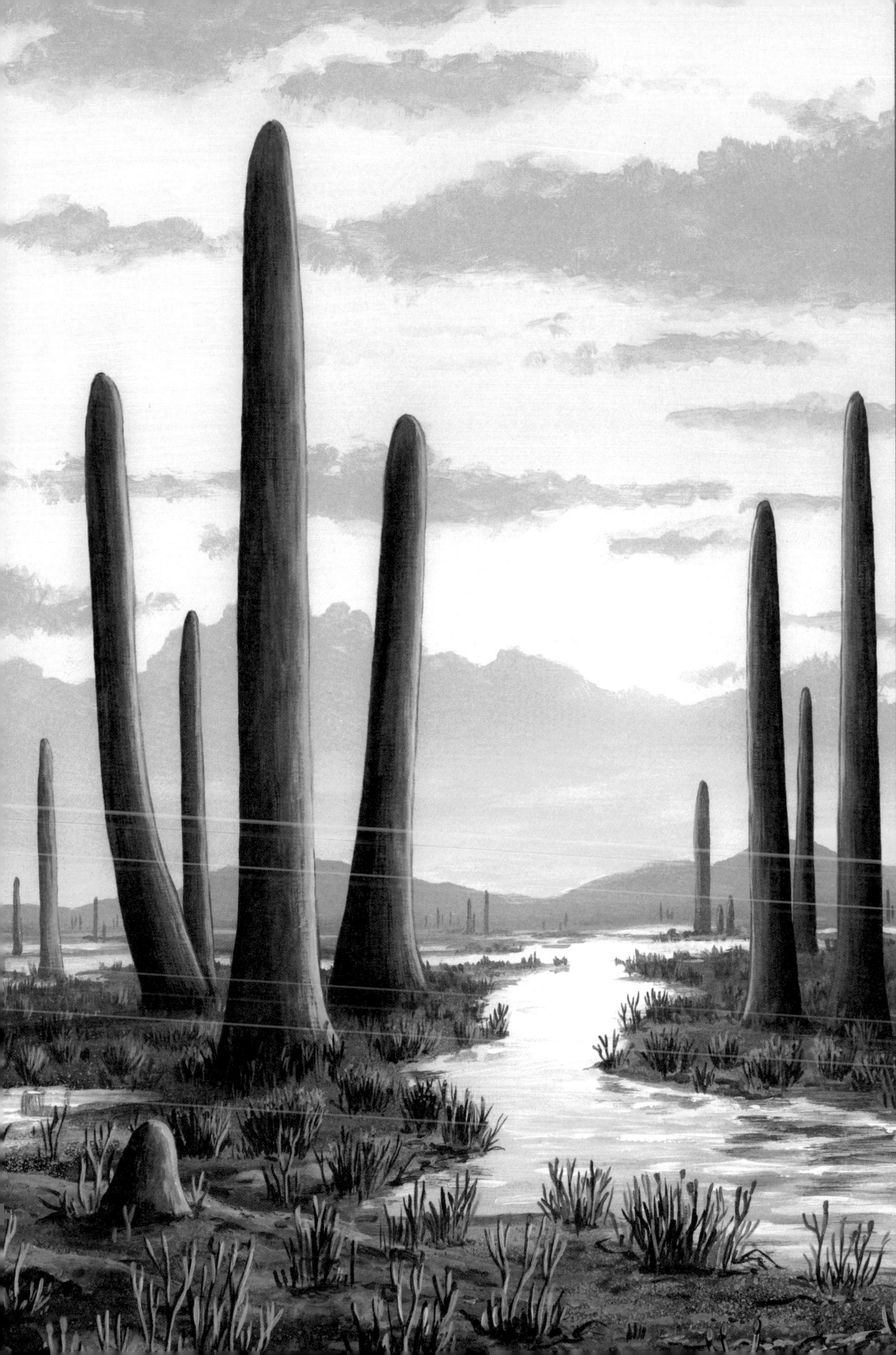

2. Land Ahoy!

470 million–252 million years ago

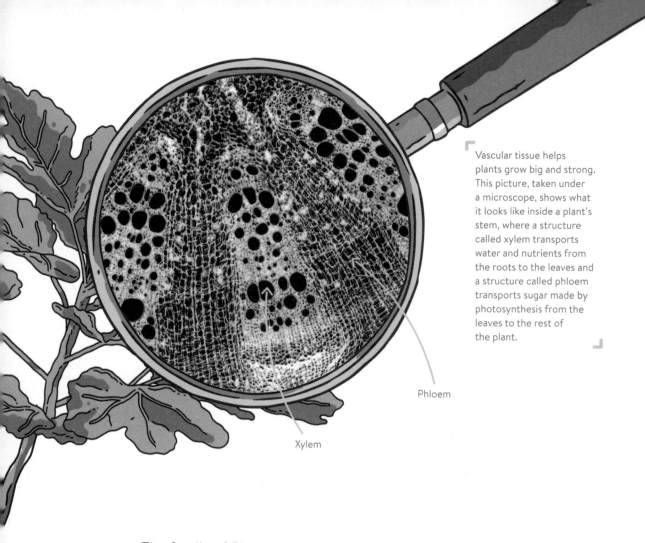

Vascular tissue helps plants grow big and strong. This picture, taken under a microscope, shows what it looks like inside a plant's stem, where a structure called xylem transports water and nutrients from the roots to the leaves and a structure called phloem transports sugar made by photosynthesis from the leaves to the rest of the plant.

Phloem

Xylem

The fossils of Rhynie are so well preserved that scientists can see exactly what these ancient plants were made of and how they worked. It is clear that they contained a substance called lignin. Lignin toughens the walls of plant cells. It makes the walls waterproof so the tubes inside the plant can carry water up to the top of a high tree. It's like having plastic tubing instead of tubing made from tissue paper.

Lignin makes trees woody and keeps them standing upright. But it took at least 40 million years for these small vascular plants to evolve into proper trees. They never could have made it to these heights were it not for another group of living things, called fungi.

Do you like mushrooms? I have to say they don't score very high on my list of tasty snacks. But researching and writing this book has turned me into a big mushroom fan. That's because without fungi (the giant group, or kingdom, of living things to which mushrooms belong) the world would be a disgusting and very smelly place.

We don't know much about the origin of fungi. We don't even know if they started life in the sea or on land. That's because their soft bodies don't leave many fossils behind. But we are pretty sure that fungi were already living on land when plants got there. Since then, fungi have developed into a huge variety of life forms, from some of the smallest to the largest living things on Earth.

Small fungi are just one cell. The yeast that makes bread rise is one of those. Large fungi are some of the biggest living things on Earth. One fungus in Oregon, United States, is estimated to stretch out underground across nearly ten square kilometres – equivalent to more than 1,300 football pitches!

Fungi feed on other organisms just as animals do. Most fungi are made up of an underground network of root-like threads called a mycelium. The mushroom is just the part of the fungus that pops up above ground. The mushroom's job is to spread spores. These tiny reproductive cells

Fungi can be found just about anywhere. They can grow in the soil, in food, on trees, on plants and animals, in fresh water, in seawater, and even in between your toes!

get blown by the wind then settle themselves and grow new fungi identical to their single parent.

Fungi are vital for all life on Earth because they eat dead things. Without them the world would be drowning under piles of the dead bodies of plants and animals – not a happy thought. They also make chemicals that help plants grow.

Sometimes nature has a real fondness for teamwork. Big networks of underground fungi pass nutrients and water to the roots of trees. In return, trees supply fungi with food. Thanks to ancient fungi, primitive plant life was able to move further inland, enriching the soil as it went.

Soil is made up of sand, minerals and the decayed remains of once-living things. Plants, tiny animals including worms, and fungi all help keep this precious life force working. They turn fallen leaves and rotting trees into nutrients to help new plants grow. They have been digging up the soil for the last 400 million years. And all that digging mixes the soil, renewing and regenerating it. This is called the soil cycle.

In fact, without living things, there would be no soil. The Earth would be nothing more than dust and rock, like the surface of the Moon, Mars or Venus.

> **THE WORLD DEPENDS ON FUNGI, BECAUSE THEY ARE MAJOR PLAYERS IN THE CYCLING OF MATERIALS AND ENERGY AROUND THE WORLD.**
>
> Edward O. Wilson, biologist

Fungi and plants were not the only organisms to move on to land. A few small crawly creatures emerged about 440–420 million years ago.

The first ever land animal was probably an arthropod. This group includes millipedes, insects, spiders, crabs, lobsters and a whole lot of other creatures with jointed legs and hard outer parts called an exoskeleton.

It took about 50 million years before another kind of animal made the move on to land. If you were a fish living in the seas back then, life could be over fairly quickly. Stinging jellyfish, sea scorpions with deadly tail spikes and giant placoderms were just a few of the dangers swimming around. If you were able to get out of the water, you might have had a better chance of surviving. After all, the shores were now full of plants and juicy worms to eat.

Fish aren't built to live on land, though. One problem is breathing oxygen from air instead of water. Another is working out how to move around. Imagine walking on fins instead of legs – it wouldn't be a simple walk in the park.

In a process called mycorrhiza, fungi supply water and minerals to a plant, and the plant provides the fungi with sugar it makes using photosynthesis.

Tiktaalik found a way around this. It used its fins to wade through shallow bogs and to heave its body out of water on to the land. Which means *Tiktaalik* is the first creature ever known to have been able to do a press-up!

Tiktaalik had wrist bones for lifting its body off the sea floor, lungs for breathing air, and a strong ribcage and neck.

Tiktaalik lived about 375 million years ago, when primitive plants were growing near the shores. Its fossils show how fish-like fins were now being used as the first real arms, shoulders, elbows and wrists.

It's bizarre to think that the reason you and I have wrists and ankles goes all the way back to creatures like *Tiktaalik*. That's because they needed hinged joints to heave their bodies up off the ground. Do a press-up yourself and you'll see just how important these hinges are!

Tiktaalik is one of the first of a group of animals known as amphibians. *Amphi* in ancient Greek means 'both' and *bios* means 'life'. They live both in the water and on the land. Not only could the first amphibians walk on land, they could also breathe through primitive lungs rather than using gills like fish. Equipped with these new features, some amphibians, such as the two-metre-long *Eryops*, became the most dominant creatures on the land. They had staying power. Their descendants include modern frogs, newts and toads.

While amphibians were growing into giants, so were plants. As we saw earlier, some plants had developed woody stems to stay upright. And thanks to fungi, they could gather food in their roots even if they weren't living near the water's edge. But to move the water and food up their tubes against the pull of gravity so they could grow tall, they needed a pumping system.

A plant's key to growing tall lies in millions of tiny holes that cover the surfaces of its leaves. Depending on the weather conditions, plants open or close these little holes, which are called stomata. When it is hot, water in the leaves evaporates through the stomata, making the sap in the stem more concentrated. This causes water to be drawn up into the leaves at the top. It is a process known as transpiration.

Can you see what looks like a pair of little lips in the magnifying glass? That's a stomata on the surface of a leaf seen through the lens of a scanning electron microscope.

Stomata

Early land plants, including trees, created spores just the way fungi do. They released the spores into the air and let the wind spread them. But spores need warm and wet conditions to grow. That's fine in damp marshes or bogs, but hopeless in dry areas. By about 360 million years ago, some plants had developed a new way to reproduce – seeds.

Seeds are stronger than spores. They have a hard, water-resistant coating called a testa. The protective coat keeps seeds from getting damaged in the air, on the water, or even inside an animal's guts. Inside the coating, there is an embryo, the part of the seed that will grow into a new plant. And with its own private stash of food in the form of sugars, proteins and fats, the seed has plenty of nutrients to grow even in a tough environment.

One of the early seed-bearing trees were cycads. They look like small palms (although they are not related) and can been traced back to about 320 million years ago. About 300 species of cycads are still living today. Like eyesight in trilobites, seeds changed the

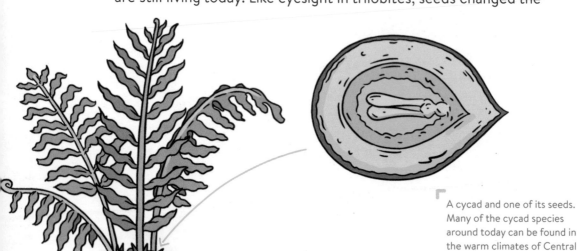

A cycad and one of its seeds. Many of the cycad species around today can be found in the warm climates of Central America, Australia and Africa.

world entirely. For millions of years they have made plants the dominant form of life on land.

Can you imagine a millipede the size of a person? Or a sea scorpion that is bigger than your outstretched arms? If, like me, you are not so sure that this is a world for you, then be grateful you were not alive 300 million years ago. Welcome to the Carboniferous Period.

How insects learned to fly is still a mystery. Experts think it probably had something to do with the arrival of tall plants and trees. Wouldn't it make sense for an insect to develop little wing flaps to jump or glide from one tree to another? That way they wouldn't have to climb all the way down and then up again. Gradually the wing flaps would have grown larger. Finally insects could glide, dive and flap their wings.

Griffinflies had a wingspan of around 75cm. They're now extinct, which is probably for the best!

Seagull-sized relatives of today's dragonflies were some of the most spectacular insects that have ever lived. Griffinflies had complete command of the skies. They could feed off smaller creatures as and when they liked. There were no birds back then to challenge them. They might even have had nearly all-round vision the way their relatives do today.

No one knows exactly why these creatures could grow so large. Some scientists think high levels of oxygen in the air (almost twice as much as now) allowed animals to get bigger. Others have shown that too much oxygen can be poisonous to tiny baby creatures. They think Carboniferous babies had to grow bigger fast so as not to be killed by the high levels of oxygen. But a giant insect fossil has been found for a period with much less oxygen. That makes some experts wonder if oxygen was the cause at all.

That's the way it is with science. Ideas that explain the evidence we have are called hypotheses. When we get new evidence, we sometimes have to come up with new hypotheses.

In a world of fierce giants, other creatures simply had to adapt or die. And adapt they did. Smaller insects evolved folding wings, just like those we see in houseflies today. This new kind of wing

> 66
> THE DRAGONFLY IS AN EXCEPTIONALLY BEAUTIFUL INSECT AND A FIERCE CARNIVORE ... [IT] CAN PUT ON A BURST OF SPEED, STOP ON A DIME, HOVER, FLY BACKWARD, AND SWITCH DIRECTION IN A FLASH.
> 99

Richard Preston,
science writer

1

2

3

Like flies, ladybirds are able to switch very quickly between walking and flying, thanks to the mechanism in their wings, which easily folds in and out.

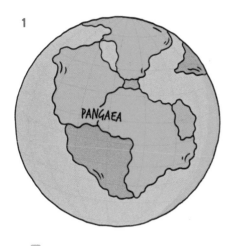

1

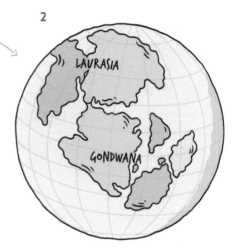

2

1. By about 250 million years ago, the Earth's landmasses had collided, resulting in a giant supercontinent, Pangaea.

2. By about 152 million years ago, Pangaea had split into two huge land masses, Gondwana in the south and Laurasia in the north, with oceans between them.

3. By about 95 million years ago, Earth's land masses had begun to resemble the layout of the continents as they are today.

meant that small insects could crawl into narrow spaces. Larger, fixed-winged griffinflies and other predators couldn't reach them there. Flying insects with folding wings are by far the largest group of insects alive today. It goes to show that the folding wing probably counts as another of nature's most successful adaptations ever.

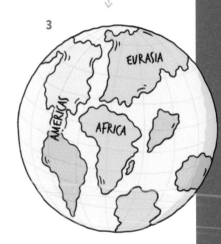

3

Just about this time, when griffinflies ruled the skies, the world's land masses had started colliding together into one giant continent. It is called Pangaea (meaning 'all Earth'). While this was happening, the climate became warmer and drier. So the ponds and puddles where amphibians laid their eggs probably started to dry up and disappear. More animals

The eggs of amphibians, like this frog egg, let water flow in and out. That's fine for laying eggs in the wet, but they're no good on dry land.

had to compete for less water. As usual when the environment changes a lot, animals changed with it.

Amphibian eggs are squishy, with a covering that lets water in and out. That's the best way when you lay your eggs in the wet. But as the land dried out, some creatures began to lay a new kind of egg, one a little like a plant seed, with all the water and nutrients a baby creature needs contained inside a leathery, soft or hard shell. Armed with these new eggs with waterproof shells, these animals could press-up their way inland as far as they liked. Then they could lay their egg right on dry land, and after a few weeks, hey presto! Out hatched a little creature. We call this group of animals reptiles.

So a waterproof egg is actually a portable pond or puddle. These little marvels of nature changed the story of animals by allowing them to give birth away from water. You may find eggs also make for some quite interesting breakfast talk.

The earliest known reptile is called *Hylonomus*. This twenty-centimetre-long, lizard-like creature lived from about 312 million years ago in the Carboniferous Period. It ate millipedes and small insects. And it was food for large amphibians and giant griffinflies.

Fast forward a few million years and reptiles ruled the land. One very cool example is *Dimetrodon*. Growing more than three metres long, this lumbering giant walked on four legs and had a long swaggering tail. *Dimetrodon* was the largest meat-eater of its time. It had a peculiar sail on its back. Some scientists think it may have been used to heat up its body and blood in the early-morning sunlight. It could then have helped to release heat and cool *Dimetrodon* in the warmth of the day.

Creatures like *Dimetrodon* roamed the land for about 60 million years. But their time came to a sudden end when life suffered its worst ever brush with death – the Permian Mass Extinction.

> " THE SHELL AND EGG MEMBRANES ALLOW GAS EXCHANGE TO AND FROM THE DEVELOPING EMBRYO, LETTING OXYGEN IN AND CARBON DIOXIDE OUT BUT RETAINING WATER. "

P. Martin Sander, palaeontologist

Dimetrodon lived around 280 million years ago. Its sail-like back may have helped it control its temperature.

That single supercontinent, Pangaea, was now fully formed. When continents collide, one thing is certain. You can expect more and bigger volcanoes to erupt. What's the biggest volcano you can imagine? How about one that spreads lava over an area the size of Western Europe and then goes on erupting for another one million years? That's what experts think happened 252 million years ago, forming the Siberian Traps, a huge area of volcanic rock in what is now northern Russia.

But that's not all. Volcanoes throw lots of carbon dioxide into the air. Carbon dioxide is one of the gases responsible for global warming. Experts think that at the end of the Permian Period, the Earth's climate became too hot for most life forms to survive. Nine out of ten species of plants and animals went extinct.

It was as if life on Earth had been struck down by a killer fever. But this was no ordinary illness because it lasted 80,000 years!

Volcanic activity may not have been the only reason for the Permian Mass Extinction. It is also possible that a meteorite strike in Antarctica added to the drama.

The volcanic activity that formed the Siberian Traps might have looked something like this Icelandic landscape with the erupting Bardarbunga volcano.

Chapter 3
DINOSAURS

252 million–5 million years ago
Terrible lizards and what comes after

○ **245 million years ago**
The age of dinosaurs
begins.

○ **220 million years ago**
Termites become the
first insects to live
in giant nests.

○ **150 million years ago**
Some feathered dinosaurs take
to the skies, becoming birds.

○ **140 million years ago**
Plants reproduce using
flowers and fruit.

65 million years ago
A massive meteorite wipes out all dinosaurs except birds.

56 million years ago
Mammals and birds dominate the land and sky.

30 million years ago
Monkeys appear.

14 million years ago
Apes appear.

Very few reptiles survived the terrible Permian Mass Extinction. But one of these survivors is very important to us. *Lystrosaurus* is a link between reptiles and mammals. If it hadn't survived, some experts think mammals may never have evolved at all. Humans are mammals. So we must be thankful that this possible distant ancestor of ours made it, even if it did look like a cross between a lizard and a pig. Then, out of disaster came a completely new generation of reptiles. These were the most fearsome creatures ever to tread the Earth. Welcome to the age of dinosaurs!

Pisanosaurus
227–221 million years ago
South America

Lystrosaurus
250 million years ago
Asia, Africa, Antarctica

Nyasasaurus
245–240 million years ago
Africa

Eoraptor
228 million years ago
South America

Fossils of about 800 types of dinosaur have been found so far, although nearly 2,000 are thought to have existed altogether. Some walked on two feet, some on four. Some ate plants, some ate animals, some ate both.

Among the first known dinosaurs were the prosauropods. These were plant eaters that could grow up to ten metres long, with small heads and long necks. They usually walked on all fours, but sometimes climbed on to two legs when reaching to nibble at the top of a tree.

At the beginning of the Triassic Period, *Lystrosaurus* was the most common animal on land. But by the middle of the period, dinosaurs had burst on to the scene. This picture shows *Lystrosaurus* and some Triassic dinosaurs along with the dates when they lived and where their fossils were found. Because they lived at different times and in different places, they would never have appeared together like this.

Plateosaurus
210 million years ago
Europe

Coelophysis
225–220 million years ago
North America

Gideon and Mary Ann Mantell were amateur fossil hunters who lived in Lewes, England. In 1822, the Mantells found several very large fossilised teeth in a forest near their home. They worked out that these teeth belonged to an animal about eighteen metres long. That's nearly as long as two double-decker buses!

After years of argument, scientists agreed about the Mantells' teeth (well, not theirs, but the ones they found). They decided they belonged to a new type of creature that had never been known before. They called it the *Iguanodon* because they thought it would have looked something like a much larger version of a modern iguana. Later fossils showed it didn't look quite like that and wasn't much more than half as big as they thought, either.

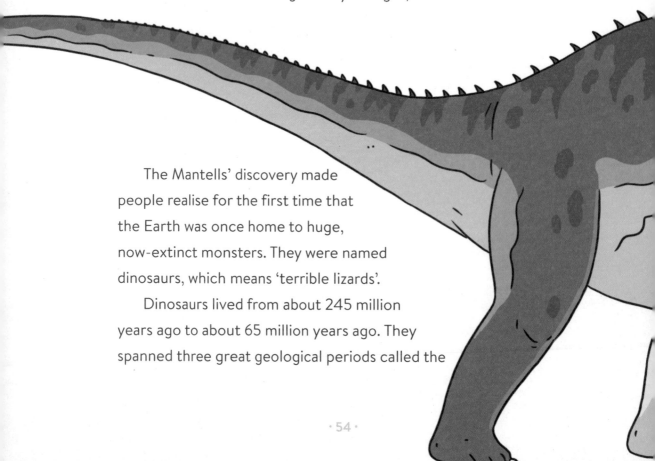

The Mantells' discovery made people realise for the first time that the Earth was once home to huge, now-extinct monsters. They were named dinosaurs, which means 'terrible lizards'.

Dinosaurs lived from about 245 million years ago to about 65 million years ago. They spanned three great geological periods called the

Triassic, Jurassic and Cretaceous. On our twenty-four-hour clock of all Earth history, they lived between 10:43pm and 11:39pm.

Some of the biggest dinosaurs were the sauropods, and one of the biggest of them was *Argentinosaurus*. This huge, heavy beast walked on all four legs. It could grow up to thirty metres long. And it may have weighed up to seventy tonnes,

Argentinosaurus could weigh up to seventy tonnes – that's the same as ten African elephants!

probably making it the heaviest animal ever on Earth. Its survival strategy was simple. It grew so large that few other creatures were big enough or strong enough to kill it. Other dinosaurs were fast. *Ornithomimus* may have been the speediest dinosaur of all. By studying footprints it left in mud, some scientists reckon it could run as fast as Olympic champion Usain Bolt. Its name means 'bird-like' because Othniel Charles Marsh, the palaeontologist who named it, noticed how much its claws looked like a bird's. And that was in 1890. He didn't have any idea that over 100 years later other palaeontologists would find fossils that show *Ornithomimus* also had feathers.

Still other dinosaurs had unusual built-in tools. *Iguanodon* was one of those. Its thumb was shaped like a terrifying dagger. Perhaps it used its thumb to defend itself, standing upright on its hind legs to fend off attackers. But some scientists think *Iguanodon* would just have run from predators and used its thumb spike for spearing food.

Of course the dinosaur with the strongest bite is the most famous dinosaur of all, the *Tyrannosaurus rex*, or *T. rex* for short. It lived in what is now western North America. *T. rex* walked on two legs and had a massive skull, balanced by a long, heavy tail. Each of its hands had just two fingers, and its upper arms were quite short compared with its massive legs and tail. At around twelve metres long and weighing more than a modern elephant, this was one big carnivore. It dined on dead carcasses or live prey – possibly both.

The most complete *T. rex* skeleton was found by fossil hunter Sue Hendrickson in August 1990. This famous fossil was named Sue after its discoverer. Sue is 12.3 metres long from nose to tail.

> " DINOSAURS REPLACE THEIR TEETH THROUGHOUT THEIR LIFE. AND T. REX REPLACED ALL OF THEIR TEETH EVERY YEAR. "
>
> Jack Horner, palaeontologist

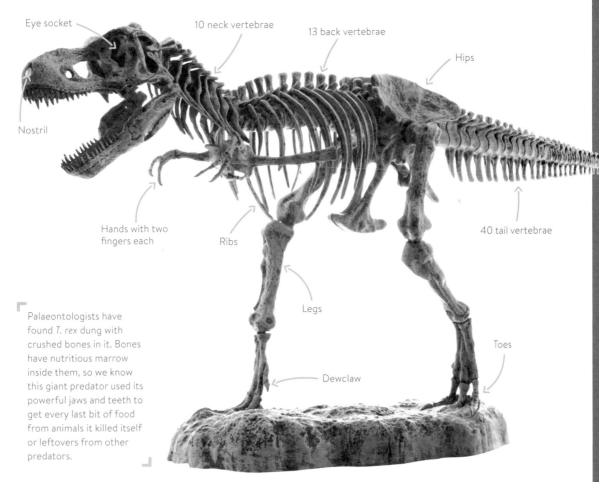

Eye socket

10 neck vertebrae

13 back vertebrae

Hips

Nostril

Hands with two
fingers each

Ribs

40 tail vertebrae

Legs

Toes

Dewclaw

Palaeontologists have
found *T. rex* dung with
crushed bones in it. Bones
have nutritious marrow
inside them, so we know
this giant predator used its
powerful jaws and teeth to
get every last bit of food
from animals it killed itself
or leftovers from other
predators.

Not all dinosaurs were big or fast or strong. One of the smallest, *Microraptor*, was a four-winged dinosaur the size of a crow. It couldn't fly but probably glided from tree to tree looking for food.

In 1861, Christian Erich Hermann von Meyer, a German fossil hunter, announced the discovery of what he claimed was the first-ever bird. He called it *Archaeopteryx*. It was about the same size as a modern magpie, and was definitely bird-like. Its feathers were arranged in much the same way as a modern bird's. It even had bird-like claws on its legs, and a wishbone. Von Meyer's fossil dated back some 150 million years, which means it lived at about the same time as the long-necked prosauropods were munching the tops of trees.

Quetzalcoatlus

For years experts were baffled as to which creatures birds were descended from. How had they learned to fly? Where did their feathers come from? Knowing about just one prehistoric bird wasn't enough to understand what happened.

Then, in 1996, Chinese scientists announced that fossil hunter Li Yumin had found a fossil that showed some dinosaurs had feathers. *Sinosauropteryx* caused a sensation. This was a 1.5-metre-long, two-legged creature with the jaws and flattened teeth of meat-eating dinosaurs. It had clawed fingers, and its legs showed it must have been a fast runner.

The puzzle of where birds came from had at last been solved. Feathers first appeared on some dinosaurs. They probably helped keep their bodies warm. Then later, some feathers evolved into the kind that helps birds fly. Many scientists think that all theropods (smart, fast dinosaurs including *Velociraptor* and *T. rex*)

had feathers, especially when they were young. So what's the difference between birds and dinosaurs? Well, not much.

Actually dinosaurs are alive and well in the world we live in today. But don't panic. Only the kind that could *fly* are still alive. It's just that we call them birds!

Another bird-like dinosaur with feathers on the back of its head, body and arms was the *Sinornithosaurus millenii*. This fossil, found in China, dates to about 125 million years ago.

Theropods and birds

Date	Name		Characteristics
228 million years ago	*Eoraptor*		*Eoraptor* had five fingers on each hand and five toes on each foot. Birds today have three fingers in each of their wings.
220 million years ago	*Coelophysis*		*Coelophysis* had a wishbone. Birds today have a wishbone too, made up of two collarbones stuck together in a forked shape.
120 million years ago	*Oviraptor*		*Oviraptor* was discovered alongside some fossilised eggs, and it had feathers. Experts think it was probably brooding over its own eggs like a chicken.
Today	Chicken		Chickens can fly! They also have feathers, talons, a beak and a wishbone. Today they are farmed worldwide for meat and eggs.

No one knows exactly how birds evolved from dinosaurs. But here are some examples of species and their characteristics that hint at the way today's birds emerged.

While dinosaurs ruled the land, two other types of animals dominated the ocean and skies. Giant sharks, underwater crocodile ancestors and nightmarish long-necked marine reptiles prowled the seas gobbling up squid and fish. And in the skies, flying reptiles called pterosaurs swooped and glided, including giant *Quetzalcoatlus*, with a wingspan of twelve metres! That's as wide as a small airplane.

Dinosaur times were pretty exciting, but for a long time they were missing one thing we now take for granted. Flowering plants are by far the most successful plants alive today. But for about 330 million years, none of the plants in the world had flowers.

The oldest flower fossils date back to about 140 million years ago. This was during the Cretaceous Period, when dinosaurs were at the height of their power. Since then, flowering plants have made a massive impact on life on Earth. In fact, more than seventy-five per cent of all our food comes from flowering plants and the animals that eat them.

Flowers are brilliant at helping plants reproduce more easily. To talk about how, we need to go back to between 1 and 2 billion years ago. At that time, a new form of reproduction started in the oceans. It is called sexual reproduction. It works by combining genetic information (called DNA) from the cells of two parents so that the baby has a combination of the parents' genes. That way, the baby is different from either of its parents. It's a great way of making sure all members of a species are different from each other.

On one journey, a bee can travel as much as 6km from its hive. When it returns, it dances to tell the other bees where to find the best flowers.

In fact, it works so well that almost all life forms you see around you reproduce this way.

But trying to mix DNA when you are a plant is quite tricky. How on earth can two plants that can't move from place to place swap cells?

Flowers are a stunning solution to the problem. They spread reproductive cells called pollen from one plant to another in many different ways. Some release them to be carried by the wind. Others attract creatures – such as beetles, bees and moths – that move from place to place. Some even partner with a very particular creature.

This is a two-way deal. Some beetles, bees and moths need flower partners as much as the flowers need them. The insects eat some of the flower pollen and also drink a sugary liquid called nectar that the flower produces. While they're eating, the insects get the pollen all over themselves, so they carry it on their bodies from flower to flower. Everyone's a winner! That's why many flowers are so brightly coloured. It's so they can attract insects. It's like a

form of TV advertising, saying, "Hey, look at me, over here! I have a sugary drink and, guess what, it's FREE!"

But even after successfully swapping their DNA, plants still have a problem. Their seeds now must be spread out so young plants don't compete for vital nutrients and water with their parents. Some seeds travel on the wind (such as the helicopter-like seeds of a sycamore tree), some by water (a coconut), and some by sticking to an animal's fur (a burr).

But the most interesting method of all is to package seeds inside a tempting, ready-made meal. That's the real purpose of all fruit, from strawberries and apples to peaches and even tomatoes! Fruits are nature's ready-made meals, designed by flowering plants to tempt animals to eat them and spread their seeds. When they've been digested, the seeds inside are randomly scattered on the ground in the animal's dung.

By the way, nothing is better for helping seeds grow than a shot of manure in the form of animal dung. It's another great example of natural teamwork in action.

Helicopter seeds – which are produced by field maple, Norway maple, sycamore and ash trees – spiral through the air, enabling them to travel out of their parent's shade.

W e are now roughly 100 million years from the present day. Let's see, that's about 11:29pm on our twenty-four-hour clock of Earth history. That leaves only thirty-one minutes to go. Any sign of humans yet?

Actually, there is a hint of humans going on, even though it's still millions of years before any sign of our ancestors can be seen wandering across the grassy plains of Africa.

Today, people live in vast towns and cities, some, like Tokyo in Japan, with more than 30 million people. But the idea of millions of the same animal species living close together first appeared long before humans. Welcome to the first insect 'cities'. These are the giant communities of bees, ants and termites.

There are about 20,000 different types of bees alive today. Some – especially honeybees – form highly social groups. It's fascinating to see the similarities between beehives and human cities. Honeybees pass on knowledge from one generation to another. They care for their young, and sometimes they even sacrifice their lives for the group. Also, these little insects do different jobs, dividing what needs to be done among them.

People have different jobs, as lorry drivers, computer programmers and palaeontologists, just to name a few. For a long time, biologists thought we were the only animals that divided work in this way. But, as any beekeeper will tell you, that is not so. Honeybees do it too. It's a good example of how things we assume happen only in the human world sometimes be seen in the lives of other creatures in the natural world.

Honeybees also communicate. They talk to each other through

Divide and rule. The queen bee lives at the centre of a hive. Worker bees are female and their job is to gather pollen and nectar to make honey. Drones are male and their job is to mate with the queen.

the language of dance. When a bee returns to the hive from gathering food, it tells the others where to look for more food by performing a certain type of dance. The 'round dance' means that food is within fifty metres of the hive. The 'waggle dance' provides details about both the distance and the direction of the food. Then there's the 'jerky dance'. This is used by the bees to decide whether to increase or decrease the amount of food gathering they need to do, depending on the hive's overall needs.

Ants belong to the same insect group as honeybees. The oldest fossils of ants' nests date from about 100 million years ago. There are many similarities between ants' nests and honeybees' hives, but ants do not dance. Instead, they communicate through sound, touch and smell. When an ant finds food it will leave a trail of scent along the ground all the way home, to lead others to its source.

Leafcutter ants are gardeners. They cut plant leaves and carry them back to the colony to feed a special fungus that grows in 'gardens' in their nest. The ants then dine off the fungus when it is ready to eat!

It finds the way back by remembering certain landmarks, often using the position of the Sun as its guide.

But the prize for the first insects to work out how to live together in giant groups goes to termites. Fossilised termite nests date back 220 million years. These tiny creatures create some of the biggest insect cities of all. They often live in colonies that number several million. A queen can lay thousands of eggs a day. She gets so large (sometimes up to ten centimetres long) that she is often unable to move. If she needs more space, a team of worker termites heaves her up and pushes her to a newly built chamber.

Dinosaurs might have been the most successful land animals of their time and insects the most sociable, but there were plenty of other creatures around and about as well. At about the same time that dinosaurs came on the scene, another type of creature was living in the shadows. Mammals are descendants of creatures related to *Dimetrodon* – the one with the sail on its back – and *Lystrosaurus*, the one that survived the terrible Permian Mass Extinction.

Mammals went a lot further than *Dimetrodon* in controlling their temperatures. The ability to keep your body warm when it's cold outside is called being warm-blooded. Because mammals were warm-blooded, they could hunt at night and sleep during the day, avoiding the worst predators. Most of them were also small. That made it much easier to hide away in the daytime, under rocks or inside a tree.

And to help stay warm, mammals grew fur. Actually, the reason we have hair goes all the way back to our rat-like mammal ancestors. They developed fur all over their bodies to keep themselves warm while hunting at night so they could escape attack from the dinosaurs. But how could they hunt in the dark?

Most nocturnal mammals have eyes that contain lots of light-sensitive cells called rods. These help animals like cats see when there's very little light. Some mammals have eyes that are great at detecting movement. They can see their prey darting around even in very low light.

Mammals also developed excellent hearing. This allowed them to detect the faintest rustle of a possible meal in leaves and grasses. Much later, a few mammals, such as bats, would develop this amazing hearing even more. They use a system called echolocation, allowing them to create a detailed mental picture of the world around them using sound.

Another way mammals became pros at night hunting was by growing the smell-interpreting part

The sabre-toothed squirrel was a shrew-like mammal with fangs.

of their brains. They used their noses to find the yummy food they craved. If you have a cat or dog, you'll know exactly what I mean.

Then disaster struck once again. Dinosaurs had dominated life on land for about 180 million years. But then they were utterly wiped out. Only the birds survived. Pterosaurs, the flying reptiles, also vanished. So did the marine reptiles, except for the turtles, which somehow survived. It was also the end of the road for the ammonites, those spiral-shaped creatures, relations of today's octopus and squid.

How could this happen?

About 65 million years ago, a humongous asteroid hurtled towards the Earth. As this dark chunk of deadly rock and ice made its final approach, planet Earth would have looked like a sparkling blue and green jewel in the black void of space. Down came the

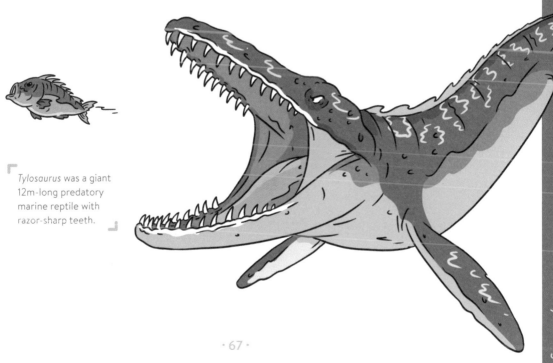

Tylosaurus was a giant 12m-long predatory marine reptile with razor-sharp teeth.

asteroid, possibly splitting up into several pieces before finally smashing into an unsuspecting world.

Asteroids and meteors fall from the skies in a constant rain even today. But usually they break up and burn as they cut through the Earth's thick, heavy atmosphere. You can sometimes see meteors yourself on a clear night. They are commonly called shooting stars. But this was no ordinary shooting star. This thing was about ten kilometres wide – that's the size of a large city!

It hit the Earth with the force of thousands of nuclear bombs, blasting a crater more than 160 kilometres wide. Everything in a 1,000-kilometre-wide area was wiped off the map in seconds, leaving behind an enormous cloud of deathly hot, toxic gas.

The noise and sight of the impact would have deafened and blinded countless living creatures. Many of those not killed by the blast would have been drowned by giant waves created by the impact. Earth was plunged into darkness by thick heavy clouds of rock and dust lasting for as long as a year. Plants all over the world died from lack of sunlight and from a cooling climate. Even on the opposite side of the globe from the impact, animals died of starvation.

Dinosaur times were over, just like that.

Mammals, well adapted for living in the dark, were quick off the block once the dinosaurs were gone. Well, it seems quick when you're moving through time as fast as we are. Within 3 million years of the meteorite catastrophe, shrew-sized mammals had evolved into creatures as large as dogs. Within 5 million years, mammals of all shapes and sizes roamed the land. This period of time, from 56 to 34 million years ago, is called the Eocene. (*Eocene* means 'new dawn' in ancient Greek.) Our twenty-four-hour clock of Earth history shows it's between 11:42 and 11:49pm.

It's now that the ancestors of modern mammals came on to the scene. There were carnivorous predators such as *Andrewsarchus*, which looked like a wolf but was twenty-two times bigger than its modern cousin. Even more amazing was the 'thunder beast' *Megacerops*. This was one huge plant eater that looked like a rhinoceros but was the size of a modern elephant. But not all Eocene mammals were gigantic. The ancestors of today's horses appeared then, too. One was *Hyracotherium*, which was only as big as a middle-sized dog.

> **THE LARGEST MAMMALS EVOLVED WHEN EARTH WAS COOLER AND TERRESTRIAL LAND AREA WAS GREATER.**
>
> Felisa A. Smith, biologist

One group of Eocene mammals is of very special interest. In fact, creatures from this group – primates – will become the main focus of the next part of our story. Modern primates include monkeys and apes, lemurs and aye-ayes. But the first primates looked more like squirrels. Early primate fossils have been found all over the world.

Monkeys emerged by around 30 million years ago in Africa or Asia. Soon after, one or more groups of these monkeys somehow crossed the Atlantic. It's a bit of a mystery how they did it. Some experts think they found themselves bobbing on a raft in the middle of the ocean, eventually to be washed ashore on the coast of what is now Brazil. We call the descendants of the monkeys that made this

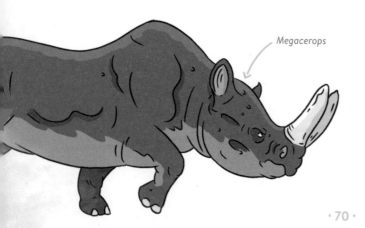

Megacerops

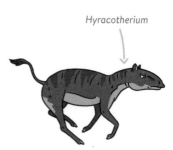

Hyracotherium

journey, the New World monkeys. And the ones which stayed behind in Africa and Asia are called Old World monkeys. These two main groups of monkeys still exist today.

The New World monkeys of South America have flat noses and use their tails to help them swing and balance in the trees. Some species can happily hang from a branch by their tail alone. It's as if they have an extra hand.

Apes evolved from monkeys. Palaeontologists have found fossils of early apes that date to about 14 million years ago in Europe, Asia and Africa. So it's hard to figure out where they first appeared. Over time, these early apes evolved into today's great apes – orangutans, gorillas, chimpanzees, bonobos and humans.

Yes, humans are apes. Biologists have discovered that the DNA in you and me is ninety-eight per cent the same as the DNA of other great apes. And they've figured out that humans and chimpanzees have a common ancestor that probably lived some time between 4 and 7 million years ago. That's not long ago when you look at our clock. After all, it's only about two minutes before midnight.

Spider monkey

Macaque

New World monkeys, including the spider monkey (top), have flat noses and can swing from trees using their tail. Old World monkeys, like the macaque (bottom), have narrow noses and sitting pads on their buttocks.

Chapter 4

HANDS FREE

5 million–65,000 years ago
Some apes walk on two feet

○ **5 million years ago**
South and North America
link up, changing the
world's climate.

○ **4 million years ago**
The first ancestors of humans
walk upright in Africa.

○ **2.4 million years ago**
Homo habilis appears in
Africa, making extensive
use of stone tools.

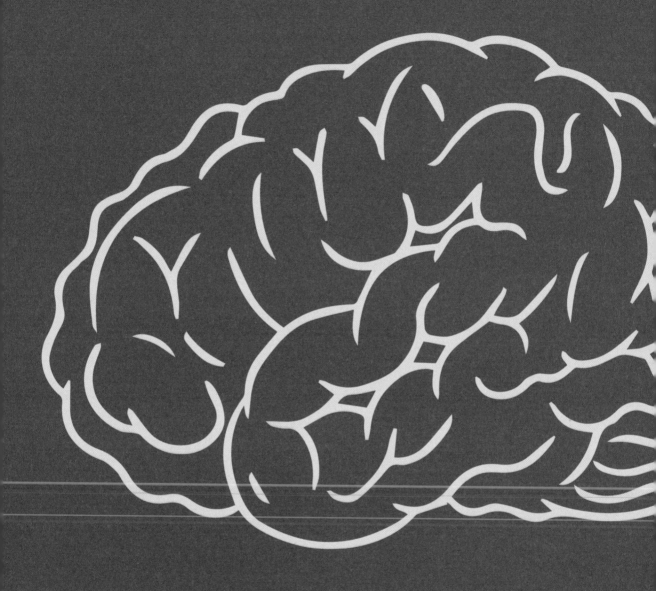

1.9 million years ago
Homo erectus appears with a brain at least twice as large as the first upright apes.

1.5 million years ago
Early humans learn how to light and control fire. They begin to eat cooked food.

400,000 years ago
Neanderthals are among several human species with brains as large as modern humans'.

A lot of people are talking about climate change these days. It's a big deal because the world is warming up and the ice caps are melting. Which is especially bad news if you happen to be a polar bear or a coral reef.

But it's fairly bad news for humans, too. The less ice at the poles, the more water in the seas. And that makes the water rise higher up on the land. One day there could be no ice left at all, and if that happens, the seas would be sixty-six metres higher than they are today. That means that if forty-two football players stood on one another's shoulders on a present-day beach, even the top one would need to be wearing scuba gear. Seas that high would swamp most of the world's coastal communities. Millions of people would have to leave their homes. That's why people are worried.

But for the Earth, being ice-free is pretty normal. For most of the Earth's history there have been no ice caps at all and the seas have been as high as that sixty-six-metre level. Every so often, things would change and the world would get colder and the seas lower (remember Snowball Earth?). Then they would get warmer again.

One of the times things began to change was about 5 million years ago. At the time, the world only had one big ice cap – on Antarctica. Then something pretty major happened. The tectonic plate that carries South America met the tectonic plate that carries North America. The two continents ended up attached by a thin piece of land that today is part of the country of Panama.

Higher temperatures are causing ice to melt earlier in spring and refreeze later in autumn. That means it's harder for polar bears to find solid ice, which is crucial for resting, breeding and standing on while hunting.

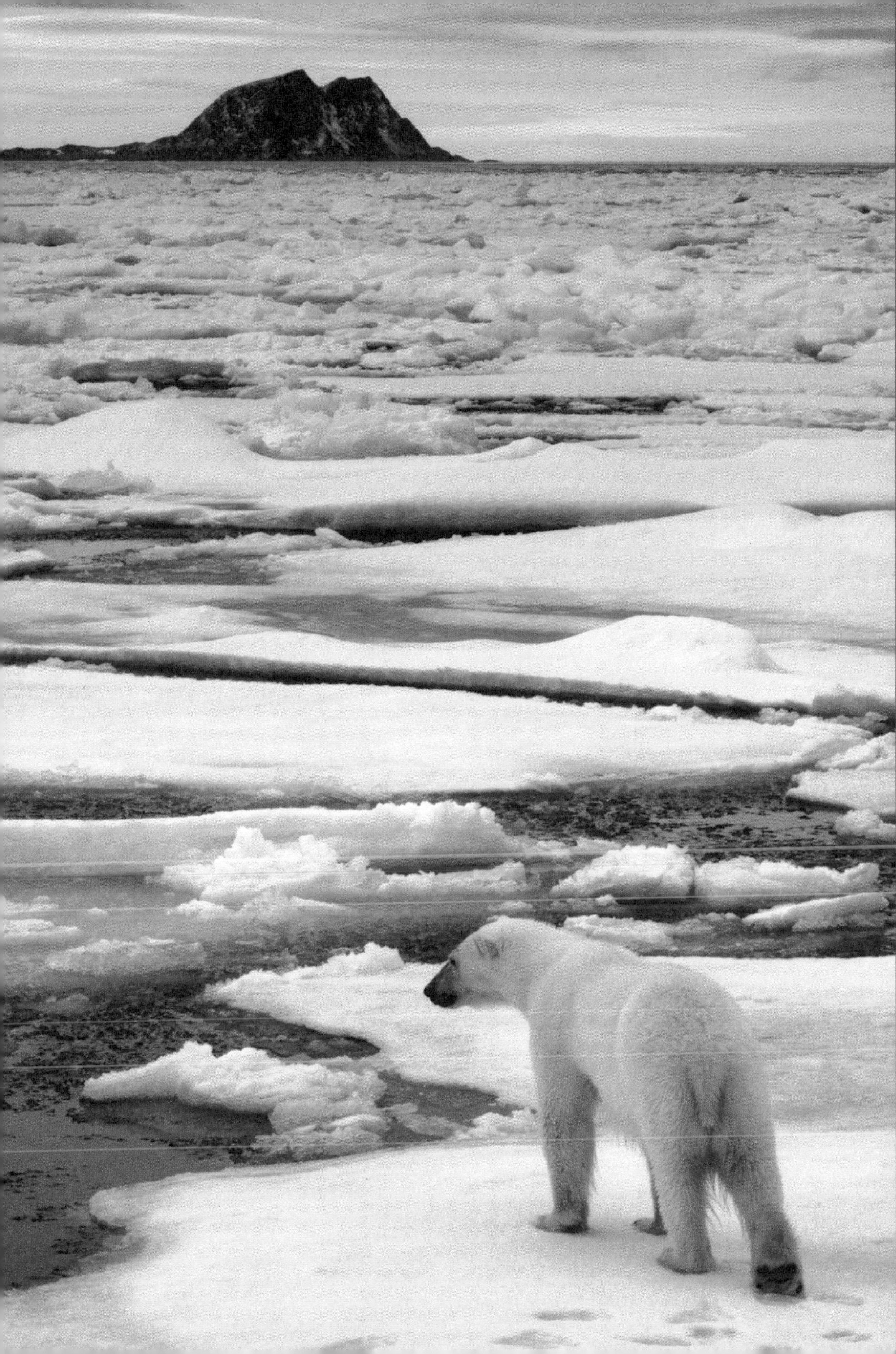

4. Hands Free

5 million–65,000 years ago

This new land connection forced Atlantic sea currents to flow northwards. As a result, a new climate system spluttered into life. It pumped warm air north and heated up winters in north-west Europe by at least ten degrees Celsius. The warmer water in the North Atlantic started to evaporate more quickly. Water vapour travelling north collided with cold air in the Arctic, where there was probably already a little ice. The vapour fell as snow, landing on the ice and the cold water around it. Over time, the snow settled in layers and formed thick packs of ice. And so by about 2.5 million years ago the Earth was wearing a second big ice cap, this time in the Arctic.

With huge ice sheets now on both poles, the Earth plunged into a super-deep freeze. Colossal ice sheets called glaciers spread southwards from the North Pole. Sea levels plummeted because so much water was trapped as ice. The Earth was in the grips of a full-

The Perito Moreno glacier in Argentina is mysterious. Experts don't understand why it is advancing while most of the other glaciers in the world are retreating because of warming temperatures.

blown ice age. And here's the amazing thing: it still is. This whole time, since the glaciers started forming almost 3 million years ago, the Earth has been in a cool spell. It hasn't stayed exactly the same temperature all that time, of course. It's got warmer and colder and warmer again. Glaciers have crept on to the continents then pulled back again then crept up again. But all that time, the Earth has had two large ice caps. Just in case you were wondering, we're now in a warm time in the ice age, what's known as an interglacial period. And it's getting warmer fast.

And you know what else happened over that time? Humans, that's what. Humans ancestors were already around a million years before the deep freeze started. But we modern humans evolved during an ice age, and that has made all the difference to our story.

Lucy was an ape who lived in what is now Ethiopia in Africa about 3.2 million years ago. She was discovered in 1974 by a team of scientists headed by American Donald Johanson. They gave her a woman's name because her skeleton was small, which

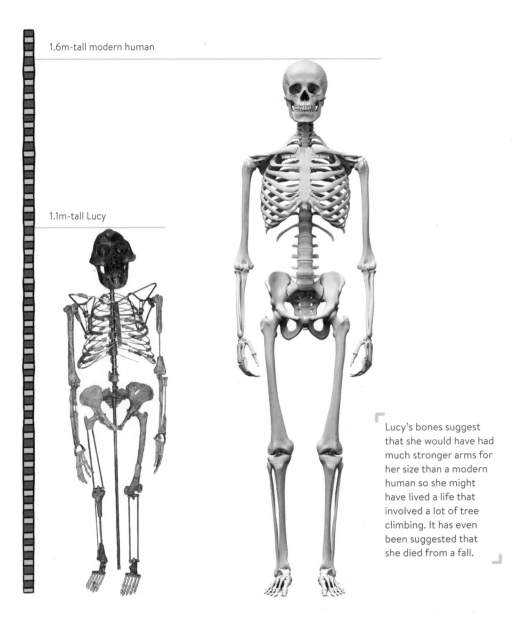

1.6m-tall modern human

1.1m-tall Lucy

Lucy's bones suggest that she would have had much stronger arms for her size than a modern human so she might have lived a life that involved a lot of tree climbing. It has even been suggested that she died from a fall.

they guessed meant she was female. They called her Lucy because when they were celebrating the find the team was listening to the Beatles song 'Lucy in the Sky with Diamonds'. Her species name is *Australopithecus afarensis*.

Lucy was about 1.1 metres tall and weighed about twenty-nine kilograms. When her discovery was announced to the world, Lucy caused a sensation. Why? Because experts could tell from the shape of her bones that she definitely walked on two feet, and humans are the only modern apes that do that consistently.

No one is quite sure what it was that made apes like Lucy stand upright, but it turned out to be a great advantage. With their hands free, they could carry food more easily, helping them survive even when times were tough. Being hands free means you can carry tools, too. And think how much easier it would be to hunt with a spear or to carry nuts wrapped in animal skin.

Since Lucy's discovery, bones and teeth of lots of other similar creatures have been found. But was Lucy human? If being human means belonging to a group of apes that walks on two feet, then Lucy counts. But if it's about having big brains, then we must wait another million years or so for our genus: *Homo*.

The first species experts feel safe calling human was *Homo habilis*. Its brain was 500–800 cubic centimetres, nearly

NOW, WHEN WE IMAGINE LUCY WALKING AROUND THE EAST AFRICAN LANDSCAPE LOOKING FOR FOOD, WE CAN FOR THE FIRST TIME IMAGINE HER WITH A STONE TOOL IN HAND AND LOOKING FOR MEAT.

Shannon McPherron, archaeologist

twice the size of Lucy's (although still only half the size of our own brains). And this species was very good at making tools. That's why *Homo habilis* marks the beginning of what is known as the Old Stone Age. It's about 2.4 million years ago and just forty-five seconds to midnight on our twenty-four-hour clock of Earth history. The age of humans has finally begun.

Now let's fast forward about 600,000 years. Enter *Homo erectus*. Skulls of these humans show a second dramatic

The stone tool above was made by *Homo habilis* about 2.5 million years ago. The one on the right was made more than 1.7 million years ago by *Homo erectus*.

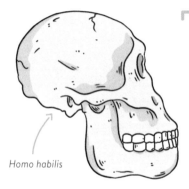

Homo habilis

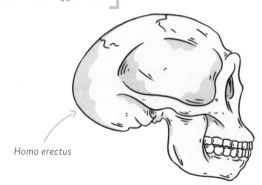

Homo habilis had large cheekbones and a small head. *Homo erectus* had a flatter face and a much bigger head.

Homo erectus

increase in brain size to about 750–1,300 cubic centimetres, almost as large as the brains of humans today. What on earth was going on?

There is an ancient Greek myth that tells the story of a divine being called Prometheus, who stole the fire of the gods and smuggled it down to Earth in the stalk of a plant.

Prometheus was severely punished for his crime. When the king of the gods, Zeus, found out, Prometheus was tied to a rock. Each day an eagle was sent to peck out his liver. Each night his liver would grow back so that it could be pecked out again when the eagle returned the next day.

The story of Prometheus is a myth. But it is a fact that no creature anywhere in the world other than human beings has ever been able deliberately to light and control fire. We don't know when they started or which species was the first. There is evidence from about 1 million years ago, but scientists think humans may have started controlling fire much earlier than that, maybe as long as 1.5 milion years ago, or even more.

Fire scares away dangerous wild animals and keeps you warm in colder climates. Perhaps that's why humans first wanted to start and control fires. But all the evidence suggests that quite quickly ancient

In 2012, researchers discovered the earliest evidence of fire in Wonderwerk Cave in South Africa. They found 1-million-year-old charred animal bones and burnt plant remains.

people started using fire for something even more important. And what they did with it changed the course of all Earth history.

Neuroscientist Suzana Herculano-Houzel studies the human brain. She has found a way to measure the number of brain cells inside our heads. And it turns out that on average a modern adult human has 86 billion neurons, the main type of brain cell. A chimpanzee has only about 28 billion.

So the question is how humans came to have so much brain. Dr Herculano-Houzel believes cooking is the key. That's because brains take a lot of energy. Modern humans use twenty per cent of all the energy we take in to fuel our big brains. Cooked food releases much more of its energy than raw food. It also takes less time to chew and digest. And because you get more energy from each vegetable or piece of meat you eat, you don't need to eat quite as much or spend quite as much

> " IF WE STILL FED LIKE OTHER PRIMATES DO — WHICH MUST HAVE BEEN HOW OUR ANCESTORS GOT HOLD OF CALORIES — WE WOULD HAVE TO EAT 9.5 HOURS EVERY DAY. "

Suzana Herculano-Houzel, neuroscientist

time finding your food. So the invention of cooking was a gigantic breakthrough, which allowed humans to develop gigantic brains.

Around the time cooking was invented, ancient humans became big travellers. The earliest *Homo erectus* fossils are from Java, in what is now Indonesia. They date to 1.9 million years ago. So either *Homo erectus* evolved in Asia from an ape that had travelled there earlier, then migrated back to Africa, or it evolved in Africa and had already made it to Asia. How could these early people (or pre-people) have gone all that way without roads and tracks, let alone cars, boats or planes? It is hard for us to imagine

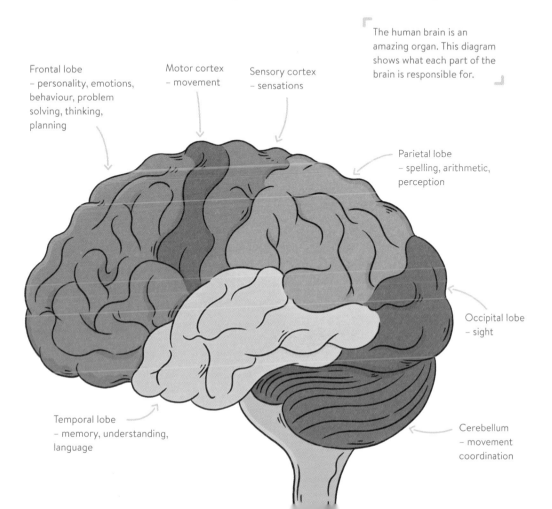

The human brain is an amazing organ. This diagram shows what each part of the brain is responsible for.

Frontal lobe
– personality, emotions, behaviour, problem solving, thinking, planning

Motor cortex
– movement

Sensory cortex
– sensations

Parietal lobe
– spelling, arithmetic, perception

Occipital lobe
– sight

Temporal lobe
– memory, understanding, language

Cerebellum
– movement coordination

walking such enormous distances. But they did have one huge advantage over us today – they were not in a hurry.

Over time, early humans made it to the farthest reaches of Africa, Asia and Europe. Fossilised footprints found near the Norfolk coast of England date back about 800,000 years. And England is almost 15,000 kilometres from southern Africa.

In 1856, quarry workers in the Neander Valley in Germany found what looked like human bones. But they weren't quite like our bones. They belonged to another species of human, Neanderthals, which first appear in the fossil record about 400,000 years ago. Since then, many Neanderthal sites have been found.

Experts think that between 400,000 and 70,000 years ago, at least five different species of humans were living on the planet. There were *Homo erectus*, *Homo neanderthalensis*, *Homo heidelbergensis*, a small hobbit-like species called *Homo floresiensis*, and *Homo sapiens* (that's us!). Did they fight? Did they live together or in their own separate communities? Could they talk? As you can see, there are still a lot of unanswered questions.

Neanderthals have had a bad press. They have been portrayed as being thick, old-fashioned or brutish. Pictures of Neanderthal people looked, until recently, more like other great apes than like humans. They were shown

Homo erectus
1.9 million–140,000 years ago, Africa and Asia

walking with a stoop and bent knees. This is all wrong! Neanderthal brains were at least the same size as those of modern humans. Some might have had even bigger brains. They also walked as upright as we do, although they were usually shorter. Neanderthals were stronger than we are and had big noses and foreheads that sloped back above jutting eyebrows.

Neanderthals were also highly skilled at using tools. Recent evidence shows that their hands were at least as nimble as ours. In 2013, bone tools they made were found in south-west France.

Neanderthals built houses from animal bones. They buried their dead with care, too. They often put precious objects in the graves

Homo neanderthalensis
About 400,000–40,000
years ago, Europe and Asia

Homo floresiensis
100,000–50,000
years ago, Asia

Homo heidelbergensis
About 700,000–200,000 years
ago, Europe, Asia and Africa

Homo sapiens
About 200,000
years ago to today

These cave drawings, found in Spain in 2018, were likely created by Neanderthals. The close-up drawing of the cave art shows animals and symbols around a ladder shape. The animals are very faded, but the artist has drawn them so we can see them well.

of those they loved, maybe to help them on to the next life. And in 2018, archaeologists discovered art on the walls of caves in Spain that dates back to 65,000 years ago, before *Homo sapiens* arrived in the area. Neanderthals were probably the artists.

And there's one more thing. In 1989, a Neanderthal bone almost identical to a bone in modern humans was found in a cave in Israel. The bone is called the hyoid. The hyoid connects our tongues to our throats and allows us to speak and sing. This means that Neanderthals could probably speak and sing, too.

Making weapons and tools, chatting, holding funerals and creating art are all things that require brainpower, creativity and skill. The evidence suggests these ancient people were asking some very important and very human questions. Is there life after death? Do my actions in this life affect the next life? What brings me good luck? These are the questions of curious minds that feel very much like our own.

Chapter 5

YOU AND ME

200,000 years ago–5000 BCE
How a single species of humans,
Homo sapiens, became the last on Earth

Timeline

200,000 years ago
Homo sapiens emerges
in Africa as a new
human species.

120,000 years ago
Modern humans begin
to trek out of Africa as
the glaciers recede.

65,000 years ago
Modern humans reach
Australia after rafting over
shallow seas.

40,000 years ago
Neanderthals go extinct.

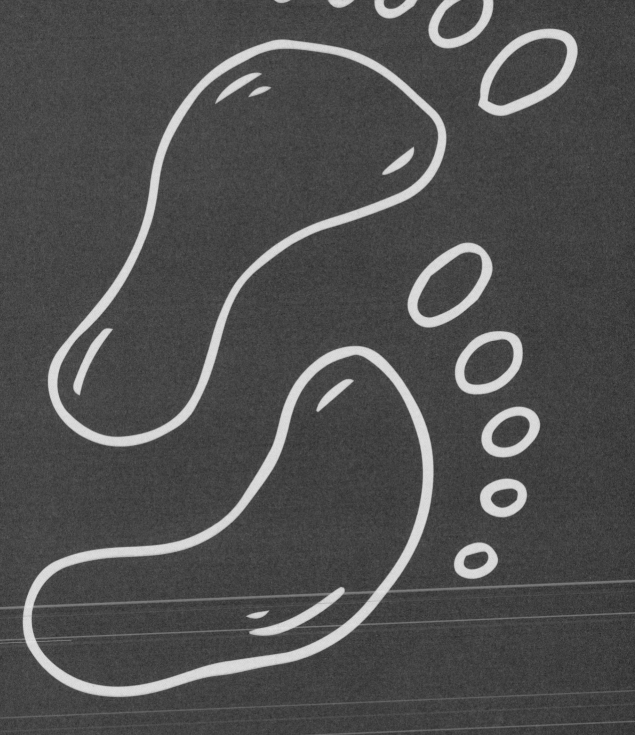

21,000 years ago
The last ice-over reaches its peak.

11,000 years ago
Farming begins in the Fertile Crescent.

11,000 years ago
Jericho emerges as one of the world's first towns.

10,000 years ago
The Pleistocene Extinction kills off most of the world's large animals.

Sit still and do nothing at all for just four seconds. Go on. Do it now …

Now sit still and do nothing for twenty-four hours. OK – I don't expect you actually to do that. But try to imagine it anyway.

The four seconds are just a little longer than how close we are to midnight on our twenty-four-hour clock. That long twenty-four hours is how much of Earth's history passed before the first *Homo sapiens* could be heard calling across the hot, dusty African plains. You see, compared with Earth, we humans are *very* young indeed. We are called *sapiens* because in Latin the word means 'wise' or 'full of knowledge'. Once you have finished this book, you can decide if you think it's a good name.

Modern humans and Neanderthals lived at the same time for many thousands of years. They mixed enough so that most modern humans have about one to four per cent Neanderthal DNA. It's involved in many things our bodies do, from how we look to how we sleep to what diseases we get.

To find the other ninety-six to ninety-nine per cent of our genetic roots, we must look to other sources. But which one is still a matter of debate. Some scientists think we're mostly descended from *Homo erectus*. Others think *Homo heidelbergensis* was involved. However it happened, the first modern humans evolved about 200,000 years ago.

We humans are a restless lot. Have you noticed that although today most people live in houses, they don't stay inside them for very long? I am reminded of this every time I sit in a traffic jam or go to the airport. Why, oh why, do so many people spend so much time

These polished eagle talons may well be a Neanderthal's necklace from about 130,000 years ago. They were discovered in present-day Croatia. *Homo sapiens* made jewellery at about the same time.

trying to move from one place to another? Now I get it. Being constantly on the move is deeply woven into our nature.

We've seen that human ancestors travelled thousands of kilometres almost 2 million years ago. About 120,000 years ago, *Homo sapiens* started to do the same thing, with different groups leaving Africa at different times.

DNA research shows *Homo sapiens* were quite diverse even before they left Africa. They may have had slightly different face shapes, hair textures and skin colours. And they also had differences that were less easy to see from the outside, such as what diseases they might suffer from. Over time those differences would evolve to become the rich diversity of humans today.

Homo sapiens travelled all over the world. They trekked to the Middle East, where they started mixing with Neanderthals. They swept across Asia.

About 65,000 years ago, people first paddled ashore in Australia. The seas were much lower back then, thanks to water being locked up in ice sheets. So the distance they had to travel on rafts was far less

than it would be today. People also headed west to Europe, arriving about 50,000 years ago.

As *Homo sapiens* settled around the world, other human species were vanishing. The last Neanderthals died out sometime between 40,000 and 28,000 years ago.

No one is quite sure why other human species who lived at the same time as *Homo sapiens* went extinct. Did we kill them off? Did we eat all of the available food? Did some deadly disease come along that affected only them and not us? Or did we just mix with them until they became part of us? We don't know. What we do know is that once Neanderthals were gone, there was only one human species left. Us.

Until about 12,000 years ago, people moved around all the time from place to place. They probaby hunted animals and gathered wild fruit and nuts. A person who travels all their life is called a nomad, and the lifestyle they lead is known as nomadic.

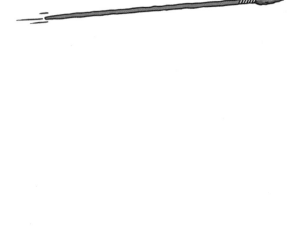

Such people had few possessions. The more they owned, the more they had to carry from one place to another. Sharing made for a better way of life.

The most important thing to carry with you on a long trek is water. You never know when you'll find a stream, but you know you are sure to get thirsty. To solve that problem, humans dried gourds, vegetables belonging to the same family as pumpkins. When they're dried, their shells harden, and the seeds and fibre inside can be removed to leave a perfect water container. Prehistoric nomads used plenty of those.

Nomadic people would also carry spears or bows and arrows for hunting. They had flint tools for skinning dead animals and lighting fires.

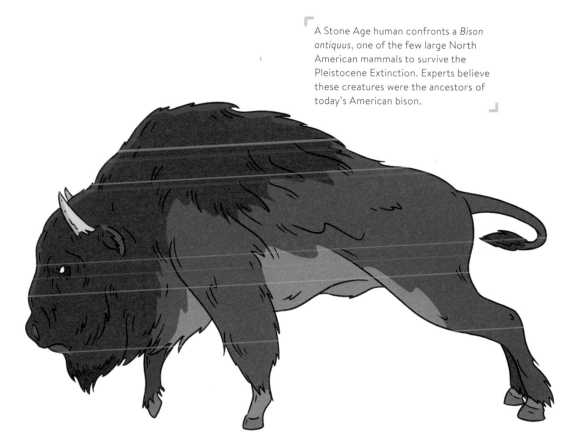

A Stone Age human confronts a *Bison antiquus*, one of the few large North American mammals to survive the Pleistocene Extinction. Experts believe these creatures were the ancestors of today's American bison.

One of the best-preserved examples of a nomad is Ötzi the Iceman. Two German holidaymakers unexpectedly bumped into him while walking in the Italian Alps in the summer of 1991. It was quite a shock to find a dead body in the ice. It turned out that this wasn't any old body but one that had been frozen in the ground, on the edge of a glacier, for more than 5,000 years.

Now 5,000 years ago is a *lot* more recent than 12,000 years ago. But still Ötzi provides some good clues as to what an ancient nomadic life might have been like.

Ötzi's body froze soon after he died, so it was preserved as a mummy. No one knows why he was walking in the mountains or where he was going, but close to his body was a prehistoric backpack. It had everything he needed for his journey. There was a copper axe, arrows for hunting and a blade sharpener. He even had a birch bark tube for carrying embers to light fires. Ötzi was clearly an expert mountaineer.

Bow and arrows, stone tools and a copper axe

Coat made out of goat and sheep hide, fastened with a belt

Backpack

Dagger

When nomadic people migrated, they changed the world as they went. Over the last 2.6 million years, glaciers have come and gone, sometimes covering the northern parts of the world for thousands of years at a time. Each time the climate has changed, individual species, including humans, adapted to different climates, hot or cold. And when one species died out, others evolved to take its place.

When the Earth was warming up from a frozen time called the last glacial maximum, the story should have been just the same. But it wasn't. Dozens of large mammals were alive and well all over the world when the warming started. Some of them had existed for tens of millions of years. Yet, between about 13,000 years ago and about 8,000 years ago, most of the biggest of them died out. This disaster is known as the Pleistocene Extinction after the era when it happened.

In North and South America, horses, big cats, elephants, mammoths and mastodons, camels, great bears, giant beavers, peccaries (pig-like mammals), giant ground sloths and the glyptodont – an armadillo the size of a pick-up truck – all mysteriously

Shoes of deer hide and bearskin

Under his warm clothes, the Iceman had several tattoos. Because they were applied over injuries such as broken bones, experts think they were part of a healing ritual among his people.

disappeared. In all, about three-quarters of the large mammals became extinct. When the Pleistocene Extinction was over, very few animals in the Americas were bigger than a turkey. Even the beavers and bears that made it through the crisis were smaller cousins of those giants that once existed.

Pretty much the same thing happened in Australia, although the extinctions there started earlier. Victims included the giant kangaroo, a rhino-sized wombat and its relatives, and a fierce marsupial lion. Huge reptiles died off, too, including the giant horned tortoise and some gigantic crocodiles.

Large animals went extinct in other parts of the world as well. The southern half of Africa lost fewer than the rest. But even there about one in every six big mammal species went extinct. Experts find this whole worldwide extinction event puzzling because no new large animals arose to take the places of those who had disappeared.

What on earth was going on? Some experts point to global warming, which changed environments worldwide, even where it had never been cold. As a result, large animals lost habitat. But climate alone doesn't explain the timing of some of the extinctions.

In many places, the extinctions followed the arrival of humans in the area. Maybe they were to blame. Could humans have hunted all these giants to extinction? Or did fire-lighting humans burn so many animal habitats so quickly that the animals couldn't survive?

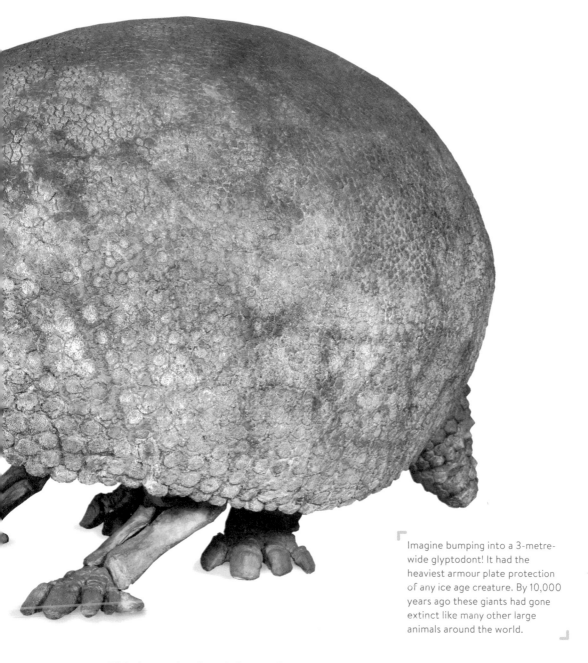

Imagine bumping into a 3-metre-wide glyptodont! It had the heaviest armour plate protection of any ice age creature. By 10,000 years ago these giants had gone extinct like many other large animals around the world.

This hypothesis might explain why elephants, rhinos and big cats survived in Africa when animals like them went extinct elsewhere. African animals and humans had evolved together over millions of years. Could they have found a balance that let both survive?

The point of having a hypothesis is to test it against other evidence, to ask questions that might prove or disprove it. For example, if humans caused the extinction, why did Africa lose any animals at all? As often happens in science, we don't know all the answers. We just have to keep making hypotheses and questioning them. There could be more than one cause. Perhaps humans and climate change are both to blame for the Pleistocene Extinction.

The part we played at the beginning of the last second to midnight on the twenty-four-hour clock of Earth history may have been our first big impact on the Earth's environment. It was not to be the last.

Percentage of large mammals that went extinct after the Pleistocene Extinction

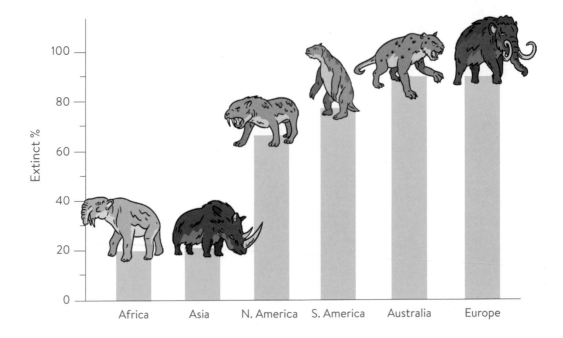

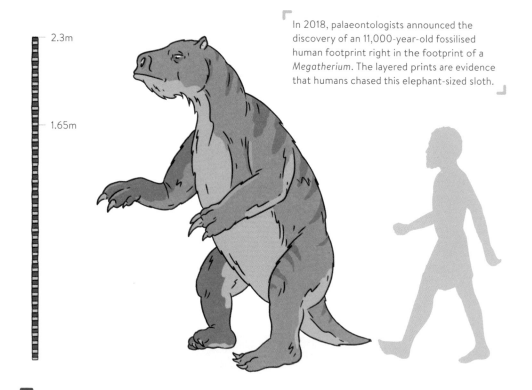

2.3m

1.65m

In 2018, palaeontologists announced the discovery of an 11,000-year-old fossilised human footprint right in the footprint of a *Megatherium*. The layered prints are evidence that humans chased this elephant-sized sloth.

Imagine living in a world where there are no shops selling food. In this world there are no fields or farms, no milk, no bread, no cakes, no cauliflower. You and your family live off wild fruits and nuts. You scavenge leftovers from animals killed by predators. You roast meat on a fire after a successful hunt. This was the way people lived for most of human history.

Some of the first people to try out a new way of life lived in an area of the Middle East known as the Fertile Crescent about 11,000 years ago. This was a rich land with just the right amount of rain for growing things. Forests of oak and pistachio trees thrived. People known as Natufians had settled near the coast in what is now Syria, Lebanon and Israel. The sea provided them with a good source of fish. They also went up into the nearby hills, where wild grasses grew.

There were so many good things to eat that the people didn't need to be nomadic. They lived in small villages in round mud and clay huts and gathered food from the land around them. In some seasons they would hunt for wild animals, such as gazelles.

Natufian people loved dogs. All pet dogs today – from a pug to a poodle – are actually part of the sames species as the grey wolf. Some wolves started to evolve into dogs as long as 40,000 years ago. Later, humans started breeding dogs to be great workers that can pull sleds, herd sheep or guard against attack. And they were also bred to be great friends. We don't know what work Natufian dogs did – or if they did any at all. All we know is that graves have been found in which they have been buried side by side with their humans. As a dog lover myself, knowing that makes me feel close to these people from the far distant past.

Descendants of the Natufians were among the world's first farmers. But the seeds they grew were very different from the seeds farmers use today.

In the wild, seeds from grasses like wheat need to be as light as possible and loosely attached to the stalk. That way they have the best chance of being blown far and wide on the wind. But small seeds that fall easily to the ground are a farmer's nightmare. Instead they want big seeds that stay firmly attached to the stalk. If a grain of wheat gets blown away by the wind, you won't be able to use it for food or for planting next year's crop, because it's gone – poof!

So how did early farmers get bigger seeds? It's pretty simple,

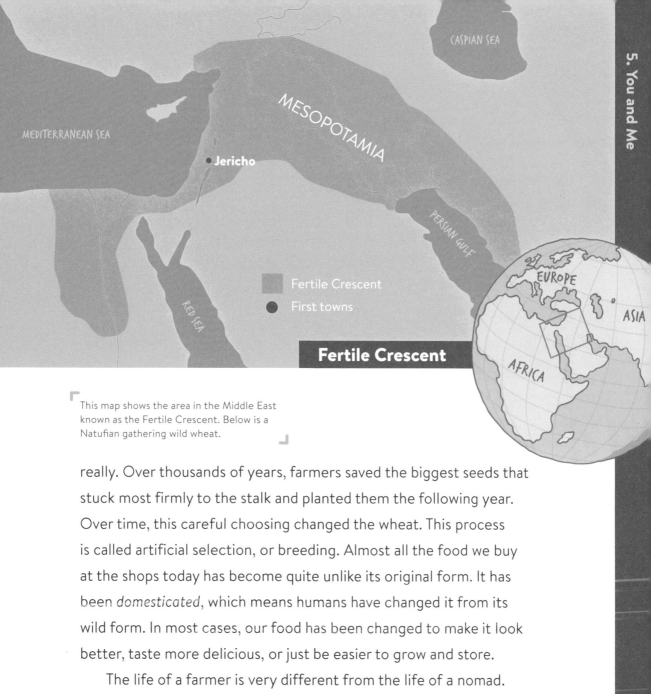

MEDITERRANEAN SEA

CASPIAN SEA

MESOPOTAMIA

• **Jericho**

PERSIAN GULF

RED SEA

Fertile Crescent

● First towns

Fertile Crescent

EUROPE

ASIA

AFRICA

This map shows the area in the Middle East known as the Fertile Crescent. Below is a Natufian gathering wild wheat.

really. Over thousands of years, farmers saved the biggest seeds that stuck most firmly to the stalk and planted them the following year. Over time, this careful choosing changed the wheat. This process is called artificial selection, or breeding. Almost all the food we buy at the shops today has become quite unlike its original form. It has been *domesticated*, which means humans have changed it from its wild form. In most cases, our food has been changed to make it look better, taste more delicious, or just be easier to grow and store.

The life of a farmer is very different from the life of a nomad. Farmers have to stick close to home so they can grow crops, harvest the fields and care for their animals. They also need to put up buildings for storing food so it doesn't get wet and go rotten. Sheds and barns are needed to protect livestock against winter cold and wild animals.

Farming 10,500 years ago was a lot harder than it is today. There were no ploughs, tractors or combine harvesters to help back then. Planting, weeding, digging, harvesting and grinding seeds into flour between slabs of heavy stone were just a few of the tasks that had to be done by hand. Skeletons of early farmers tell the grim story. They often have twisted toes, buckled backs and knobbly knees.

Jericho is one of the world's oldest towns. It was founded by Natufians and has been lived in continuously for about 11,000 years. Round houses from 9,000 years ago had more than one room and open spaces for cooking and washing. These early buildings were built on solid foundations, with stone floors and walls made of clay bricks. Each home had its own special corner for storing grain and other food. For these people, the days of living on the move were long gone.

As farmers bred better crops, they were able to make enough food to do more than feed their families. They could swap any extra food for useful or beautiful things other people had made. That meant some people didn't have to farm at all. People made things that could be given to farmers in exchange for food.

Some people made pots, pans, jewellery and clothes. Others developed tools and technologies such as wheels, chariots and armour. They mined metals from the ground and figured out how to process them to make objects out of copper, bronze, tin and iron.

Obsidian is natural glass that forms when lava from a volcano cools quickly. It was a very precious material because it was brilliant for cutting animal skins to make clothes. Obsidian occurs naturally in the rocky hills of central Turkey, but experts have found carefully shaped pieces hundreds of miles away in ancient Jericho. How did they get there?

Well, what if you had been alive back then? Perhaps you might have thought about swapping some of your precious seeds for that natural glass found only in some far-off land?

Merchants are people who buy goods and then sell them. This is called trade. When merchants started trading across long distances, they needed carts and ships to transport their goods. And of course they needed plenty of goods to trade. Eventually, trade led to a form of exchange very familiar to us today. We call it money.

When a lot of people live close together doing different jobs and trading with one another, you have what is called a civilisation. So that means it's almost time to meet our first kings and queens.

These super-sharp tools, dating from 5,000 years ago, are made out of a natural glass called obsidian.

Chapter 6

CIVILISATION BEGINS

5000–1500 BCE
Writing kicks off a new era

5000 BCE
The Nabta Playa
stone circle in
Nubia is built.

5000 BCE
Megalithic buildings
– giant temples and
stone circles – begin
being built in various
sites across Europe.

3500 BCE
Sumerian civilisation
is the first to develop
writing and the wheel.

3300 BCE
People living in the Indus
Valley start to build trading
settlements that turn into
towns and cities.

3000 BCE
Norte Chico people build their first pyramids.

2550 BCE
The Pyramid of Giza is built in Egypt to house the tomb of the pharoah Khufu.

1700 BCE
The Minoan civilisation reaches its peak on the island of Crete.

30 BCE
The rule of phaorahs in Egypt ends for ever when the Roman Empire defeats Cleopatra's armies.

S I L O P

= PTOLMIIS

The name of Egyptian king Ptolemy V
is inscribed in the Rosetta Stone. Here
is his name in hieroglyphics.

I

magine someone said they had invented an amazing new mind-reading technology. This person claimed that their system could transfer the thoughts from your brain into the mind of someone else. It would work from thousands of miles away. You could even use this system to find out what they thought long after they were dead. Would you believe them?

Amazingly, that technology really does exist. And, believe it or not, it was invented more than 5,000 years ago. Here's how it works.

You take a thought in your brain, convert it into a code and put the code on to an object. Now you give the object to someone else who already knows the code. They read the code and, hey presto, your thoughts are now inside their brain!

This mind-reading technology is called writing.

If you were imagining some kind of fancy ancient helmet with wires sticking out of it, you may feel a bit disappointed. Sorry about that. But many of the things we take for granted as ordinary today are extraordinary achievements developed in the ancient past. Writing is just that. No other creature on the planet can do it. Only we humans.

Technically, history begins with writing. It's what we learn about the past by reading what people have written down. Everything before is prehistory, or prehistoric.

The Rosetta Stone, found in Egypt in 1799, contains the same text written in three scripts, including Egyptian hieroglyphics and Ancient Greek. Since historians knew Ancient Greek, they used the stone to decipher the hieroglyphics.

No one knows who invented writing. It is highly unlikely that any one person did. But from about 3400 BCE, we see the first clear use of written symbols. That's one-tenth of a second from midnight on our twenty-four-hour clock.

If you're wondering what the BCE stands for, it means Before the Common Era. The Common Era begins at the year 1. Anything before is BCE. Anything after is CE. For example, my dad was born in 1936 CE. Pharaoh Cleopatra, who we'll meet later in this chapter, died in 30 BCE. We tend to leave the letters CE off dates with four numbers in them, such as 2018.

Writing began with merchants of the Middle East, who drew simple pictures on clay tablets to represent the things they were buying and selling. Next to each picture, they made marks for how many of these things changed hands. These tablets were baked in

Sumerian language

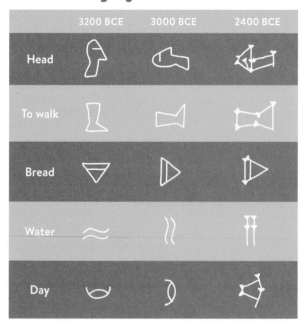

Sumerian script evolved over time. Also at first, the direction of the writing went from top to bottom but later changed so it was read from left to right.

This clay tablet, carved by an Assyrian merchant, is written in cuneiform text. It says that about 3kg of silver is owed to him by two men and explains how he would like it paid.

ovens to make their marks permanent, creating an unchangeable set of records. This meant that merchants could trade without losing track of what they had bought and sold.

Over time, wedge-shaped marks replaced the pictures. This style of writing is called *cuneiform* (which means 'wedge-shaped'). It forms the basis for three of the oldest written languages in the world – Sumerian, Assyrian and Babylonian.

Sumeria was an ancient civilisation in the south of Mesopotamia, a land in the heart of what is now Iraq. Experts believe writing first appeared here.

Sumeria grew up along two rivers called the Euphrates and the Tigris. Fresh water from these rivers meant the people could flood their fields. That made just the right conditions for their crops to thrive. The river valley also provided two long flowing superhighways. People could use wooden boats to carry themselves and their goods from one riverside city to the next.

We know a great deal about this very old civilisation, in part thanks to an extraordinary discovery.

It was the 1840s in England, and Austen Layard wasn't having any fun being a lawyer. So, he decided to go on an adventure. He headed for the distant island of Ceylon, now Sri Lanka, off the southern tip of India. But he never got there. His trek took him through the Middle East, where he got very interested in archaeology, studying the remains of ancient civilisations. He worked on several important digs and even wrote a book. Then, about ten years after he first left London, he decided to investigate a mound of earth across the Tigris River from the town of Mosul.

> ON ALL SIDES, AS FAR AS THE EYE COULD REACH, ROSE THE GRASS-COVERED HEAPS MARKING THE SITE OF ANCIENT HABITATIONS.

Austen Layard,
archaeologist

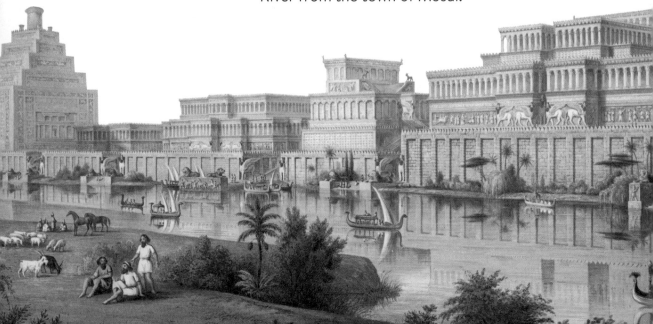

The mound turned out to be the ancient Assyrian capital of Nineveh, which had been destroyed in 612 BCE. Layard and his team uncovered a giant palace. Even more important, they found a huge royal library. We call it the Library of Ashurbanipal after the ruler who we think built it. It contained a staggering 30,000 clay tablets covered with cuneiform writing. These tablets have transformed our understanding of life in ancient Mesopotamia.

The most famous tablets from the ancient library tell of the adventures of Gilgamesh, an early Sumerian king. Gilgamesh had been a real-life king who ruled one of the first Sumerian cities, called Uruk, located on the bank of the Euphrates River. Uruk was the largest city in the world at the time. As many as 80,000 people lived there.

The Epic of Gilgamesh, probably first written down in about 2000 BCE, is a poetic fantasy. It tells the story of a character called Gilgamesh, who was two-thirds god, one-third human. Gilgamesh goes on an epic journey in search of a way to live for ever. It is the very first written work of fiction that we know of.

This statue shows Gilgamesh taming a lion. It depicts the ruler's power and strength.

It isn't just writing that we owe to these creative people. They also loved maths. The Sumerian counting system was based on the number sixty. It's a great number to base a maths system on because there are so many ways to divide it (by two, three, four,

After his amazing discovery, Austen Layard made drawings of the palace of Nineveh. In 1853, architect James Fergusson used the drawings to create this painting of what it may have looked like.

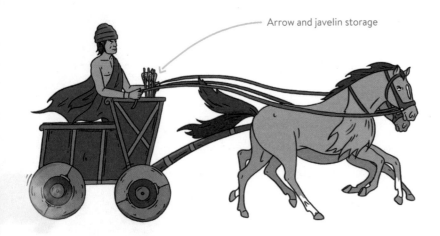

Arrow and javelin storage

Wheels gave Sumerians the ability to attack enemies from a moving chariot, pulled by horses.

five, six, ten, twelve, fifteen, twenty, thirty). It's thanks to the Sumerians that we have sixty seconds in a minute, sixty minutes in an hour and 360 degrees in a circle.

As if that weren't enough, these ingenious people came up with the most revolutionary invention of all time – the wheel. The first wheels we know about were potters' wheels, used to make clay pots. These were invented in about 3500 BCE, around the same time as writing. By about 300 years later, Mesopotamians had wheeled chariots. Who made the leap from making pots with wheels to carrying pots on carts? We don't know.

Like all human civilisations, Sumer didn't last for ever. About 2200 BCE, a terrible drought lasting over 200 years devastated the region. Land around river mouths became impossible to farm because seawater made it too salty. In a bid for survival, the Sumerian cities were fighting among themselves and with their neighbours. Finally, in 1787 BCE, Babylon conquered Sumeria and made it part of the Babylonian empire.

> **THEY DEVISED SUCH USEFUL TOOLS, SKILLS AND TECHNIQUES AS THE POTTER'S WHEEL, THE WAGON WHEEL, THE PLOUGH, THE SAILBOAT, THE ARCH, THE VAULT, THE DOME, CASTING IN COPPER AND BRONZE, RIVETING, BRAZING AND SOLDERING, SCULPTURE.**
>
> Samuel Noah Kramer, Assyriologist

magine you are a mighty ancient king and a genie pops out of a magic lamp.

"You can have as many wishes as you want!" says the spirit.

How would you respond? Would you ask for all the money in the world? To be able to boss everyone around? Or how about some all-powerful magic ring that would make you live for ever?

History is full of stories about people who have wanted power and riches. But the first rulers who believed they could have it all came from ancient Egypt.

Ancient Egypt

Ancient Egyptians built some of the most incredible monuments and cities in the ancient world, most of them along the banks of the Nile River.

These all-powerful rulers were called pharaohs. More than 150 of them reigned over ancient Egypt from about 3000 BCE to 30 BCE. That's about 3,000 years!

The Egyptian people believed pharaohs were living gods and that when they died they joined all the other gods in heaven. These divine rulers took full advantage of their power. They had some amazing palaces, temples and tombs built for them.

Have you heard of the seven wonders of the ancient world? Only one of them still survives today. It's called the Great Pyramid of Giza and was built as a tomb for one of the earliest pharaohs, called Khufu, who died in 2566 BCE.

This giant construction originally towered skywards 147 metres. That's about as high as a fifty-storey building. It is made of more than 2 million blocks of stone, each one weighing as much as a minivan. Experts are still puzzled at how these ancient people could have cut, transported and hauled into place so many huge stones. They didn't even have wheels. And it was all to create a grave for one man-god.

The pharaohs may have believed they were gods, but their power depended on something quite natural – a giant river. The Nile is one of the longest rivers in the world. It flows north from central Africa into Egypt. Along the way, it picks up lots of fresh, nutrient-rich mud, which it dumps on Egypt's fields when it floods every year. Mud like this is just the right stuff for growing an almost unlimited supply of food. And plentiful food made Egypt rich and the pharaohs powerful.

Another natural feature helped the pharaohs hold on to that power. The little strip of fertile land next to the Nile was surrounded by desert. Today we know this huge dry area as the Sahara. This giant desert protected Egypt from invaders. The pharaohs didn't need fancy walls, towers or castles to keep their country safe. Invaders could only approach in one of three ways. They could cross hundreds of miles of desert. Or they had to come by sea and wade through the boggy, reedy marshes of the Nile where it flows into the Mediterranean. Or they could come down the Nile from what is now Ethiopia and Sudan. The first two ways were well protected by nature. The third less so.

Up the river lay Egypt's most regular trading partners, the Nubians, who were sometimes friends and sometimes foes. Egypt imported gold, ivory, copper, incense and animals from people living in the tropical areas of central Africa. All of those goods

More than 70m long, the Great Sphinx has the face of a human and the body of a lion. Notice the pyramid of Khafre in the background? It's the second largest of the ancient Egyptian pyramids of Giza and was built for Pharoah Khafre, son of Pharaoh Khufu, whose own pyramid is nearby.

came through Nubian traders. Nubians were also famous as brave warriors who were brilliant shots with a bow and arrow.

Nubians came from a very old civilisation. As early as 5000 BCE, their ancestors had constructed a ring of stones that may have been the very first structure built to study the stars and planets. This astronomical observatory dates from 2,000 years before England's famous ancient stone circle, Stonehenge.

At times the Egyptians conquered parts of Nubia. At other times members of the two countries' ruling families married. And once Nubia – at that time called Kush – conquered Egypt. Their leaders became Egyptian pharaohs for 200 years.

Egypt's relationship with its southern neighbours was made easy (and sometimes dangerous) by another accident of nature.

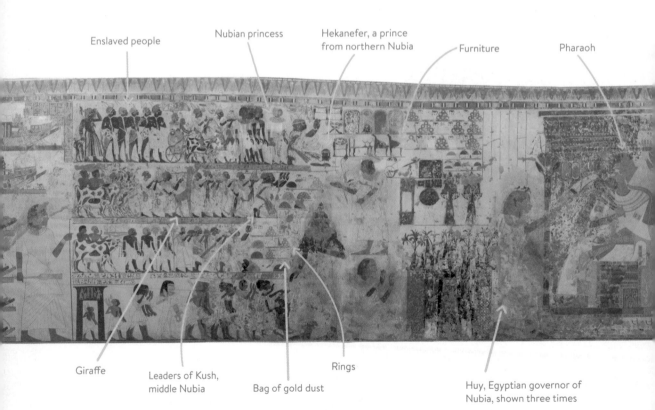

Enslaved people

Nubian princess

Hekanefer, a prince from northern Nubia

Furniture

Pharaoh

Giraffe

Leaders of Kush, middle Nubia

Bag of gold dust

Rings

Huy, Egyptian governor of Nubia, shown three times

The winds in Egypt usually blow from north to south, the opposite direction from the flow of the river. That means people could float downstream in wooden boats. Then, when they wanted to return home, all they had to do was raise a sail and let the wind blow them back upstream. What could be more convenient?

Do you believe in life after death? How about your friends and family? If you ask them, I expect you will find some do and some don't. And among those who do, there are lots of different ways to believe in an afterlife. Some people believe in heaven and hell. Others believe in reincarnation. That's the idea that your spirit comes back to Earth in another person or even as a different living creature.

In the days of ancient Egypt, everyone believed in life after death. And they believed they were going to need to pack some things to take with them when they went to the afterlife.

A pyramid showed off how rich and powerful a pharaoh was. But it also provided a safe place to store all the things the pharaoh would need in the next life. And that included his or her body.

In the mid-1920s, before the invention of colour photography, museum artist Charles Wilkinson copied paintings on the walls of the tomb of Huy, the Egyptian governor of Nubia during the time of Pharaoh Tutankhamun (1336–1327 BCE). We are lucky he did because many of the originals have been damaged or destroyed since. This painting shows a group of Nubian leaders bringing gifts (including gold, exotic animals and enslaved people) for King Tut. Nubia was very ethnically diverse, as you can see from the wide range of skin colours shown here.

A rotten body wouldn't be of much use, though, even in a fancy tomb. So, the Egyptians invented a way to preserve dead bodies by turning them into mummies. It was a complicated process that could take as long as seventy days.

Mummification wasn't just for pharaohs. Anybody in ancient Egypt who could possibly afford it made absolutely sure they were mummified when they died. Some people even had their pets mummified.

The expert who performed mummifications was a special priest called an embalmer. First, the embalmer removed the stomach, intestines, lungs and liver from the body. He then dried them out and placed each in its own container called a canopic jar.

Usually, the embalmer removed the brain, too. Herodotus, an ancient Greek writer who saw a mummification, wrote that to get

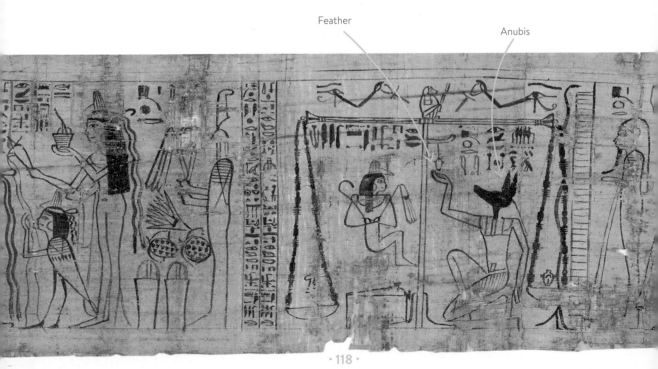

Feather

Anubis

the brain out of the skull, the embalmer punched a hole from inside the nose into the brain cavity. Then he pulled the brain out with a hook. For centuries people thought this was how it was done. But now it looks as if he didn't understand what he was seeing.

Two American researchers, Bob Brier and Ron Wade, did an experiment in 1994 that showed brains are too soft for a hook to work. So probably what happened was this: the embalmer stuck a stick through the hole in the back of the nose into the brain and gave it a good stir. Brains are very soft, sort of like yogurt. When the embalmer stirred hard, the brain turned to liquid and oozed out through the nostrils.

The heart was the only organ the embalmer left in the body. The ancient Egyptians believed that this was the seat of the soul, where people did their thinking and feeling. They thought that in the next

Anubis, the jackal-headed god of the dead, weighs a dead person's heart against a feather to see if the person's soul should enter the afterlife.

life the gods would weigh it to judge if the person had lived a good or bad life on Earth.

Once the organs were removed, the embalmer packed the corpse with a special salt called natron to dry it out. When it was dry, he stuffed the corpse with linen and sawdust, added fake eyes, and wrapped it in strips of cloth. The finished mummy was packed inside a coffin called a sarcophagus and placed in a tomb. In the case of a pharaoh, that tomb might be a pyramid.

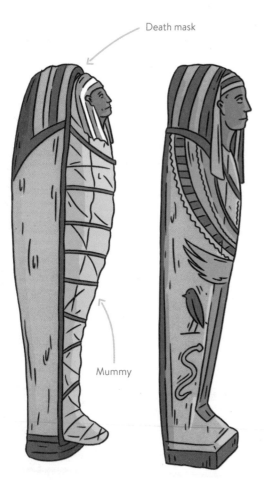

Death mask

Mummy

Sarcophagus bottom   Sarcophagus lid

All around the body was everything that the dead pharaoh could possibly need in the afterlife. Archaeologists have found food, drink, crowns, tableware, weapons, clothes, books, pictures and even games and toys in tombs. The tombs of important people contained teams of servants. Luckily these weren't real people. They were wooden or stone dolls, called shabti. Their purpose was to come to the dead souls of their masters or mistresses whenever they needed help.

Experts know a lot of this because the ancient Egyptians had writing. They used a system called hieroglyphics. They might

A sarcophagus was a metal or stone container that housed a mummy to protect it from tomb robbers and animals.

have got the idea of writing from the Sumerians, but nobody knows. In any case, they wrote down their burial rituals in The Book of the Dead. This collection of texts also includes magic spells, which were written and illustrated on scrolls and placed in tombs. The spells were meant to help the souls of the dead pass through the dangers of the underworld and into an afterlife of everlasting joy.

You see, writing really does allow us to see inside the minds of people who have been dead for thousands of years.

In about 2040 BCE, the capital of Egypt was moved south to a city called Thebes. Here the burials continued. But there was one important difference. Pharaohs no longer built grand pyramids for all to see. Instead their tombs were carved into rock underground. They showed off above ground by building temples.

Hundreds of underground tombs have been discovered in the Valleys of the Kings, Queens and Nobles, near Thebes. Remarkably, some have survived almost completely intact.

Maybe you have seen a film or read a book about someone finding treasures buried in ancient tombs? Most of these stories are fiction. Here is one that is true.

Howard Carter was a British archaeologist who had been working in the Valley of the Kings on and off for fifteen years. One day, on 4 November 1922, a member of his team found some steps leading into what he hoped was the tomb they had been looking for.

The team spent the next three weeks very carefully removing the sand and rock that covered the doorway of the tomb. Once they got inside, they saw Carter had been right. They were standing in the burial chamber of boy-king Tutankhamun. King Tut had become pharaoh when he was only nine and died when he was nineteen.

A huge hoard of treasure was packed inside the chamber. The most famous object of all was the boy-king's funeral mask, made out of solid gold. It was placed on Tut's face underneath three layers of gold coffins inside a stone sarcophagus.

In the end, even the natural defences surrounding ancient Egypt weren't enough to save it. The last true pharaoh, Cleopatra VII

Howard Carter (left) and one of his assistants examine the mummy of King Tut. The discovery of the boy king's tomb wasn't important because King Tut was a super important Pharaoh. He probably wasn't. It's because most of the things buried with him were still there. All of the other Egyptian tombs ever found by archaeologists before this had been mostly empty, their treasures stolen by tomb robbers.

Philopater, is usually known simply as Cleopatra. She ruled Egypt mostly by herself even though she was supposed to be co-pharaoh with her younger brother Ptolemy. When her army was defeated by the Romans, she killed herself rather than surrender. The story is that she took her own life by letting a poisonous snake bite her. But probably she committed suicide some other way, though some think she was murdered. No one knows for sure.

Cleopatra was a brilliant politician. No one can be sure what she looked like because portraits of her done during her lifetime, including this 2,000-year-old coin, look very different from one another.

Once Cleopatra was gone, independent Egypt was no more.

At about the same time as the all-powerful pharaohs were ruling in Egypt, a totally different type of civilisation was thriving in what is now Pakistan, India and Afghanistan.

Once again it was formed along the banks of a giant river. This one is called the Indus. But this civilisation covered an area twice the size of either Egypt or Sumeria. At its height, it was as large as modern Western Europe. It is known as the Indus Valley civilisation.

Archaeologists have found about 1,000 cities and settlements in the Indus Valley. They date to between 3300 and about 1900 BCE. That's about the same time period as Sumeria.

One of the two big cities was Mohenjo-Daro. It was laid out in regular blocks like a modern city. Each street was connected to a water supply and sewers. Excavations have unearthed large public buildings, including a meeting place that could hold up to 5,000 people.

These people wove cotton, made beautiful pottery and crafted copper and bronze into fine jewellery and statues. And they seem to have lived mostly in peace. Lots of toys and games have been found, but very few weapons.

Unlike in Egypt and Sumeria, there were no royal tombs here. And there were no fancy pyramids or big palaces that usually come with rich rulers. Plus there is no evidence of a single all-powerful king or queen.

But here's the thing – we can't be completely sure. The Indus Valley civilisation had writing, probably inventing it just after the Sumerians. But nobody has yet figured out how to read it. For that reason, we only know what we can learn from the objects the Indus Valley people left behind. Their stories are still waiting to be decoded.

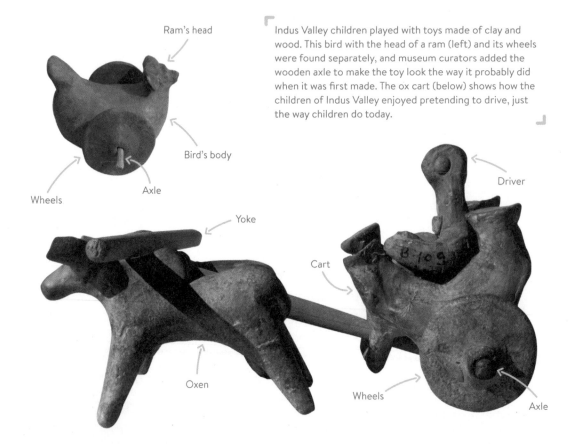

Ram's head

Bird's body

Wheels

Axle

Indus Valley children played with toys made of clay and wood. This bird with the head of a ram (left) and its wheels were found separately, and museum curators added the wooden axle to make the toy look the way it probably did when it was first made. The ox cart (below) shows how the children of Indus Valley enjoyed pretending to drive, just the way children do today.

Driver

Yoke

Cart

Oxen

Wheels

Axle

While the Egyptians were building their pyramids, the Sumerians were inventing the wheel and the Indus Valley people were laying out their efficient cities, another major civilisation was doing some of the same things. Norte Chico in what is now Peru included dozens of cities along rivers. They built irrigation canals to water their fields. Like the Indus Valley people, it seems the Norte Chicoans were peaceful people, with no sign of weapons, defences or war injuries.

And like the Egyptians, these people had mummies and pyramids. Their mummies may have been naturally dried rather than being embalmed by priests, though. And they built their first pyramids in around 3000 BCE, even before the Egyptians built theirs. The mummy of a leader we call the Woman of the Four Brooches was found inside one of the biggest pyramids.

But there were important differences. The Norte Chico people farmed in different ways to the farmers of the other three cultures. They grew vegetables, including squash, beans, avocados and sweet potatoes. Their main crop was cotton, which was farmed inland and traded to coastal groups in exchange for fish and other seafood. Fishermen then used the cotton to make nets.

Because cotton was so important, some experts think these people made beautiful textiles like later Peruvian cultures did and still do. They played music on decorated flutes and had gatherings in huge plazas. They wore carved jewellery and drew figures that might have been gods on gourds. But they didn't paint their buildings or build large sculptures. And they didn't have pottery, which meant they had to roast their food rather than cooking it in water.

As far as we know, the Norte Chico didn't have a written language. They used a set of strings called quipu to keep track of numbers for trade. Some archaeologists think quipu were also used to record language. If that's true, it's yet another language we don't know how to read.

These major civilisations were not the only ones to leave remarkable remains between 5000 and 1500 BCE. Cultures all over the world were creating communities, trading with their neighbours and making art. Europeans are famous for building massive structures near their graves. These were usually made from enormous blocks of local stone. This is why their culture is known as megalithic (*mega* means 'big' and *lithic* means 'stone').

Many of these stone structures were set upright in circles, like Stonehenge in England,

Was Stonehenge in England a venue for royal ceremonies, a site for worshipping the dead or or a way to predict solar eclipses? No one knows for certain.

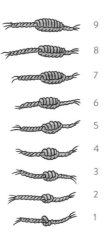

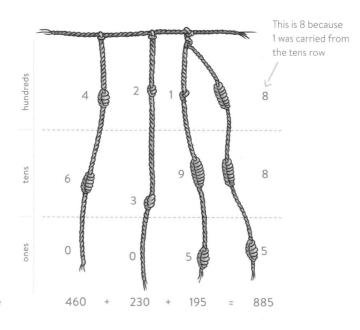

This is 8 because 1 was carried from the tens row

hundreds	4	2	1	8
tens	6	3	9	8
ones	0	0	5	5

460 + 230 + 195 = 885

Quipu could have up to 1,500 wool or cotton strings hanging down. The number of turns in each knot, their position and the number of knots on the string add up to a value.

which dates back to about 3000 BCE. In other places they were constructed as temples, with altar tables at one end or in the centre. Famous surviving examples include Hagar Qim on the Mediterranean island of Malta. Sometimes the structures were lined up with the rising and setting Sun or arranged in other ways that helped people keep track of the seasons.

Most ancient rulers we know about were men. And in most societies men had more power than women. So it's easy to assume that's always the way it was, everywhere and at every time.

But that's not quite true. There were some women pharaohs in Egypt. Many early civilisations had powerful female gods. And in Ancient Egypt and Sumeria, women were men's equals under the law and could run businesses and own property. We know from the way women were buried in Norte Chico that they held important roles in society. But nowhere in this period were women and men more clearly equals than in the Minoan civilisation on the Mediterranean island of Crete from about 2000 to 1600 BCE.

Accounts from ancient Greek historians and images on vases and wall paintings describe a society in which both men and women participated in all daily activities. There were no special roles for one or the other, and priestesses were some of the most important people in society. One of the most striking examples of equality on Crete is sporting contests where women and men both competed.

A favourite sport was bull-leaping. A gymnast (a woman or man) would grab the horns of a bull and somersault on to its back. Then, in a second somersault, she or he would leap off its back and land upright back on the ground.

> " AT THE BIRTH OF SOCIETY AND CIVILISATION I FIND A RELIGIOUS LANDSCAPE LITTERED WITH FEISTY FEMALE DEITIES WHO MAKE WISDOM THEIR BUSINESS. "
>
> Bettany Hughes, historian

It's possible women were actually more important than men in Minoan society. And some experts think their goddesses were more important than their gods. When Minoan writing – the first ever in Europe – is deciphered, perhaps we'll know for sure.

Unfortunately, this society was not to last after men on horseback, equipped with metal weapons, swept across Asia, Europe and the Middle East.

But before we get to them, let's turn our attention to two civilisations in Asia that would beat the odds and last even longer than Ancient Egypt.

Chapter 7

MEANWHILE, IN ASIA

3000–200 BCE
More powerful civilisations thrive

○ **2697 BCE**
Legendary beginning
of silk-making

○ **1600 BCE**
The Shang dynasty
begins.

○ **1500–1200 BCE**
The Hindu Vedas are
composed.

○ **500 BCE**
Confucius and Buddha
teach new ways to live.

500 BCE
People in China develop the blast furnace to make cast iron.

300–200 BCE
Steel is invented in India.

261 BCE
King Ashoka converts to Buddhism and works to build a kingdom of peace.

221 BCE
Qin Shi Huang becomes the first emperor of China.

W hat if Olympic medals were given to countries? In that contest, the two biggest contenders would be China and India. Today China is home to more than 1.4 billion people. India is close behind with more than 1.3 billion. Together, that's more than one-third of all the people in the whole world. What's more, India and China are home to some of the most amazing civilisations ever.

On the list of ancient Chinese inventions are paper, gunpowder, the compass, printing and umbrellas. Indians invented the number zero and the game of chess. They wrote the longest poem in history. They founded the very first university. And they were the first people to produce high-quality steel in large quantities.

Jump back to about 2500 BCE. Sumerian and Indus Valley civilisations are at their height, and the Egyptian pharaohs are about 500 years into their long rule. Two other civilisations are thriving in China. The Longshan live along the banks of the Yellow River in the north, and the Liangzhu live next to the enormous Yangtze River, further south.

It was the ancestors of the Liangzhu who first started to farm rice. It happened about 10,000 years ago in a place called Shangshan. Rice is an incredible crop. It can grow in both very wet and fairly dry

The first game of chess was played in India. It was called chaturanga. The pieces included a king, elephant, horse and soldier.

areas, so that means many kinds of land can be turned into rice fields. Rice gave China the ability to support a large population.

Rice farming also started very early in India, at the time of the Indus Valley civilisation. Some scientists think that rice farming spread to India from China. But recently archaeologists have found a different kind of rice grain in the Indus Valley. So maybe India started farming rice separately from China.

At about the same time that rice farming appeared in the south, people along the Yellow River started growing millet, another grass. Remember how farmers in Mesopotamia used selective breeding to make their wheat seeds bigger? These rice and millet farmers did the same thing with their seeds.

Archaeologists know what ancient people grew and ate because they have found remains of their food. These are usually just a few grains mixed with other finds. But sometimes they find a whole meal. In 2005, archaeologists working along the Yellow River found some 4,000-year-old millet noodles still in the pot. It's things like this that make us realise ancient people were just like us.

Rice is the most important crop for more than half of the world's population today.

Silk is extraordinary stuff. It reflects the light, making it look shiny and glamorous, and it's very strong. So it's a perfect fibre for clothing. Do you know where these lovely fibres come from?

The caterpillar of the moth *Bombyx mori* is the key. It munches the leaves of the mulberry tree for twenty to thirty-three days. Then it oozes out a continuous strand of silk more than a kilometre long, wrapping it around itself to make a cocoon. After ten to fourteen days, the caterpillar has changed into a moth, and out it comes. The common name of *Bombyx mori* is silkworm, but it's not a worm at all.

Archaeologists have found evidence of ancient people using silk. It was being farmed in China by about 3300 BCE and in the Indus Valley very soon after. And the very first writing in China talks about the silkworm spirit. Silk was very important even then to those who cared for the caterpillars and who wove their cocoons into cloth.

Thousands of years after the beginning of the silk trade, a story began to be told in China about the origin of silk-making. It stars

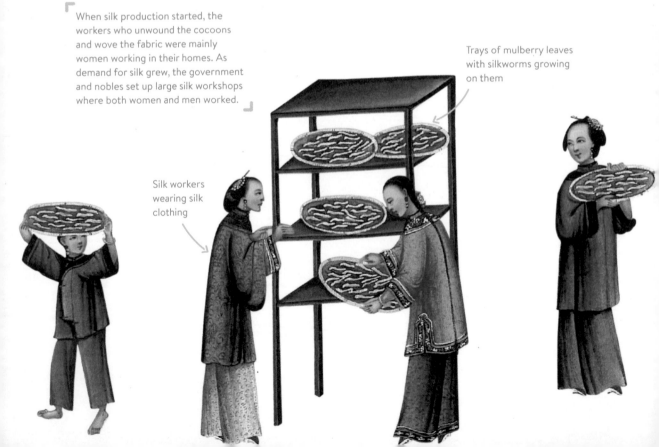

When silk production started, the workers who unwound the cocoons and wove the fabric were mainly women working in their homes. As demand for silk grew, the government and nobles set up large silk workshops where both women and men worked.

Trays of mulberry leaves with silkworms growing on them

Silk workers wearing silk clothing

Leizu. She was said to be the wife of the legendary Yellow Emperor, who is said to have lived from 2697 to 2598 BCE. Here's the story.

Leizu was out walking in the emperor's garden. There she saw thousands of caterpillars causing a great deal of damage by eating their way through the leaves of a grove of mulberry trees.

Curious to know more about these creatures, Leizu collected some of the cocoons and sat down to drink a cup of tea. While she was looking at one of the cocoons, she accidentally dropped it into the steaming water and a fine thread started to uncurl. Leizu found she could wrap this thin, strong cord around her finger. She persuaded the emperor to plant more mulberry trees. She then helped develop a process for making silk cloth.

Silk-making declined in India after the Indus Valley civilisation ended. That left China as the only place where people knew how to make this precious cloth. And for over 2,000 years they managed to keep the secret. That way anyone who wanted silk always had to buy it from China.

Legendary
Empress Leizu

Silk was so popular that the trade routes connecting China to the rest of the world became known as the Silk Road. The cloth's fine texture and shimmer made it one of the greatest luxuries of the ancient world.

Of course, the secret was bound to get out one day. As the story goes, in about 550 CE, some monks smuggled silkworms to Constantinople (now Istanbul, Turkey). From there it spread around the world, including to India, which is now a major producer of silk.

The first rulers of ancient China who we know for sure are real and not just legendary belong to the Shang dynasty (about 1600 to 1046 BCE). A dynasty is a series of rulers belonging to the same family. So in this period, China was ruled by the Shang family.

In the 1920s, archaeologists dug up a site called Yin. There they found eleven major royal tombs and the foundations of a giant Shang palace. Inside were tens of thousands of beautiful bronze, jade and stone objects. They also found impressive weapons that had helped the Shang conquer the land for hundreds of miles around.

We know a lot about the Shang dynasty because they wrote things down. But in their case, this writing wasn't records of trades or long stories. Rather, it was a way to communicate with the spirits.

Here's how it worked. If you were a king and had a question for the gods, you could write the question on a piece of turtle shell or ox bone. You might ask, *When will it rain? Will we win the next battle? Will we have a good silkworm crop this year?* Then you would hold a hot metal rod against the shell or bone until it cracked. You would interpret the length and direction of the cracks to reveal the gods' answers to questions. Sometimes

Bronze is a strong metal made from a mixture of copper and tin. Skilled Chinese metal-workers made this axe blade in the 1000s or 1100s BCE. It was made by heating bronze until it melted and then pouring it into a mould. This process is called casting.

you would write down your interpretation on the same bit of shell or bone.

Archaeologists have found more than 200,000 pieces of turtle shell and ox bone. About a quarter have questions and answers written on them. They are called oracle bones. Experts have found it easy to read some of these inscriptions because they match up pretty closely to modern Chinese writing.

Ancient Chinese people took great steps forward in iron production, too. Metallic iron is extracted from a rock called iron ore. The Iron Age is the name for the time when people first started doing this. It started around the Mediterranean Sea and in India in about 1200 BCE, in Nubia in about 1000 BCE, and in China in the 700s BCE.

One of the Shang kings, Wu Ding, asked the oracle bones about all parts of his life. He wanted to know the weather, whether he would win upcoming battles, whether he should give certain commands and even the cause of his toothaches.

To get the metal out of iron ore, workers mixed the ore with charcoal and heated it in a kind of furnace we now call a bloomery. The iron oxide in the ore reacted with carbon in the charcoal. That reaction produced the gas carbon dioxide. When the gas went up the furnace chimney, it left metallic iron behind, without ever melting the iron.

What came out was a lump of spongy metal that had to be heated and hammered for a long time to get the impurities out. Iron made this way is called wrought iron. It's a lot of work and can only be made into very simple shapes. But iron is stronger than bronze, the metal that was most common before. Iron swords introduced a new era of dangerous weapons all over the world.

Then, sometime about 500 BCE, someone in China made an enormous discovery. They figured out that if you can create a furnace that gets hotter, you get the same reaction between charcoal and iron oxide. But now the iron that comes out is hot liquid metal, which you can pour into moulds to make almost anything you like. The breakthrough invention is called a blast furnace. And iron made this way is called cast iron. We still use blast furnaces today, but it took a long time for the technology to appear

Iron ore and charcoal

Chemical reactions

Pump

The first blast furnaces were simple but revolutionary. Iron ore and charcoal were put in at the top. A human-powered pump pushed oxygen into the furnace to keep the fire hot. Inside the furnace, the ore and charcoal reacted, and molten iron poured out of the furnace into moulds to make tools or weapons.

outside China. The first European blast furnaces were built over a thousand years later.

Some of the most important objects made out of iron were used in farming. Cast-iron ploughs did a great job of turning huge areas of land from scrubby waste into productive fields. Iron ploughs cut heavy soil better than wooden ones. And casting allowed metal workers to design a shape that pushed the dirt away from the row instead of letting it pile up in front of the plough.

So cast iron meant more food. And the more food the Chinese grew, the more people could be fed. The more people, the stronger and bigger Chinese civilisation became.

At more or less the same time the Chinese were inventing the blast furnace, someone in India came up with something even better than cast iron. They heated iron, charcoal and glass together until the iron melted. It absorbed the carbon from the charcoal and turned into high-carbon steel. Steel is stronger and more flexible than iron, and it doesn't rust or crack. You can imagine how useful it is for buildings, pots and pans and weapons, among many other things.

> " VERY LIKELY, THE CAST IRON FOUNDRY WORKERS ADOPTED AND ADJUSTED THE ORIGINAL BRONZE PRODUCTION TECHNIQUES... "
>
> Wengcheong Lam, anthropologist

The Iron Age in China happened during the Zhou dynasty. The Zhou came right after the Shang and lasted a long time, from 1046 to 256 BCE. The Zhou set up a system with regional noblemen – leaders of city-states outside the capital. These leaders were in charge of their states but loyal to the king. However, over time these nobles gained more and more power and began fighting the king and one another for control.

As the king's power fell apart, educated people who had once worked for the government lost their jobs. Some of them became philosophers. These thinkers travelled from city to city teaching and advising kings on how to rule wisely and on how society should work. The ideas they developed are known as the Hundred Schools of Thought.

One of these thinkers was Kong Fuzi, also known as Confucius. We don't know very much about Confucius as a person, but one story says he was minister of justice in the state called Lu. When he was in his fifties, he left his job and began trekking around the kingdoms of northern China. He taught his view of the right way to lead a good life and the best way to rule a kingdom. As fights between rival states got worse, Confucius made it his life's mission to try to sow the seeds of peace.

Confucius believed that a good society was one where everyone followed the rules and was kind to others. He advised kings that if they set a good example to their people, the people would obey them. He taught the same about parents and children, high-born people and ordinary people, men and women.

The leaders (kings, parents, high-born people and men) should respect the people they were in charge of as human beings. In turn, their inferiors (subjects, children, ordinary people and women) should always do what they were told even when they didn't agree.

Extreme respect for parents and elders is central to Confucian philosophy. In one Confucian story (above), a tiger charges at a father and teenage son walking in the mountains. The son jumps in front of the father to protect him. Seeing the son's bravery, the tiger is so impressed that he doesn't attack after all.

In the case of children, he included grown-up children. If you were forty years old and your father was seventy, you were still his child and should always obey him. Confucius believed heaven wanted people to live in this orderly way. And he believed that if you did right, heaven would take care of you.

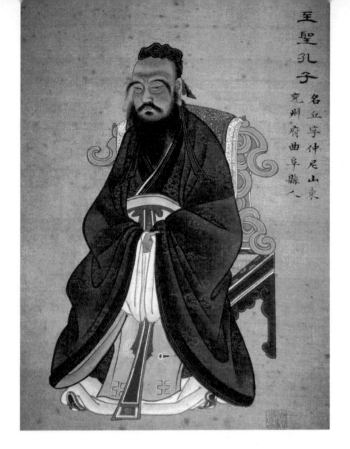

至聖孔子
名丘字仲尼山東
兗州府曲阜縣人

Confucius is thought to have lived from about 551 to 479 BCE. His ideas about family, morality, behaviour, authority and traditions are still influential in Chinese society today.

As part of his rules about kindness, Confucius is quoted as saying, "That which you do not desire, do not do to others". Do you recognise this saying? Often called the golden rule, this idea is part of nearly every religion in the world. It asks us always to remember that others are human beings and deserve to be treated as we would want to be treated in their situation, even when the other person is very different from us. You can see why he was, and is still, considered a very wise person.

Around the same time Confucius and the other thinkers of the Hundred Schools of Thought were teaching in China, another very important thinker was teaching on the other side of the great Himalaya Mountains in India. His name was Siddhartha

Gautama. You have probably heard of him. His followers call him the Buddha.

Siddhartha was a Hindu. The Hindu religion is the oldest of the five major religions practised in the world today (that's Hinduism, Buddhism, Judaism, Christianity and Islam). It probably started during the time of the Indus Valley civilisation. It then developed for thousands of years. The first holy books of Hinduism are called the Vedas. They were composed by the culture that came after Indus Valley. We don't have any examples of written versions of the Vedas until long after they were composed. The Vedic culture passed these important verses along through the generations by memorising them and teaching them to others.

> "
> RAISE THYSELF UP, GROW THICK BY THY OWN MIGHT, O GRAIN! BURST EVERY VESSEL! THE LIGHTNING IN THE HEAVENS SHALL NOT DESTROY THEE!
> "
>
> A blessing for the planting of grain from the Atharva-Veda

The central idea of Hinduism is that each person has an eternal soul or self that is reincarnated after death into another being. This being can be an animal or a person. Hinduism also includes a caste system. People are born into a particular caste or level in society. They stay in that caste for their whole life. The highest caste, Brahmins, were priests in Siddhartha's time, and it was their right to demand food and whatever else they needed to live from other people. The lowest castes then were servants or slaves. People in the middle worked in the government or were farmers or traders.

In Hinduism, everything you do in life creates karma, which is sort of like positive points and negative points. If you follow the

Hinduism is said to have 33 million gods, each with its own job to do. All of them work together under the leadership of Krishna, the Supreme Being, to keep the universe running. Here are two important ones. Brahma is the creator of the universe. Ardhanarishvara is a combination of the god Shiva and the goddess Parvati and represents the Hindu belief that female and male energy must work closely together to make the universe work.

Brahma

White lines cover a third eye of spiritual power

Jewelled crown made of bamboo strips

Prayer beads for the many substances needed to create the universe

Book for knowledge of the world

Lotus flower for divine beauty and purity

Animal skins represent a simple life

Shiva (the male side of Ardhanarishvara)

Parvati (the female side of Ardhanarishvara)

rules, then you collect good karma. And good karma allows you to be reincarnated at a higher level in the next life. The rules include being kind and compassionate to others, performing the rituals to the gods and meditating. Over many lives you can move up from being an animal to being a low-caste person to being a high-caste person. Finally, you reach moksha, when you are free from the hardships of the cycle of birth and death. For some Hindus, this means your soul is reunited with the soul of the whole universe or it becomes one with God.

Siddhartha rejected some parts of Hinduism that he thought were wrong. He created his own religion, now called Buddhism. We don't know very much about Siddhartha's life, but we believe he lived from about 560 to about 480 BCE. And we think he was born in Lumbini, in what is now Nepal.

According to one legend, Siddhartha was born a prince. His mother, Queen Maya, died a few days after his birth. Siddhartha's father was very protective of him and had three palaces specially built in his son's honour. The idea was that Siddhartha would live all his life in these palaces. That way he would be hidden away from the poor, desperate lives led by most ordinary people.

But, at the age of twenty-nine, Siddhartha's curiosity to see the world for himself overcame him. So he sneaked out of his palace. He met old people and people with diseases and people who were dying. He was so upset by what he saw that he decided to leave his luxuries behind and join ordinary people in their suffering.

This period in northern India is called the Second Period of Urbanisation. City-states covered the area along the Ganges River. The time was full of thinkers, much like the Hundred Schools of Thought in China. In Hinduism, one of the new ideas was that an important way to live a holy life is to become what's called an ascetic. Ascetics give up all possessions, pleasures and family connections. They focus entirely on prayer and meditation. Siddhartha decided to become an ascetic. At one point he ate no more than a single leaf or nut a day and almost starved to death.

This is obviously not a good idea, and Siddhartha figured that out in time. He concluded that starving himself was adding suffering to the world, not taking it away.

It is said that Siddhartha sat down under a tree to meditate for forty-nine days. After all of this time quieting his mind, he gained

This statue of the Buddha was made in the late 1400s or early 1500s CE in Thailand.

what is called enlightenment or nirvana. He could see the truth of all things and felt lasting peace and joy. From then on, he was known as the Buddha, meaning 'awakened one'.

The Buddha said that all people are equal and that castes don't matter. He also stopped thinking about karma and earning points for the next life. But he continued to believe in reincarnation and the importance of meditation and selflessness. He taught a middle way between a life of always wanting more and a life of rejecting everything. He believed if you were kind and compassionate to others, meditated to stay calm, and lived simply, you could find your way to nirvana.

For the next forty-five years, the Buddha walked along the Ganges River in what is now north-east India and southern Nepal. He talked to everyone who would listen, from kings and queens to robbers and beggars. He explained to them that anyone can gain enlightenment. After attracting thousands of followers, the Buddha died at about the age of eighty.

Some rulers were afraid of Buddhism and other new ideas popping up at the time, so they tried to stop them. Others put up with them. But then, something amazing happened that started the

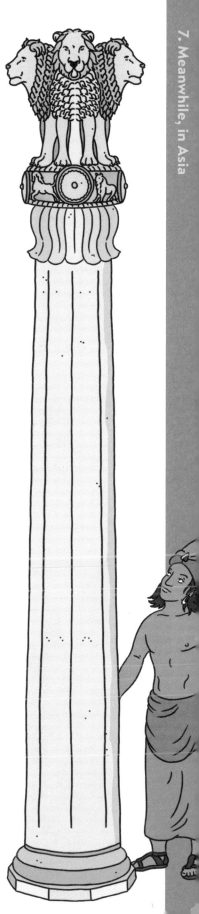

process of making Buddhism the major religion
it is today.

About 200 years after the death of the Buddha,
the Maurya Empire unified India by conquering all
its different kingdoms. This was at about the same
time high-carbon steel was being invented. The
third Maura king was named Ashoka. When he came
to power in about 260 BCE, there was just one
undefeated kingdom left. It was called Kalinga.
Of course, Ashoka attacked the Kalingans.

The last battle of that war is known as the Battle
of Kalinga. According to some stories, it left more
than 100,000 people dead on the battlefield. The
day after winning the battle, it is said that Ashoka
walked out across the city. All he saw were burned-
out houses, dead horses and scattered bodies. Ashoka
was a very tough guy. His name even means 'without
sorrow'. But the sight of all this carnage is said to have
made him weep and cry, "What have I done?"

Horrified at the appalling loss of life, Ashoka
became a Buddhist. Over the next twenty years,
he tried to help his people live in peace. The best
information we have about King Ashoka is from a
collection of instructions to his subjects that he had

The Lion Capital of Ashoka sits on
top of a pillar built around 250 BCE.
Its four lions were adopted as the
official emblem of India in 1950.

carved into pillars and rocks all around his kingdom. They are called the Edicts of Ashoka. In them, he asked people to be kind and generous to others, to work to improve themselves, to be honest and to be grateful.

Following Ashoka's reign, Buddhism spread to many other countries. His children Mahinda and Sanghamitra took Buddhist teachings to what is now Sri Lanka. By 100 CE, Buddhist monks had reached China. From China the religion spread throughout Korea, Vietnam, Thailand and eventually into Japan. Nowadays more people practise Buddhism in other countries than in India itself.

About forty years after King Ashoka finished bringing together all of India, a warrior named Ying Zheng led the Chinese state of Qin (pronounced 'Chin') in defeating the rest of China. When Ying became emperor in 221 BCE, he took the name Qin Shi Huang, which means 'first emperor of China'.

Around 8,850km in length, the Great Wall of China is the longest structure ever built by humans. It was built to protect against invasions from the north.

Qin Shi Huang wanted to make sure the country didn't fall apart again. He took back power from the nobles and built up a strong army. He also ordered a set of walls to the north of some Chinese states to be connected together. The idea was to defend the country against attacks from nomads. This job took thousands of workers and long after his death became the Great Wall of China.

Qin Shi Huang decided that China needed shared systems to make it easy for different parts of the empire to work well together. He created money that could be used all over the country. He ordered a system of standard weights and measures to make trade easier. He also created a written language that would allow educated people to communicate clearly with one another.

The emperor rejected almost all ideas from the Hundred Schools of Thought. The one he kept was called Legalism. It worked for him because it upheld the emperor's right to harshly punish or even kill anyone who disobeyed him. Other ideas, including those of Confucius, were strongly discouraged.

As you might imagine, not everyone liked Qin Shi Huang. In fact, he survived several attempts to kill him. As he got older, the emperor became desperate to find a magic potion that would make him live for ever. Remember the story of King Gilgamesh from Sumeria, who went in search of the same thing?

Qin Shi Huang was on a tour of eastern China, looking for this potion, when he died. It is thought that his doctors made up some pills which they believed would give everlasting life. Unfortunately, they contained mercury, a highly poisonous metal.

For over 2,000 years, no one knew where Qin Shi Huang was buried. Then, one day in 1974, some farmers who were digging a well struck an unusual object buried deep underground. What they found led to one of the most incredible archaeological discoveries of all time.

It was an enormous necropolis, or tomb city, that took up ninety-eight square kilometres. That's a big as the city of Coventry, in England.

When archaeologists dug up a part of the necropolis, they found a huge army of clay soldiers. Like the shabti of the Egyptians, these figures were meant to help the emperor in the next life.

But these aren't miniature figures. They are life-size statues, at least 8,000 of them. Each soldier is an individual work of art. They are made of terracotta, a kind of red clay. They carry bronze weapons and are lined up all ready for battle. And with the soldiers are 600 clay horses and more than a hundred life-sized wooden chariots.

By 100 BCE, both China and India were at peace. But, sadly, humans are not that good at making peace last. In fact, that's exactly what we're about to see as we turn our gaze towards Europe and the Middle East, where several of the world's greatest classical civilisations are in full swing.

Experts think Emperor Qin Shi Huang employed as many as 700,000 workers over a period of forty years to create the Terracotta Army to protect him in the afterlife.

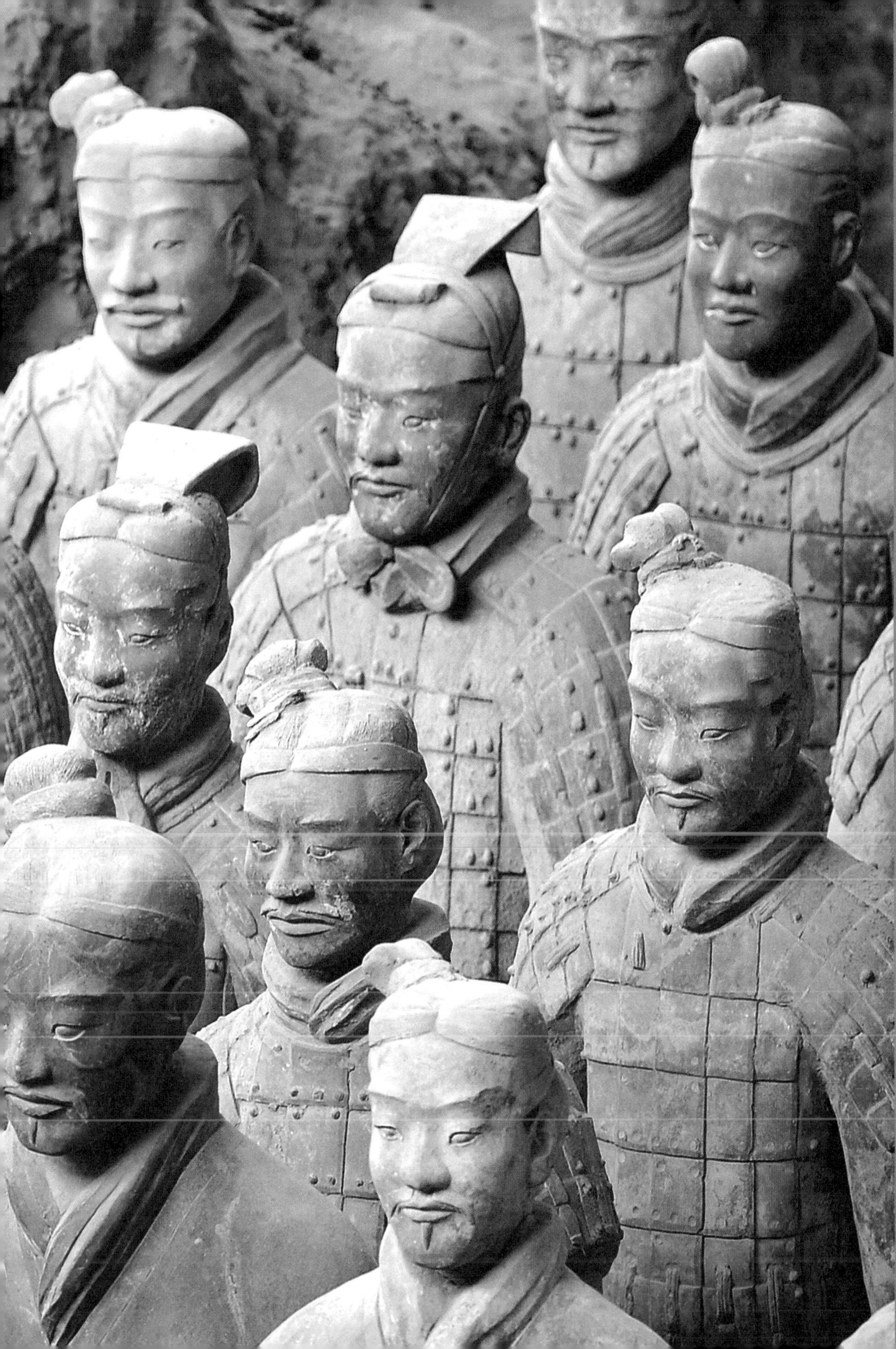

7. Meanwhile, in Asia

3000–200 BCE

RISE AND FALL

1400 BCE–476 CE
Classical empires come and go

○ **1260–1180 BCE**
According to legend,
Trojan Wars are fought
between Greeks
and Trojans.

○ **1200 BCE**
Israelites begin writing
down pieces of what
will become the
Hebrew Bible.

○ **776 BCE**
The first ever Olympic
Games take place in
ancient Greece.

○ **585 BCE**
Thales successfully
predicts a solar
eclipse.

549–530 BCE
Cyrus the Great
creates the
Persian Empire.

336–323 BCE
Alexander the
Great builds the
Macedonian
Empire.

30 CE
Jesus is executed.

120 CE
The Roman
Empire stretches
all the way from
Mesopotamia to
England.

476 CE
The western Roman
Empire falls.

D o you like olives? When I was young I used to stay at a fine old English house that belonged to my great-uncle and namesake. I remember he always offered us olives in front of his roaring log-fire before dinner. I still love olives, maybe because they remind me of Uncle Christo.

Olives were first farmed by the people of ancient Greece. They were a very important crop. Ancient Greeks didn't have iron ploughs the way the Chinese did. And they didn't have the rich soil of China either. So it was harder to make a living from farming grains like wheat, barley or rice. Olive trees grew well, though, and olives mattered.

That's because everyone wanted olive oil. It was as precious as gold is today. Squeeze out the oil from olives and you could use it for lighting lamps to see in the dark, for cooking food, or even to make soap for scrubbing yourself free of grime.

You could also trade your olives to buy something that meant you would never again need to work in the fields. And you'd never need to make your bed or even do the washing-up after dinner. Can you guess what that incredible something was?

The answer might be pretty disturbing. It ought to be. Because that incredible thing that could do all your work for you was another person – a slave.

In all of ancient Greece, we know the most about the city-state of Athens. That's because so much was written about it. The state of Athens included both the city itself and the surrounding countryside. In Athens (and probably

Olive branches

in other places in Greece), two opposite ideas seemed to go hand in hand. One was democracy. The other was slavery. It is one of the saddest truths of human history that millions of people have had to spend their lives enslaved. Being enslaved means having to work without pay and be treated with harsh, often cruel, disrespect by people who think you are worth a lot less than they are.

In ancient Greece, every free family who could possibly afford it had slaves. In fact, not having even one slave was a mark of extreme poverty. Enslaved people worked on farms and in people's houses. They also built buildings and roads, made pottery, and mined metals. And not only families and businesses owned slaves. The government of Athens did, too. It rented them out to companies, and the money they made went to pay the government's bills.

Until about 600 BCE, in Athens anybody could be enslaved. All you had to do was fall on hard times and take a loan you

Pots can tell us quite a bit about life in ancient Athens. The one on the left shows a race at the Panathenaic Games, which took place every four years in Athens, along with other competitions including the Olympian Games. The pot on the right shows women chatting and filling pitchers at a public water fountain.

couldn't pay back. Or you might be travelling and be kidnapped and sold into slavery in another country. Or you could be captured in war. That made free people very aware of their freedom and also very nervous when they felt it was being taken away.

In about 594 BCE, a new leader came to power in Athens. His name was Solon, and according to the stories told about him much later, he was a great warrior and a poet. Solon is famous for making some very big changes.

One thing Solon did was to set up a system where all citizens could vote to decide exactly what the government should do. This is called direct democracy. Other Greek states also set up direct democracies.

It was an exciting moment if you were a citizen of Athens. But there was one catch. You only counted as a citizen if you

In ancient Greece, soldiers used wooden devices called siege engines to break down castle walls. A siege engine could be as large as a small house and might be covered in damp horse hides to protect it against flaming arrows. Some experts think these machines were the inspiration for Homer's story of the Trojan horse.

were free, male, Athenian and rich enough to own property. If you were a slave, female, foreign or poor, forget it. So actually most people who lived in Athens couldn't vote. But the idea of elections in which the people had a say, the origins of democracy, did begin right here.

Because they had so many slaves, Athenian citizens had something worth even more than olive oil. They had time, bags and bags of it. Because other people were doing all the hard work, Athenian men could use their time to learn, think, write, invent and discover. They even had time to go to giant outdoor theatres to see plays performed and to listen to storytellers.

A Trojan soldier

Some of the most famous ancient Greek stories were written by the poet Homer. In his two book-length poems, *The Iliad* and *The Odyssey*, he tells of the legendary Trojan wars, which are supposed to have taken place around 1260–1180 BCE in what is now Greece and Turkey. You might know one of the stories.

According to Homer, Paris, prince of Troy, kidnapped Helen, queen of Sparta. Sparta was a city-state of Greece, so Greece went to war with Troy to get Helen back, and they came up with a clever trick.

They built a huge wooden horse and hid a team of crack troops inside it. Naturally, the Trojans were very curious about this giant

Athena

horse parked outside their city walls. So they dragged it into the city to take a closer look. In the dark of night, the Greek soldiers snuck out of their hiding place, opened the gates of Troy and let the Greek army flood in to destroy the city and its people.

Homer's poetry and the work of other ancient writers also tell us about Greek religion. The Greeks believed in a group of gods known as a pantheon. There were twelve main gods, or Olympians.

Zeus was the king of the gods and the ruler of their heavenly home, Mount Olympus. Hera was queen of the gods and the goddess of women and family. Poseidon was the god of the sea. Demeter was the goddess of nature, farming and the seasons. Athena was the goddess of wisdom, knowledge, science, literature and war. Greek myths tell the stories of these gods and their interactions with humans.

> DURING THE BATTLE THE DAY WAS SUDDENLY TURNED TO NIGHT. THALES OF MILETUS HAD FORETOLD THIS LOSS OF DAYLIGHT TO THE IONIANS, FIXING IT WITHIN THE YEAR IN WHICH THE CHANGE DID INDEED HAPPEN.
>
> Herodotus, *Histories*

Ancient Greek thinkers didn't always just follow the explanations in these myths, though. Thales was a Greek philosopher who lived in a city called Miletus, on the west coast of what is now Turkey. It is said that in 585 BCE he stunned his neighbours by correctly predicting that the world would be plunged into pitch darkness right in the middle of the day.

The obvious explanation back then was that the gods were angry. The not-so-obvious (and correct) explanation was that there had been a solar eclipse. This happens when the Moon passes between the Earth and the Sun, blocking out the daylight for a few minutes.

Zeus

Thales is sometimes called the father of science. He believed nature is what makes things happen, not gods such as Zeus or Hera. And he taught that if you observe the world closely and make hypotheses and test them, you can better understand how the universe works.

In the ancient world, science and philosophy were closely related. They both have to do with how the world works. One famous Greek philosopher was Socrates. Like the Buddha, Socrates thought a person's soul could be improved over time. But Socrates believed the way to improve yourself is not through meditation but through problem-solving, discussion and debate.

The original Olympic Games started as far back as 776 BCE. The games were a series of athletic competitions among the Greek city-states. Athletes ran and jumped and rode horses in honour of their gods, the Olympians. All wars paused to let competitors pass through battlefields on their way to the games.

Poseidon

Spartan fighters wore helmets like this one (above), with a crest down the middle. The small bronze statue (right) of a girl about to take part in a race was made in Sparta in about 500 BCE.

Poems were written about the winners and statues made in their honour. The most prestigious prize was a crown made from the leaves of that most precious tree of all – the olive.

Not all Greek city-states were the same. While Athens was developing democracy and philosophy, Sparta was more interested in military might. There, baby boys were inspected to see if they were strong enough to become soldiers. The weakest were abandoned and left to die on the lonely slopes of a nearby mountain range.

If you were a boy who made it to the age of seven, you were sent off to a military training camp to learn how to become a fearless warrior. There, you weren't fed enough at meals. The idea was that you to learn to steal. However, if you were *caught* stealing, you would be punished because you were too clumsy to get away undetected.

Girls in Sparta had it better. If you were a girl, you were well fed, given a lot of freedom, and encouraged to take part in sports and ride horses. You were educated at home and were supposed to grow up to be a good mother to strong future warriors. And because men were so busy fighting, grown-up women also had more power than they did in Athens and other places in Greece. They were equal citizens and could own property.

The Spartan idea was to create a super-race of strong, intelligent humans that would triumph over every other culture in the world.

Remember the Natufians? Their descendants were those first farmers who lived on the eastern shores of the Mediterranean Sea. Well, fast forward about 5,000 years to 1200 BCE. The region is now called Canaan, and it's home to city dwellers, farmers, herders and nomads.

This was an important place at an important time. That's because several things were going on there at once. One was a major trading civilisation called Phoenicia. It had city-states just like Greece, and with an incredible navy, it created colonies all along the southern coast of the Mediterranean to the Atlantic Ocean, over 2,400 kilometres away.

A second amazing thing going on in Canaan was the development of the first alphabet. Canaanites didn't write their language in symbols that represented

The Phoenician alphabet had just twenty-two symbols. This meant it was easier for people to learn than other alphabets, which had hundreds of symbols.

words or ideas, the way the Chinese and Egyptians did. Instead the they came up with a system of symbols that represented the smallest possible sound units in speech. These first alphabets just included consonants, though. A reader had to guess at the vowels.

This alphabetic way of writing spread like wildfire because the Phoenicians took it with them and used it as they traded with people all over the region. The Greeks adopted it and added vowel symbols.

The third big thing going on in Canaan is that one of the cultures there was just starting to use the new alphabet to write down some of their beliefs. This culture was called Israel.

We know about Israel in this time mostly from its scriptures, which are now called the Hebrew Bible or the Old Testament. They

Amen giving Merneptah a sword, mirrored and shown twice

Khonsu, child god, son of Amen and Mut

Mut, mother goddess

The Merneptah Stele, a stone slab created in about 1230 BCE, is one of the ways we know that the ancient Israelites were real people, not legends. Under a picture of the patron gods of Thebes helping him in war, Egyptian Pharaoh Merneptah brags about his conquests in Libya and Canaan, including saying that "Israel is laid waste and his seed is not", meaning that his army had completely wiped out the Israelites. This turned out to be quite an exaggeration.

are a combination of rules for how to live and stories that tell of the legendary founders of Israel.

One of the most dramatic stories of the Bible has to do with Egypt. It is called the Exodus. It begins with the Israelites enslaved in Egypt. In the story, God helps Moses, the leader of the Israelites, convince an Egyptian pharaoh to set his people free. To do this, God sends Egypt a series of ten horrible plagues. The great Nile River – source of Egypt's wealth – turns to blood. Frogs fall from the sky. Giant clouds of locusts eat all the crops in the fields. It gets dark in the daytime. All of the first-born sons of the Egyptians die in the same night. And more.

Once he understood that the Israelites had a very powerful god on their side, the pharaoh agreed to free them, though at the last minute he sent his army to chase them as they fled. The Israelites' god made a path of dry ground appear in the middle of the Red Sea so the Israelites could walk across. Then he let the sea flow over the path, drowning the Egyptian army.

The story of the Exodus from Egypt is a legend. And there is no archaeological evidence so far that the Israelites ever lived anywhere but Canaan. But a story that involves an escape from slavery makes a whole lot of sense if your people are enslaved at the time you're writing it, which these people were.

Locusts – one of the plagues in the story of the Exodus – mostly live quietly on their own. But they can suddenly group together into a swarm of hundreds of thousands of individuals and destroy crops, leaving people to starve.

In 586 BCE, the empire of Babylon invaded Canaan and destroyed Jerusalem, the capital of Judah, one of the Israelite kingdoms. Many of the people of Judah, called Judahites, were enslaved and taken to Babylon. It was there that Judaism began to take shape, as enslaved Judahite scholars collected and wrote down their scriptures in one place, probably for the first time.

A remarkable belief emerged from this process. The idea is that there is only one god. All-powerful and all-knowing, God created the world and is actively involved in the life of his creation. This belief is called monotheism. Judaism was the first religion that we know of to embrace it.

The Judahites spent about forty years in Babylon and in other parts of the empire. Then along came a king who truly earned the word 'Great' in his title.

Cyrus the Great founded the first Persian Empire, based in what is now Iran, in about 549 BCE. He expanded the empire until it was one of the largest the world had ever seen. It is believed that Cyrus treated all the people in the empire with respect, at least after he conquered them. He didn't enslave the people. He didn't force them to change their beliefs. This was an extremely radical idea at the time, but it helped make people happier to live under his rule.

Huge columns were built all over Persepolis in Persia to show people how mighty was the power of the Persian Empire. They still stand tall today in the remains of the walled city in what is now Iran.

After capturing the city of Babylon in 539 BCE, Cyrus freed the Jewish people from slavery and allowed them to return to Jerusalem if they wanted to. Not only that, he also had a new Holy Temple built to replace one the Babylonians had destroyed when they invaded Jerusalem.

> **I AM CYRUS, KING OF THE WORLD, GREAT KING, MIGHTY KING.**
>
> Cyrus the Great

Darius I ruled the Persian Empire from 522 to 486 BCE, when the empire was at its biggest, stretching all the way from eastern Europe to the Indus Valley. He built a magnificent new capital city called Persepolis.

At the beginning of Darius's rule, Persia mostly got along with Athens. But as Darius's armies took over more and more of Greece, Athens got nervous and started supporting revolutions against Persia. Darius responded by attacking, which led to over ten years of war between Greece and Persia. Athens won its first big victory at the Battle of Marathon in 490 BCE and finally stopped the Persian efforts to take over Greece at the Battle of Salamis ten years later.

Though no longer a threat to Greece, the Persian Empire continued to rule much of the Middle East and Mediterranean world for about the next 100 years. But then along came Alexander, King of Macedon.

Cyrus the Great

Prince Alexander was a good student and great with horses. At least he was great with his own horse, Bucephalus. His father, Phillip II, was king of the northern Greek city-state of Macedon and was busily creating an empire by defeating other states. So of course he could afford the best education for his son. When Alexander was thirteen, his dad hired a great philosopher to run a small school for Alexander and his friends.

That teacher was called Aristotle, and he ended up as probably the most famous Greek philosopher of all time. He thought and wrote about everything from nature to space and from city politics and public speaking to poetry, music, memory and logic.

Aristotle's thinking led him to a very important idea. He wrote that a basic set of natural laws could explain everything to do with everything. Understanding these rules was the key to unlocking the meaning of life. The best way to achieve this was using your senses to carefully observe the world around you. He probably taught some of these ideas to Alexander and his classmates.

Alexander's father was just getting ready to invade the Persian Empire to expand Macedon even more when he was assassinated. It was 336 BCE, and Alexander was twenty years old. Suddenly he was King Alexander. As king, his number one goal was to finish conquering the world.

Aristotle (right) taught Alexander the Great (left) when he was a boy at Mieza in Macedonia. Maybe it was Aristotle's teachings that inspired Alexander to extend his empire across parts of Europe and the Middle East and into Asia.

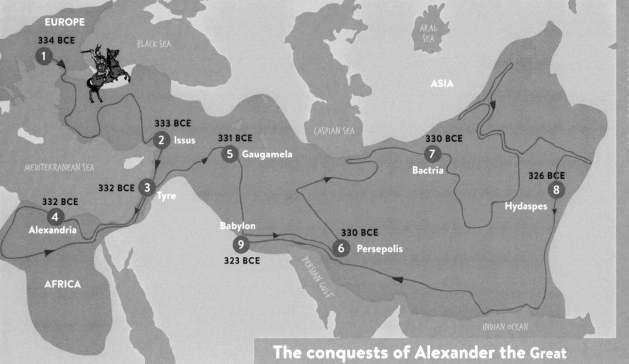

The conquests of Alexander the Great

 The Empire of Alexander the Great

〜 Alexander the Great's route

1 Alexander set off with 48,000 soldiers

2 Victory at the Battle of Issus

3 Tyre captured after seven-month siege

4 Alexandria founded

5 Victory at Battle of Gaugamela against Darius III

6 Alexander storms the Persian Gates at Persepolis

7 Persian Emperor Darius III is killed before Alexander reaches him

8 After battle of Hydaspes, Alexander conquers part of India

9 Death of Alexander in Babylon

Incredibly, he turned out to be really, really good at it. For the next twelve years or so, he led an army of something like 40,000 Greek soldiers. They crossed Persia, Egypt and even parts of India, defeating any army that stood in their way. Alexander, now known as 'the Great', expanded the Macedonian Empire until it was almost as big as the Persian Empire had been. And wherever he went, he brought Greeks with him. Thousands of them moved abroad, taking with them Greek ideas about drama, philosophy, politics and science.

Greek ideas mingled with Egyptian ideas and Persian ideas and Babylonian ideas and Indian ideas. As a result, a great wave of creativity broke over the empire. Euclid, who lived in Egypt, developed a new type of maths called geometry. Archimedes, who lived in Sicily, invented a water pump and a pulley system. And there was Eratosthenes from Egypt. He calculated the distance around planet Earth using nothing more than a stick, a well and a shadow.

Alexander died in Babylon at the age of thirty-two. Some think he died of disease, others think he was poisoned. But it didn't take long after his death for those he had left behind to start fighting for power. By 320 BCE, the Macedonian Empire was in pieces.

The next big empire to come along was like a gigantic hurricane, one that lasted around 1,000 years. The Romans, who came from what is now Italy, had a lot in common with ancient Greece. They had very similar gods, but with different names. Zeus was Jupiter, Hera was Juno, Poseidon was Neptune, Demeter was Ceres and Athena was Minerva. They picked up the Greek alphabet and changed it to work for Latin, their language. Then they spread it all around Europe, where it was used to write almost all of the European languages.

Adopting ideas from other cultures was a Roman speciality. That's how they captured Carthage, a powerful city in northern Africa. Carthage was a colony of Phoenicia, that seafaring civilisation based in Canaan. They were hard to beat at sea because they had such advanced ships. So the Romans simply captured a Phoenician ship and studied it. Within about two months, they had built themselves an entire fleet.

Alexander the Great was a role model and hero to the Romans, and by 200 BCE, the Roman war machine was expanding all around the Mediterranean. With each conquest they brought home huge piles of treasure and prisoners of war to become slaves. By 120 CE the Roman Empire was vast. It covered a large part of Europe, the Fertile Crescent, North Africa and Turkey.

It's one thing to conquer a huge empire but another to keep it under control. The Romans managed it for hundreds of years, though. One of the secrets of their success was sheer brutality.

Ancient Roman soldiers protected themselves in battle by holding their shields above them to form a huge screen. This formation is called a testudo.

In 73 BCE, slaves probably accounted for nearly half the population of the capital city, Rome. That year, Spartacus, an escaped gladiator, led thousands of slaves in a rebellion. They fought hard, but they were no match for the Roman army. When they

Most gladiator contests were between two gladiators, but sometimes gladiators were forced to fight hungry wild animals. These contests were called *venationes*, which means "wild beast hunts" in Latin.

were finally captured, the Romans decided to make an example of them. More than 6,000 rebels were nailed to wooden crosses and left to die. This form of execution is called crucifixion.

The corpses of the rebels were left hanging on their crosses for years. It was a gruesome reminder of what could happen to those who rebelled against Roman rule.

Another way to keep people from rebelling is to keep them very busy. Ruins of huge building projects such as the Colosseum and Circus Maximus in Rome still stand as a reminder of the Roman slaves who built them.

These enormous buildings were designed to increase the power of the emperor, and make him seem like a god. When the giant Colosseum was opened in 80 CE, the new emperor, Titus, celebrated by giving the people of Rome 100 days of spectacular drama in the form of mock battles, gladiator fights, animal hunts and executions in the new stadium.

The emperor came to the games so his people could admire him in all his glory. He was only too happy to see the most violent, bloodthirsty people of Rome all safely surrounded in one location under the watchful eye of his imperial troops.

Roman slaves also built Europe's first road network, which by about 100 CE criss-crossed over 7.5 million square kilometres of the empire. Most of the roads ran in straight lines. Everything that got in the way, from forests to farms, was razed to the ground.

I t's not surprising that in the midst of all this mayhem people began to think about better ways to live. Jerusalem was humming with these new ideas. One of the preachers there really grabbed people's attention. His name was Jesus.

Like the Buddha some 500 years before, Jesus's message was simple. Be peaceful. Love your neighbour as yourself. If someone

The Colosseum could seat more than 50,000 spectators when it was open for public entertainment. It has survived more than 2,000 years although earthquakes and natural erosion have caused parts of the building to collapse. This picture shows it as it stands now, in modern-day Rome, Italy.

strikes you, do not hit back. Do not worship false gods such as money. And if you follow the rules, God will reward you. It might not happen today or even during your lifetime. But on Judgement Day at the end of time, everyone who has been good and faithful will be rewarded in heaven. Those who haven't will end up in the fires of hell.

Some Jews came to regard Jesus as the son of God. They believed he was the last Messiah and would bring the end of days as foretold by Biblical prophets. But others continued to practise the traditional Judaism of the Temple or belonged to other sects.

The people of Jerusalem were deeply unhappy with Roman rule. So there were a lot of uprisings. Of course the Romans cracked down on any possible rebels. At about the age of thirty, Jesus was arrested and accused of claiming to be a king, which was an insult to Roman authority. The Romans executed him by crucifixion in around 30 CE.

Most of our information about Jesus comes from scriptures written after his death. According to these scriptures, known as the New Testament, his mother was named Mary. But his father wasn't Mary's husband Joseph. His father was God himself. The New Testament also tells of many miracles Jesus performed during his lifetime. It is written that he walked on water, healed sick and injured people, and turned five loaves of bread and two fish into enough food to feed 5,000 hungry followers.

This famous painting by Leonardo da Vinci shows the last meal Jesus (centre) had with his followers – known as apostles – before he was arrested and executed. Each of the apostles is reacting in his own way after Jesus predicts that one of them is about to give him up to the Roman authorities.

But the biggest miracle of all happened after he died. It is said that three days after his body was placed in a tomb, it disappeared. Then, his followers began to see visions of Jesus and believed he had come back to life. They wrote about this miraculous event, which they called the Resurrection. And they set out to spread their good news about the son of God coming down to Earth and dying on a cross so that everyone who believed in him might have everlasting life.

About forty years after Jesus's death, the Jews of Jerusalem rebelled against Roman rule. The Romans crushed the rebellion and burned down the Temple. Most of the ways Judaism was practised in Jerusalem depended on the Temple, so when it was destroyed, so were those ways of worshipping God.

Two new religions emerged from the rubble. One was rabbinic Judaism, the kind most Jews practise today, where people worship at local synagogues, following local religious leaders called rabbis. The other was the one founded by Jesus. It is called Christianity and is now the most popular religion in the world.

J esus's story went on to inspire millions all over the Roman Empire and beyond. It was particularly attractive to enslaved people who bitterly hated the cruelty of Roman rulers. The Roman government did its best to stamp out this upstart religion. Emperor Diocletian is famous for ordering in 303 CE that all Christians abandon their beliefs and instead pray to the traditional Roman gods. Anyone who disobeyed would be executed.

And they were. As many as 20,000 Christians may have been killed for their faith at this time. After he came to power in 306 CE,

The city of Constantinople (now Istanbul) was famous for its impenetrable walls. They were eventually breached by Ottoman invaders in 1453.

Diocletian's son Constantine stopped the killing. Then, in 380 CE, Emperor Theodosius I made Christianity the official religion of the entire Roman Empire. Now it was against the law to worship the old Roman gods! The whole world had been turned on its head in less than 100 years, and that was just the beginning.

By now, the Roman Empire was already falling apart. In 285 CE, Emperor Diocletian had split his vast territory into two parts. The eastern half was ruled from Constantinople, now Istanbul in Turkey. The western half was ruled from Rome. Then, in the late 300s, Rome's northern enemies started chipping away at the western part of the empire. The most powerful of these Germanic foes was the Hunnite Empire, led by a brilliant warrior called Attila. In 452 CE, his troops approached Rome but couldn't take it. The Italian harvest had been so poor that there was no food to feed his soldiers.

But Rome's collapse was only a matter of time. In 476 CE, an army of rebel soldiers led by a soldier named Odoacer defeated the last western Roman Emperor, Romulus Augustulus. Odoacer took over as ruler of a brand-new kingdom he called Italy, and the western Roman Empire was no more. Although the western Roman Empire was in ruins, the eastern empire – now called the Byzantine Empire – lasted for about another 1,000 years. But eventually it, too, got swept away by forces beyond its control, as we will see.

Odoacer was a warrior from Germany. His revolt led to the defeat of Romulus Augustulus in 476 CE, which is the date historians traditionally use to mark the fall of the western Roman Empire.

Chapter 9

MEANWHILE, IN THE AMERICAS

1500 BCE–1530 CE
More empires rise and fall

○ **8000 BCE**
The peoples
of the Americas
start farming.

○ **2000 BCE**
Mesoamericans are
drinking chocolate.

○ **1200 BCE**
The Olmec invent
rubber.

○ **500 BCE–500 CE**
Nasca people
create giant images
in the desert.

250 CE
The Maya develop
a complex of
city-states.

1350 CE
The city of Cahokia
is abandoned.

1428 CE
The Aztecs
establish an empire.

1530 CE
The Inca Empire is at
the height of its power.

At about the same time Chinese farmers started growing rice and millet, the first farmers in North and South America were gathering their own harvests. Just like the farmers of the Middle East and Asia, they found wild plants they could grow and breed. Soon they were producing enough food to feed towns and cities with houses and government, art and religion.

But as we saw with Norte Chico, Americans didn't have wheat, barley or rice. The first crops they farmed were potatoes, beans, squash, peanuts and corn.

Corn, also known as maize, was probably domesticated in southern Mexico, starting with a grass called teosinte. A teosinte ear has just five to ten seeds. Each seed is coated in a hard shell. That was great for wild teosinte. Its seeds could survive a journey through the insides of the most acidic animal stomach. It wasn't so great for people who wanted breakfast, though.

So farmers chose those plants with an unusually large number of seeds as well as those with the softest shells. Eventually they were able to turn teosinte into the highly nutritious crop we know today as corn.

Domesticated corn seeds spread north and south. People of the Andes Mountains in South America grew it. And so did the later Iroquois all the way up in what is now upstate New York in the United States.

Teosinte

Teosinte, a wild grass, is the ancestor of corn.

Corn

Nowadays, people and animals both eat corn. And it's also an important source of the fuel known as biodiesel. It's the biggest grain crop in the world and is grown on every continent except Antarctica.

In the 1500s, the Spanish Franciscan friar Bernardino de Sahagún studied Mesoamerican people. Here are some of his illustrations of corn farming.

Over thousands of years, farmers the length and breadth of the Americas developed more and more food crops. The list is astonishing. They grew chillies, sunflowers, pumpkins, peppers, avocados, aubergines, sweet potatoes, tomatoes, quinoa, cranberries, strawberries, pineapples, walnuts, peanuts, pecans, cashews and vanilla. Oh, and cacao, the main ingredient in chocolate.

Chocolate is produced from the seed pods of the cacao tree. It has a chemical called theobromine in it, which wakes you up. The word theobromine means 'food of the gods' and it gets this name because it was sacred to the Mesoamerican people, the cultural group that lived in southern Mexico and parts of Central America. Remember those 4,000-year-old noodles that archaeologists found in China? Well, something similar happened with chocolate. Archaeologists working in Chiapas, Mexico, found pieces of 4,000-year-old pottery with the remains of a chocolate drink in it.

Cacao seed pods are harvested twice a year. The beans and pulp inside are scooped out and left to ferment to develop the flavour. Next, the beans are dried out and roasted. Their little shells are removed, leaving behind 'nibs'. Grinding the nibs results in cocoa mass and cocoa butter. Nowadays, additional ingredients such as sugar and milk (for milk chocolate) are added to create chocolate.

If you have ever sneaked a taste of baking chocolate, you know that chocolate by itself is very bitter. That's how the Mesoamericans liked it. They drank it unsweetened for thousands of years before Europeans came along and decided to add sugar and extra fat and later to make it into bars.

We've already visited Norte Chico, the oldest civilisation we know of in the Americas. The second-oldest American civilisation was founded by the Olmec of south-central Mexico. Their name means 'rubber people', and they got this name because they figured out how to make rubber, by mixing rubber tree sap (called latex) with sap from morning glory vine.

If you mix equal parts of those liquids, you get a very flexible substance. Shape it fast, before it dries, and you have a great bouncy ball. Spread it on cloth, and you get a waterproof poncho. You can also mix seventy-five per cent latex and twenty-five per cent morning glory sap and get a very long-lasting, sturdy material, sort of like plastic, that can be shaped into waterproof containers.

The Olmec civilisation lasted from about 1200 BCE to about 400 BCE. So they were around in King Tutankhamun's time and at the time of the Shang and Zhou dynasties in China. They were making rubber while the Phoenicians were sailing around the Mediterranean and the Israelites were just starting to write down some of their beliefs. They were worshipping their gods when the Olympic games were being held in Greece and Cyrus the Great was building the Persian Empire.

The Olmec are famous for more than rubber. Like the Egyptians and Sumerians, they were great at counting and maths. They were possibly the first people in the Americas, and one of the first in the world, to use a symbol for zero as a place holder, to show a number's value.

They also sculpted what we now call colossal heads. These were huge

Rubber is extracted from the rubber tree by using a tool to scrape off a section of bark. Sap then drips out and is collected in a bucket, often tied to the tree.

This Olmec head was discovered near Lake Titicaca on the Peru-Bolivia boundary. Imagine how you would feel if you found this on a day out!

portraits carved into boulders. Some were taller than a basketball player and weighed more than twenty tonnes. But they looked like individual people. So archaeologists think they are portraits of powerful rulers.

No one knows why the Olmec built these heads. Did their rulers want memorials to themselves, the way the Egyptian pharaohs did? Were the giant faces intended to grab the attention of the gods?

The Olmec invented a ball game now called ulama, which spread throughout Mesoamerica and north into what is now northern Mexico and the south-western United States. Just as the original Greek Olympics were a combination of athletics and religious worship, so was ulama. Dozens of ancient ball courts have been unearthed.

Major issues and disputes between rival kingdoms could be decided in a ball game, too. It was the gods' decision who would win and who would lose. Winning was very good news. Losing, not so much. That's because the losing side might be sacrificed and their bodies buried underneath the court to honour the gods.

Ulama (which is still played in some parts of Mexico today) is like a mix between football and basketball. A stone ring hangs high above each end of the court, and each side tries to send the ball through the other team's ring and protect its own ring. Players aren't allowed to touch the ball with either their hands or their feet. They have to pass it using their hips, thighs, forearms and heads.

The Olmec may also have had their own form of writing. In the late 1990s, road builders in south-eastern Mexico found a stone block engraved with sixty-two symbols that look like they represent animals, plants, insects and fish.

Some archaeologists think the Olmec were what is called a mother culture. That means they passed their culture and beliefs along to later cultures in their area, including the Maya and Aztecs.

The Maya arose about 600 BCE in the Yucatan Peninsula in what is now south-eastern Mexico. Their civilisation extended across what is now Belize, Guatemala and parts of Honduras and El Salvador. Maya cities easily compare in size and complexity to ancient cities in other parts of the world.

The Maya built huge pyramids and temples. On their walls, they carved scenes from their mythology and inscriptions in the Maya language. In Maya writing, some symbols represent entire words. Others represent the sounds of syllables. Their writing has been decoded, so we can read it.

> " THERE WAS NEITHER MAN, NOR ANIMAL, BIRDS, FISH, CRABS, TREES, STONES, CAVES, RAVINES, GRASSES, NOR FORESTS; THERE WAS ONLY THE SKY. "
>
> The Popul Vuh

The Maya calendar is really a combination of several ways to keep track of time. One – called the Haab cycle – tracks a year made up of 18 months of 20 days each plus one month with only 5 days. (18 months x 20 days) + (1 month x 5 days) = 365 days, or one year.

The Maya also invented an accurate calendar that kept track of time from 3114 BCE all the way to 2012 CE, the end of a great cycle.

Crops and farming lay at the very root of Maya beliefs about the creation of the world. The Popol Vuh is a collection of Maya mythology. Its name means 'Book of the People', and it was passed down by word of mouth for many generations.

According to the Popol Vuh, three gods, in the form of water-dwelling feathered snakes, created humans to keep them company. First they tried to make them out of mud, but that didn't work. Next they used wood, but that didn't work either. Finally, 'true people' were modelled out of corn. Their bodies were made of white and yellow corn. Their arms and legs were cornmeal. This story shows how reliant the Maya were on corn for their survival.

Around 900 CE, the mighty cities of the Maya were abandoned, maybe as a result of severe drought caused by climate change. The Maya themselves didn't disappear, though. They stopped living in cities and instead lived in villages and small towns. They continued to work the land. They are there to this day.

Of course, the local people of Mesoamerica always knew they were living near the ruins of their past. But either they weren't telling outsiders about it, or the outsiders weren't listening. Finally, in the 1830s, Juan Galindo, governor of Petén in Guatemala, paid attention. Galindo explored the ruins of several of the great Maya cities and wrote about them. He also noticed that the people portrayed in ancient Maya art looked very much like modern local people, so were probably their ancestors. Once Galindo's writing made its way into the wider world, other

explorers and archaeologists started studying this incredible ancient civilisation.

But not all ancient Maya ruins were easy to find. Some of them had became so overgrown with jungle that not even the local people remembered them. Then, in 2017, archaeologists using a new technology called Lidar uncovered a vast Maya city in Guatemala. Houses, forts and pyramids surrounded by networks of canals and fields show that around 15 million people lived in these Maya lowlands. The strongly built forts suggest that the Maya were involved in significant wars with their neighbours.

This example shows exactly why history has to keep on being written over and over again. It's easy to think we know everything about the past, but that's impossible. New discoveries like this remind us there's always so much more to find out.

Chichén Itzá was a powerful regional Maya capital and trading centre on the Yucatan peninsula in what is now Mexico.

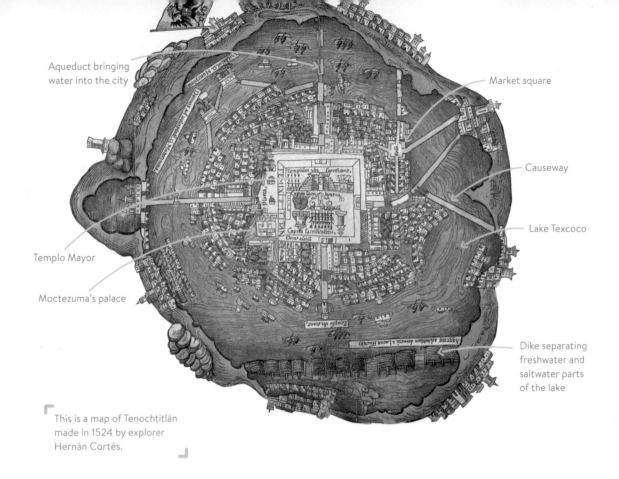

Aqueduct bringing
water into the city

Market square

Causeway

Lake Texcoco

Templo Mayor

Moctezuma's palace

Dike separating
freshwater and
saltwater parts
of the lake

This is a map of Tenochtitlán
made in 1524 by explorer
Hernán Cortés.

n about 1325, more than 400 years after the decline of the
Maya cities, another civilisation known as the Aztecs built a
majestic capital city called Tenochtitlán in central Mexico on an
island in Lake Texcoco, at the site of present-day Mexico City.
Tenochtitlán was connected to the mainland by causeways built up
from the bottom of the lake. Each one had gaps allowing boats to
pass through. Over those gaps, the Aztecs built bridges that they
could take down in times of war. It was like having a city surrounded
by a giant moat.

A huge sixty-metre-high Templo Mayor, or Great Pyramid,
was built at the heart of the city in honour of Tlaloc, god of rain
and fertility, and Huitzilopochtli, god of war and the Sun. Special

opening ceremonies, which took place in 1487, are said to have involved human sacrifices. The hope was that all of these precious gifts would persuade the gods to send good luck and lots of rain so the Aztecs' crops would grow.

The Aztecs spread out and conquered most of south-central Mexico, creating an empire that made the capital richer and richer. At its height, it had aqueducts bringing water in for its citizens, busy city markets, and a zoo full of animals, some brought from more than a thousand kilometres away. The zoo was so big that it took 300 zookeepers to care for all the animals.

Mesoamerica was not the only hotspot of ancient civilisation in the Americas. One mysterious culture in the Andes Mountains, the Nasca, created works of art that baffle experts even today. They are called the Nasca Lines. They were probably created between 500 BCE and 500 CE.

If you look down on the Nasca Desert from an aeroplane or from the surrounding hills, you can see straight lines nearly fifty kilometres long. You can also spot more than seventy enormous pictures of animals, insects and humans, some of them as big as 370 metres long, as long as three football pitches. But look at them from the ground, and all you can see are paths in the dust.

When modern Peruvians first noticed these drawings from aeroplanes in 1927, they couldn't understand how ancient people could have created them without being able to see the desert clearly from above. But archaeologists have since found wooden

stakes in the ground at the ends of the lines. That suggests the Nasca people strung string between stakes to draw the figures.

But the big question is not how the Nasca people made these, but why? Some archaeologists believe the lines are related to astronomy the way Stonehenge may have been. Others believe that they directed people to water in a desert where it only rains twenty minutes per *year*. And still others think they were gifts to the gods, offered in exchange for the hope of enough water to fill the Nasca people's irrigation canals so crops could grow.

The biggest of the Andes mountain civilisations was the Inca from Cusco, in what is now Peru. About a hundred years before Europeans arrived in the Americas, the Inca united the whole region through a combination of warfare and cooperation. At its height around 1530 CE, this great empire was the largest in the Americas, and possibly the largest in the world.

One of the Inca's biggest achievements was a 30,000-kilometre network of footpaths and trails, some of them crossing mountains more than 5,000 metres high. Many of these trails are still in use today. In Inca times, there were stations about every twenty-five kilometres along the major trails. Runners stood ready at each station to carry messages as in a relay race. That way, Inca rulers and officials could send messages as fast as possible along the whole length of the empire. With each runner having to cover only a short distance, the system could keep up top speed.

Instead of paper, parchment or clay, the runners carried quipu, those pieces of string that contained messages written in rows of

The subjects of the Nasca Lines include monkeys, hummingbirds lizards and spiders such as this one.

knots. Like the pharaohs of ancient Egypt, the Inca emperor was believed to be divine. He was regarded as the son of Inti, the Sun god. The Inca revered Inti so highly they believed that precious shiny gold itself was his sweat.

Back when the Maya were building pyramids and playing ulama, 3,800 kilometres to the north the Mississippian people were building their own civilisation. Their largest city was Cahokia, near what is now St Louis, Missouri, but they lived across the whole mid-west and south-east of what is now the United States.

The Cahokians were brilliant city planners. Like the Indus Valley cities, Cahokia was laid out in straight lines, with streets running east to west and north to south. And even before they built the city, the Cahokians moved dirt from hilly areas to low-lying areas to create a flat space for building. The city had 120 large mounds of earth, the largest ten storeys tall. Cahokia also had a circle of wooden posts that lined up with the movements of the Sun throughout the year, another structure very much like Stonehenge.

Cahokia lasted from 600 to 1350 CE. At its height in the 1200s, between 10,000 and 40,000 people lived there. But by 1350, the city had been abandoned. Was a cooling climate the cause? Or did the large population pollute the rivers with their waste, making the city an unhealthy place to live? No one knows.

By now you may have noticed that history is very good at telling the stories of dramatic events that have been written down or have left lots of physical evidence, like giant buildings, earthworks or sculpture.

> " THERE WAS A BELIEF [IN CAHOKIA] THAT WHAT WENT ON ON EARTH ALSO WENT ON IN THE SPIRIT WORLD, AND VICE VERSA. SO ... EVERYTHING HAD TO BE VERY PRECISE. "
>
> James Brown, archaeologist

But what history is not so good at is telling the stories of ordinary, everyday people. About 2,000 years ago at least a third of the world's population wasn't living in cities at all. They were hunter-gatherers, nomadic people herding animals as they moved from place to place, or just people living in tiny communities farming in the countryside.

The Hohokam, who lived in what is now the south-west of the United States, traded scarlet macaws, a type of parrot, buying them

Some of the mounds of earth in Cahokia were platforms for temples or houses of important people, and some were burial mounds.

The Thunderbird, symbolising power over nature

Grizzly bear, representing strength, family, courage and health, protects a human

The nations of the Pacific Northwest of North America carved totem poles from large cedar trees. Traditionally, each clan, or extended family, placed its pole at the front of its longhouse. The symbols carved into the pole and their order on it tell of a mythical or real event. This is an illustration of the Thunderbird house post that stands in Stanley Park in Vancouver, British Columbia, Canada.

from the Maya and selling them around North America. The Taino people of the Caribbean tied suckerfish on the end of a fishing line. They waited for the fish to stick themselves to turtles, which they would then haul in to cook for dinner. The Calusa of what is now Florida, United States, ate so many shellfish that they could build their multi-family houses on the top of giant mounds made out of the shells. In the Pacific Northwest of North America, Haida, Tlingit and other communities built giant totem poles from cedar trees to honour their gods.

These and other cultures of the Americas shared a common belief that everything in nature has a spirit.The Inuit in northern Greenland, Canada and Alaska believed the polar bear, which they called Nanuq, had a powerful spirit even after it was dead. They respected these creatures by hanging the bear skin in an honoured place inside their homes for several days after it had been hunted and killed. If the bear was male, the hunter offered the bear's spirit knives and bow-drills. If female, the hunter offered knives, skin-scrapers and needle cases.

Legend held that if a dead polar bear was treated properly by the hunter, its spirit would share the good news with other bears so they would be eager to be killed by him. If the bear was not properly treated after death, other bears would be told to stay away.

Such beliefs were not exclusive to native peoples of the Americas, however. Similar ideas can be found around the world, including among the Aboriginal Australian people. Their creation story tells of the Dreamtime, when the dramatic landscape of Australia was formed by supernatural 'ancestor beings' who broke through the crust of the unformed Earth. These beings created everything from the Sun, Moon and stars to mountains, trees and water. They made people and animals, too. Because they were created by the ancestor beings, all things – living and non-living – are related.

All people living in the ancient world had one thing in common. Their ways of life were shaped by the natural world surrounding them.

The stories of Dreamtime explained the Australian landscape. The Maya creation story showed how close the people felt to their corn. The Incas had expert knowledge of the mountains that made up their empire. The Greeks treasured olive oil because their land was too rocky to grow grain. The Chinese grew rich making silk from creatures that lived in their native mulberry trees. This is what defines ancient cultures, the connection between local environment and societies and their beliefs.

But this thread was not to last. After all, if you want to eat corn for lunch, you don't have to be in Mexico. You can buy it in a local supermarket almost anywhere in the world. Or if you want to speak to your auntie on the other side of the globe, you don't have to go there yourself. Just pick up the phone, or call her via the Internet.

Food Origins

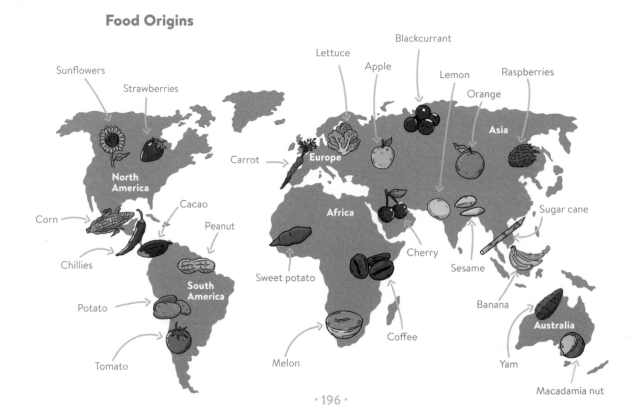

And if you want see unfamiliar places, you don't have to spend years walking as our ancestors did when they left Africa. You can drive or take a train or plane.

How on earth did the world become so connected? So small? To my mind, that's the biggest difference between the ancient and modern worlds. Some world-shrinking had already started in ancient times. Egyptians and Greeks and Babylonians shared ideas. Corn farming spread the length of the Americas. People across Asia, Africa and Europe bought Chinese silk.

But about 1,500 years ago cultures started to fuse together much more quickly. And that's what created the foundations of the world we live in today. Now it's time to turn to the hot dusty deserts of Arabia where we'll meet a man who got things moving – fast.

Food migrates right along with people. Rice, which was first farmed in Asia, is now grown in North America. Peanuts, which started in South America, are now an important part of both Asian and African cooking. Bananas, which started in Asia, are important to South American cuisine. This map shows where some of our foods originally came from.

Chapter 10

INVENTION CONNECTION

570–1279 CE

Powerful ideas emerge in the
Muslim world and East Asia

○ **570 CE**
Prophet Muhammad, the
founder of Islam, is born
near Mecca.

○ **751 CE**
According to legend,
the Muslim world learns
the secrets of paper
making from captured
Chinese soldiers.

○ **868 CE**
The oldest known printed
book is made in China.

○ **950 CE**
Gunpowder weapons
are in use.

○ **1000 CE**
Muslim Spain is a
powerful cultural
and commercial
region.

○ **1127 CE**
The Song dynasty is
attacked by raiders
from the north.
China splits in two.

○ **1202 CE**
Italian merchant Fibonacci
publishes *Liber Abaci*, bringing
Arabic numerals to Europe.

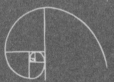

○ **1279 CE**
The Mongol Empire
is at its height.

About 1,400 years ago, a merchant in the city of Mecca in Arabia was seized by a series of visions.

He shared them and, in that way, invented a new religion. His full name was Abū al-Qāsim Muḥammad ibn ʿAbd Allāh ibn ʿAbd al-Muṭṭalib ibn Hāshim. He is known simply as Muhammad, or the Prophet Muhammad. He is the founder of Islam.

Muhammad was born in Mecca in about 570 CE. He was orphaned at about six years old and two years later adopted by his uncle, Abu Talib, who was the head of their clan. The family were traders who bought, sold and transported goods such as spices, salt, gold and ivory.

Abu Talib took Muhammad on trading trips to teach him the family business. When he grew up, Muhammad married, had children, and continued to travel and trade.

When he was about forty years old, Muhammad began to spend a few weeks each year alone in a cave, praying. It was in the cave that he had the first in a long series of visions. The Archangel Gabriel revealed to him the final and absolute word of God, the same one that Jews and Christians prayed to. Gabriel is the angel who is said to have visited Mary, Jesus's mother, to tell her that she would have a child who would be the son of God.

In Arabic, the word for God is Allah. The angel told Muhammad that there was only one Allah, not many. He said that Allah was in heaven, not on Earth. He also said that Allah

The Kaaba, a black building at the centre of the al-Masjid al-Harām mosque in Mecca, Saudi Arabia, is considered by Muslims to be the house of Allah. Muslims all over the world face in its direction during their daily prayers. A pilgrimage to Mecca at least once in a lifetime is one of the five pillars, or requirements, of Sunni Islam.

had revealed his word many times before through prophets of the Jewish and Christian scriptures. These included Adam, Abraham, Moses, Jacob, Joseph, Elijah, Jesus and more than fifty others. But, the angel said, over time humans had mistaken Allah's true words and as a result had created false religions.

Out of Muhammad's visions came a new religion called Islam, whose followers are called Muslims. There are branches of Islam, each with a slightly different set of beliefs and rules for life. The basic requirements for Sunni Muslims (the largest group) are called the Five Pillars of Islam. Shia Muslims also have pillars, but some have more than five and others have five that are a bit different from the Sunni five.

Five Pillars of Islam	
Shahadah	Believe in Allah as the one and only true God.
Salah	Pray to Allah five times a day.
Zakat	Give generously to the poor.
Hajj	Make a pilgrimage to Mecca at least once in your lifetime.
Fasting	If you are a heathy adult, fast (don't eat or drink anything) between sunrise and sunset during the holy month of Ramadan.

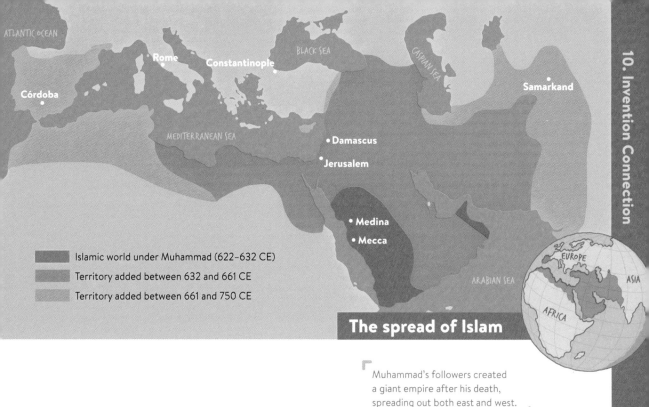

Islamic world under Muhammad (622–632 CE)

Territory added between 632 and 661 CE

Territory added between 661 and 750 CE

The spread of Islam

Muhammad's followers created a giant empire after his death, spreading out both east and west.

Muhammad was a fierce defender of his new faith. Under threat from the tribes around him, he raised an army of followers. First they took over his home town of Mecca. Then they went on to conquer the rest of the Arabian Peninsula. After Muhammad's death in 632 CE, his followers went further, adding Mesopotamia, Syria, Egypt and large parts of the Persian Empire to their new territory. Within 150 years, Islam had spread as far east as what is now Pakistan and west across north Africa into Spain.

By then, Islam was both a huge empire and easily the largest and fastest-growing religion in the world. Today there are more than 1.8 billion practising Muslims. And Islam is the second-most popular religion in the world, after Christianity. But it would be wrong to think of the Islamic Empire as just warriors on horseback. As we will soon see, it was so much more.

It's tricky to imagine a world without paper. We use it today for everything from books and magazines to tea bags and toilet rolls. Remember China's First Emperor Qin Shi Huang – the one who built himself that giant Terracotta Army? Well, after his death a new dynasty called the Han came to power in China.

In 140 BCE, Han Emperor Wu ordered that 100 jobs as government officials should be awarded based on how young men performed in a written test. But the jobs were open only to rich and well-connected families. More than 500 years later, in 693 CE, Wu Zetian, one of China's only female rulers, changed the system so that anyone could apply, even poor country people. Landing one of these high-paid jobs came to be a huge honour for the successful candidates' families and villages.

But to study for and take these civil service exams meant having to write things down. Fortunately, ingenious Chinese inventors had found a neat way to do this. There's a legend that in about 104 CE a bright court official called Cai Lun came up with a brilliant new cheap material for writing on – paper. According to the story, the

Ancient Chinese paper-makers experimented with many different materials, including grasses, hemp, old rope, silk rags and bamboo. This picture shows the process using mulberry tree bark.

1. Chopped-up mulberry bark boiling over a fire

2. Pounding the boiled bark to make pulp

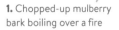

emperor at that time was very impressed by Cai Lun's paper-making system. He awarded Cai with vast wealth and a nobleman's title.

It wasn't long before Chinese people began to use soft, inexpensive paper for almost everything, from wrapping up precious objects to making umbrellas. Wallpaper, kites, playing cards and lanterns all made their first appearance in China. Even the modern habit of using toilet paper started right here.

Wu Zetian was only able to expand the exam system because paper was available for students to use for studying. And the possibility of passing the civil service exams gave poor people more hope for wealth, privilege and prestige.

Buddhist monks, originally from India, were paid by local people to pray for and educate their sons. That way people hoped to increase the chances of them passing the civil service exams. The range of subjects included everything from war strategy and law to farming and geography. And remember Confucius of the Hundred Schools of Thought? His ideas of loyalty and obedience to the family and the state ran through everything.

3. Mixing the pulp with water to the consistency of pea soup

4. Dipping a screen into the water and filtering out a thin layer of pulp

5. Drying the pulp into a sheet of paper

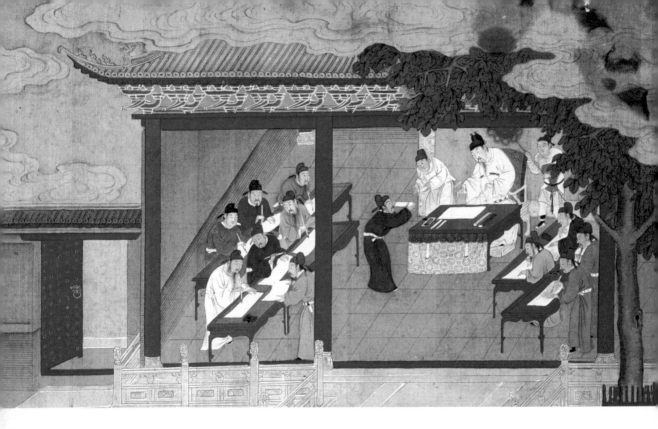

Civil service exams gave ordinary people the chance to get high-paid government jobs. A good education became the best route into Chinese high society.

Paper was so simple and so useful that it spread to Vietnam, Korea, Japan and India, but as far as experts can tell, it wasn't until the mid 700s that people outside east and south Asia knew how it was made. Which brings us back to the Muslim Empire. A wonderful story is told about how the Islamic world got the secret of paper. Here's how it goes.

In 751 CE, Muslim forces won a key battle against the Chinese on the banks of the River Talas, in central Asia. In the battle they captured a lot of Chinese prisoners. Well, it turned out that some of the captives were experts in paper-making. Islamic forces had a policy of releasing any prisoner who taught at least ten Muslims something important. These captives bought their freedom by revealing the secret of how to make paper.

Islamic inventors changed the process to make it easier. And they designed new machines that allowed them to create a lot of paper at a time. By 794 CE, paper mills were opening in Baghdad, then the capital of the Muslim Empire (now the capital of Iraq). From there, paper-making skills spread all across the Muslim world. Cheaper, easy-to-make paper began to replace expensive papyrus, silk and parchment.

Paper super-charged the spread of Islam by allowing its message to be received not just by word of mouth, but also through the holy book called the Koran, a record of what Muhammad learned in his visions. So everyone could know what the angel had said to Muhammad, all Muslims were encouraged to learn to read, and schools were set up to teach them.

Muslim rulers valued learning of all kinds. This set off a blossoming of science and literature known as the Islamic Golden Age. Ancient texts, including works by famous philosophers like Aristotle, were respected, too. Hundreds of volumes were collected in the House of Wisdom, an enormous royal library in Baghdad.

This is a fragment of one of the earliest examples of the Koran, written on a paper scroll. It was made in the 700s or 800s CE.

Muslim scholars met at the House of Wisdom in Baghdad. They translated ancient texts into Arabic and shared knowledge and scientific ideas.

The Caliphs ordered that these ancient books be translated into Arabic from their original Greek, Latin and Persian. They summoned translators, philosophers and scholars to their courts to do the work. They even tried to find ways of merging the wisdom of philosophers like Aristotle with the divine revelations of Muhammad.

It's lucky for us that the Muslim Empire cared so much about learning. Over the centuries, many of the original books have been destroyed. But thanks to these learning-loving rulers, Arabic translations of them have survived and we can read important ancient books today.

Caliphs of Islamic Spain, which was called Al-Andalus, were determined not to be outdone by their rivals in Baghdad. They set up their capital city at Córdoba, and brought in experts from all over the Islamic world.

Arabic knowledge of how to irrigate fields using underground canals and waterwheels transformed the countryside. Oranges, lemons, apricots, mulberries, bananas, sugar cane and watermelons were all crops that had never been grown in Europe before. Muslim traders even introduced rice from India, making the popular Spanish dish paella possible.

Traders brought gold and ivory from across the Sahara. Córdoba's craftspeople turned them into coins, jewellery and luxury goods for the Caliph and his court. Builders constructed a spectacular mosque called the Mezquita. With more than a thousand columns made of jasper, onyx, marble and granite, this giant house of worship could hold as many as 40,000 Muslim faithful for their five-times-a-day prayers.

By about 1000 CE, the number of people living in Córdoba had grown to more than 100,000. It was one of the biggest cities of its day. One enthusiastic chronicler claimed the city had

The Mezquita was one of the largest mosques in the world. It was converted into a Christian church in the 1200s, after Christians drove the Muslims out of Córdoba.

Mansa Musa's Mali Empire was one of the biggest in the world at the time. He is said to have remarked that it would take a year to travel from one end of it to the other.

1,600 mosques, 900 public baths, 213,077 private homes and 80,455 shops. Even if this was a slightly colourful exaggeration, Córdoba sounds like it was a pretty bustling place. The enormous riches of the Islamic world are wonderfully told through the African kingdom of Mali. Its most famous king, Mansa Musa, was probably the richest man in the world. In 1324 he went on a pilgrimage to Mecca, taking with him more than eighty camels heavily laden with gold. A devout Muslim, Musa was very generous, making donations to the poor and to governments along his route. He stopped on the way to do some shopping in Cairo, Egypt. According to historians of the time, he spent so much gold and gave so much away that gold was worth less after his visit than it had been worth before.

Following his pilgrimage, Musa built an enormous palace in Timbuktu. This Mali city became famous as a centre for learning, with a giant university of 25,000 students and a library of up to 700,000 manuscripts.

Islamic courts like those in Baghdad, Córdoba and Timbuktu propelled ideas and inventions around a huge area that connected the Far East with the West. As a result, world-changing ideas from India and China began to filter through to Europe.

For example, an Italian merchant called Leonardo of Pisa (also known as Fibonacci) travelled to Islamic Algiers in north Africa. There he saw the awesome power of doing maths using a pencil and paper rather than an abacus, a sort of calculator made with beads strung on wooden rods.

The idea of number symbols on paper had come to Algiers from Baghdad. At the House of Wisdom there, two scholars named al-Kindi and al-Khwarizmi explained in about 825 CE how to do arithmetic using a new set of symbols. There were 1, 2, 3, 4, 5, 6, 7, 8 and 9 that stood for numbers of things, plus one more, 0, that stood for no things at all. These could be arranged in rows and columns to allow fast calculation. They came to be called Arabic numerals. But they weren't actually Arabic.

As we saw earlier, the Maya were some of the earliest people to use the idea of zero, but of course there was no contact then between them and the people of Asia, Africa and Europe. So that knowledge couldn't have found its way to Baghdad.

The Sankore Mosque (below) was one of the main centres of learning that made up the famed University of Timbuktu in Mansa Musa's time.

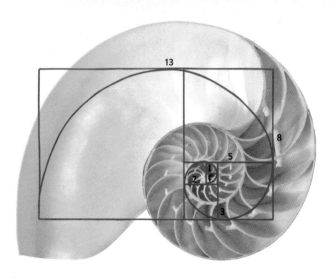

Fibonacci's book *Liber Abaci* (published in 1202) didn't just talk about the importance of Arabic numerals. It also explained number sequences and patterns, the most famous of which is called the Fibonacci sequence. This is a series of numbers where each new number is the sum of the previous two, as in 1, 1, 2, 3, 5, 8, 13 ... These ratios are often found in nature, as seen in the dimensions of this nautilus shell.

In about 628 CE, an Indian scholar called Brahmagupta wrote a maths book that showed how to use the digit 0 to write large numbers. For example, 2 can be turned into 20 just by adding a single new digit, a zero. Or 2 can be changed into 200 with two zeros. It was Brahmagupta's idea that had found its way to Baghdad.

When Fibonacci saw those Islamic merchants using numerals in north Africa, he decided he must take the ideas back to his homeland in Italy. The abacus was great at adding, but this new number system made subtraction, multiplication and division much simpler. And it was far easier than Roman numerals such as IV, XII and CVC, which were widely used in Europe at that time.

Within 200 years, Italian merchants and bankers had abandoned their old-fashioned ways and converted entirely to paper-based arithmetic using so-called Arabic numerals. This gave bankers more confidence to lend money, knowing they could easily keep track of loans and payments. Over time, banking families such as the Medici of Florence got so rich they could pay for fabulous works of art. All this money going to art triggered a renaissance of European art and culture, including works by Michelangelo, Leonardo da Vinci, and other famous painters and sculptors.

Modern medicine also owes much to Arabic scholars. Brilliant doctor Ibn Sina was born towards the end of the 900s in Bukhara, in what is now Afghanistan. He wrote about 450 books that we know of, many of them on medicine. Just stop for a second to think of what it means to write 450 books. Ibn Sina only lived to about the age of fifty-six. If we assume he started writing when he was sixteen and kept it up without stopping until he died, that means he wrote over eleven books per year. That's almost one book a month for forty years!

Ibn Sina's *Book of Healing* and *Canon of Medicine* were the most important medical textbooks in Europe for more than 500 years. The five-volume *Canon of Medicine* included the first detailed description of how the human eye works. It even told surgeons how to cure cloudy eyesight, a condition now known as cataracts.

Ibn al-Haytham, who lived at about the same time as Ibn Sina, was an Arab scientist who worked out the laws of light

Ibn Sina understood that the brain is divided into parts with different functions and that the spine connects the brain to nerves that run through all parts of the body. This illustration is from his work *Canon of Medicine*.

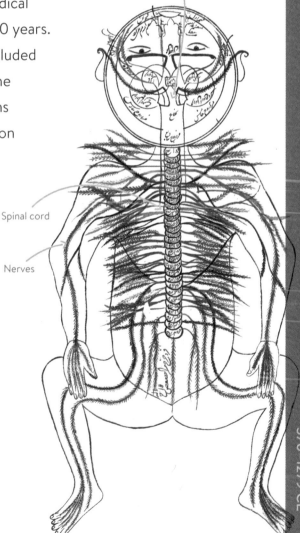

Brain

Spinal cord

Nerves

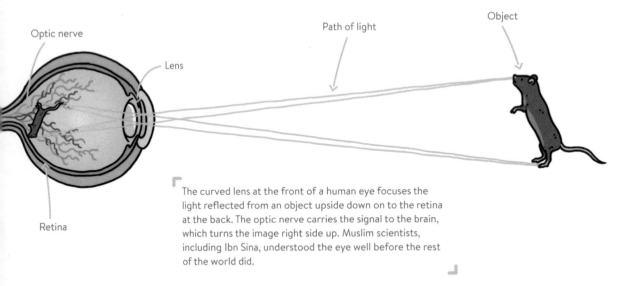

Optic nerve

Lens

Path of light

Object

Retina

The curved lens at the front of a human eye focuses the light reflected from an object upside down on to the retina at the back. The optic nerve carries the signal to the brain, which turns the image right side up. Muslim scientists, including Ibn Sina, understood the eye well before the rest of the world did.

and optics – about 600 years before Isaac Newton. Al-Haytham was born in Basra, in what is now Iraq, and spent most of his life in Cairo, Egypt. His book showed how rays of light can be reflected and bent, or refracted. It was later used by European scientist Galileo Galilei when he was building the world's first telescope for studying the stars and planets.

One reason these ideas spread so easily is because all of those thinkers were able to write on paper. But making books, and especially making more than one copy of a book, was still an enormous amount of work. Scribes, who were educated people with great handwriting, worked all day long copying books. Imagine how hard it was not to make mistakes. But that was the only way to do it. A new method of making multiple copies was desperately needed. Again, the answer came from China.

The world's oldest known complete, dated, printed book is now kept at the British Library in London, England. It is a Buddhist text called the Diamond Sutra, printed in 868 CE.

It was made in China using a technique called woodblock printing. Printers carefully carved wooden blocks with words and illustrations. They brushed the blocks with ink and pressed them on to sheets of paper. It was hard work to carve the wooden blocks, of course. But once they had been created, the number of copies that could be printed was almost limitless.

Now China's golden age of advances in science and technology was ready

Over five metres in length, the Diamond Sutra was named by the Buddha himself. Diamonds are the hardest substance we know of. The Buddha believed these teachings would cut like a diamond through life's illusions and reveal universal truths.

for take-off. Printing meant ideas, designs and creativity could spread even more easily from one place to another. Which is exactly what happened after a wise emperor called Taizu seized the imperial throne in 960 CE and founded a new dynasty called the Song.

One of Taizu's first acts was to increase dramatically the number of ordinary people who could take the exams to get government jobs – to about 30,000 a year.

Printers worked overtime. More than 500 classic texts, dictionaries, encyclopedias and history books were carved on to thousands of blocks of wood to provide mass-produced books for studying. At least a thousand new schools were opened throughout China to help prepare students for civil service exams.

But then, in 1127, disaster struck.

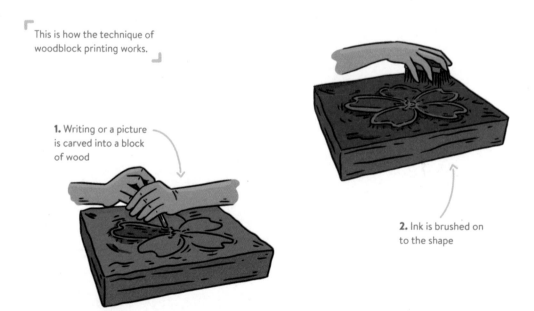

This is how the technique of woodblock printing works.

1. Writing or a picture is carved into a block of wood

2. Ink is brushed on to the shape

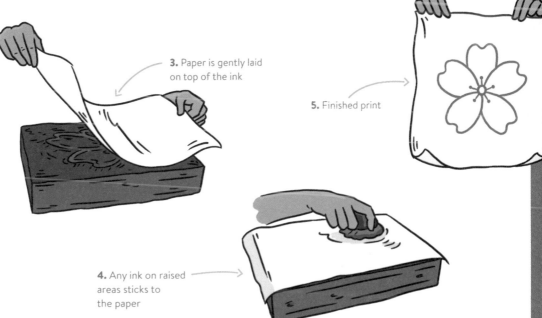

The ingenious Song government was rudely interrupted by violent gangs of people on horseback. They were a group called the Jurchens, and they came from Manchuria in the north. Well, that is how the Song saw it, anyway. The Jurchens would point out that they were the recently united Jin dynasty and that they were just expanding their empire by taking land from their weak neighbours to the south. And while they were at it, they were taking over most of the rest of northern China.

However you tell it, the result was that China was split between the northern Jin dynasty and what remained of the Song dynasty. The Song were forced to move their capital south of the Yangtze River. They were now known as the Southern Song dynasty.

Rulers of the Southern Song were angry. They challenged their people's best scholarly brains to come up with every possible way of making new weapons, with the aim of guaranteeing victory if their northern enemies attacked again.

3. Paper is gently laid on top of the ink

5. Finished print

4. Any ink on raised areas sticks to the paper

Charcoal, sulphur and a mixture of minerals had first been ground into a primitive form of gunpowder by Chinese monks during the Tang dynasty, in the mid 800s CE. These men had been ordered by their rulers to find a potion for bringing everlasting life. (Is this quest starting to sound familiar?) It's one of history's biggest ironies that during those experiments they stumbled across a combination of chemicals which could result in instant death. Brilliant minds at the court of the Southern Song were able to build on gunpowder technology to create an arsenal of powerful new weapons, ranging from catapult bombs to flame-throwing cannons.

And just when you might think the genius of these people must surely have some limits, they also pioneered the use of the most amazing navigation device of all time – the compass. The idea of

Can you see the devil with a snake weaving through his eye sockets to the right of the Buddha's head? He's about to throw a flaming bomb on to the Buddha. Above him and to the right, another demon is using a flame-thrower. This silk banner, dating to about 950 CE, is the earliest known illustration of the use of firearms.

magnetising a needle by rubbing it against silk and then floating it in water to make a primitive compass had been known in China since at least the first century CE. But in 1044, a Song dynasty military book called *Wujing Zongyao* described how this knowledge was used to create a south-pointing chariot to help guide troops in gloomy weather and on dark nights.

An even bigger breakthrough came a few years later. Song court scholar Shen Kuo worked out how to suspend a magnetised needle from a piece of silk thread and use it for navigation. His compass is known to have been used on Chinese ships from around the year 1100.

If there's one thing that history has taught us, it is that no empire can last for ever – however ingenious its people. And as we've seen before, climate can play a part in their rise and fall. In this case the climate that mattered was the one on the grasslands of central Asia north and west of China – the land of the Mongols.

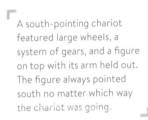

A south-pointing chariot featured large wheels, a system of gears, and a figure on top with its arm held out. The figure always pointed south no matter which way the chariot was going.

We know about year-by-year climate changes in Mongolia because in 2014 scientists Neil Pederson and Amy Hessl figured out something quite amazing. If you've ever looked at the end of a log, you can see rings. Each of those rings is the new growth of a particular year, so you can count the rings to know how old a tree is. And you can see by the width of the rings how warm and wet (or cold and dry) each year was.

Pederson and Hessl looked at very old trees in Mongolia and worked out that there was an intense drought in the area from 1180 to 1190. During this time, we know that Mongol groups were fighting one another. These were people who depended on horses, and horses depend on grass. So maybe the drought at least partly caused the conflict.

Then, from 1211 to 1225, there was a warm and rainy period which would have made the grass grow better than ever before. Suddenly there was plenty of grass for all. And what happened then was

astonishing. All those tribes united under the command of one man, Genghis Khan, and became one of the most successful conquering armies the world has ever seen. Did this happen at least partly because of good weather and plenty of grass? That's what Pederson and Hessl think.

Grass or no grass, Genghis Khan was a brilliant and brutal military planner who demanded toughness, dedication and loyalty from all his people. Soldiers who performed well in battle rose through the ranks. Cowards were killed. Each unit of ten men had a leader who reported up to the next level. If one soldier deserted, his unit of ten was executed. You can understand why people never disobeyed.

The Mongols were ruthless, but they were also open to new ways of thinking. They promoted people when they did a good job, not because they were from powerful families or even because of what country they were born in. Of course there was just one exception. Genghis Khan and his family were always in charge. The Mongol Empire was one of the most ethnically diverse in history. And many cultures were included in government. The Mongols created an international postal system. And they did research to improve farming.

Careful planning in military councils

> " THE TRANSITION FROM EXTREME DROUGHT TO EXTREME MOISTURE ... MUST HAVE CREATED THE IDEAL CONDITIONS FOR A CHARISMATIC LEADER TO EMERGE OUT OF THE CHAOS, DEVELOP AN ARMY AND CONCENTRATE POWER. "
>
> Amy Hessl, dendrochronologist

This painting shows Mongols invading a Chinese city. It is from a world history book by Persian historian Rashid-al-Din, who in 1314 assembled a team of artists from all over the Islamic world to illustrate it.

(called kurultai) and excellent spying using speedy horses were the key to Mongol military success. Whenever Genghis Khan faced an enemy city, he gave them a simple choice: surrender or die. And, as you can imagine, he was a man of his word.

By 1215 the Mongols had besieged and sacked the Jin Chinese capital at Yanjing (now Beijing). Genghis Khan then headed north and west, where his forces split into two and conquered Georgia and Crimea. On their way back to Mongolia they defeated a Russian army led by six princes. As was the Mongol custom, the defeated princes were crushed to death under the weight of a banqueting platform while the Mongol generals ate their victory feast on top.

Genghis Khan died in 1227 – no one knows how. Some say he fell off a horse. And there is a legend that he was stabbed by a Tangut princess from northern China in revenge for the murder of so many of her country's people.

Genghis Khan's children expanded the massive Mongol Empire across Russia, Siberia and deeper into central Asia. Even the Southern

The modern country of Mongolia honours Genghis Khan as their founding father. This sculpture of him sits outside the nation's Parliament building.

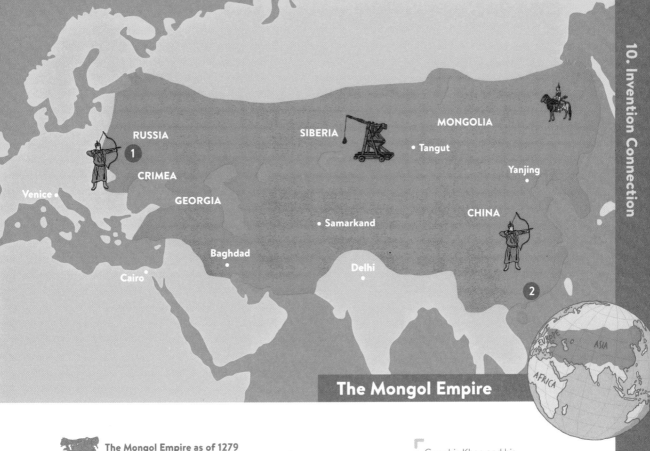

The Mongol Empire

The Mongol Empire as of 1279

1 **Battle of Mohi (1241)**
The Mongols defeat Polish, German and Hungarian forces.

2 **Battle of Yamen (1279)**
Genghis Khan's grandson Kublai defeats the Song dynasty.

Genghis Khan and his children and grandchildren created the Mongol Empire. It was the largest empire composed of one large land area the world has ever seen.

Song dynasty with its gunpowder weapons could not hold out for ever. It was one of Genghis' grandsons, Kublai Khan, who eventually defeated them.

The Song's last stand took place at the battle of Yamen in 1279, just outside what is now Hong Kong, China. When a loyal court official saw that the Song fleet had been destroyed, he knew what he had to do. Grabbing the nine-year-old Song emperor, Zhao Bing, he lifted the boy up off his feet and together they jumped from a cliff to their deaths in the sea below.

Chapter 11

MEDIEVAL MISERY

476–1526 CE

Christian Europe struggles following
the collapse of the Roman Empire

○ **542 CE**
The bubonic
plague reaches
Constantinople.

○ **800 CE**
Charlemagne is crowned
Holy Roman Emperor
by Pope Leo III.

○ **1006**
The Vikings stumble
upon the coast of
North America.

○ **1204**
Christian troops sack
Constantinople in
the Fourth Crusade.

1453
Ottoman forces capture Constantinople.

1215
King John of England is forced to agree to a set of rules called Magna Carta.

1347–1351
The Black Death kills 40 million people in Europe.

1526
Ottoman leader Suleiman the Magnificent invades Hungary and almost takes Vienna.

One of the joys of zooming out to connect together the dots of the past is that every so often you see interesting patterns. Here's a perfect example. Remember how over millions of years the world's tectonic plates go through a cycle of converging into one giant supercontinent and then split into small fragments? Well, zoom out over hundreds of years of human history and you'll see the same cycle. Empires form and split apart. Then new empires form and split apart again.

That splitting apart is exactly what happened in Europe following the fall of the western Roman Empire in 476 CE. Everybody was fighting everybody else. Europe was in a mess. About fifty years later, Byzantine Emperor Justinian I began making a huge effort to take back Europe and other parts of the former western Empire.

He sent armies and generals to
Spain, Italy and north Africa and
took lands seized by Germanic peoples
including the Huns, Vandals and Visigoths.
Justinian's success was short-lived, though.
Just three years after his death, another wave
of raiders called Lombards came streaming
down from the north. By 568 they were the
new masters of Italy.

Bubonic plague is caused by
bacteria carried inside blood-
sucking fleas. In the Middle
Ages, the fleas travelled on
the backs of rats and then
bit humans, spreading the
devastating plague.

The real losers in all of these wars were
ordinary people. They had to deal with army
after army crashing through their homes. Sometimes, they were
forced to move to a whole new place. Soldiers destroyed towns and
villages, hurt and killed innocent people, and stole food. But that
wasn't all the people had to suffer.

A terrible disease called bubonic plague broke out in about 541
and reached Constantinople in 542 CE. There it killed as many as
5,000 people a day, leaving forty per cent of the population dead. It
then spread across much of Europe. There were repeated outbreaks
over the next 300 years, killing as many
as 25 million people across western Asia,
north Africa and Europe. That's more
than the entire population of Australia
and New Zealand today.

Emperor Justinian I (centre)
stands between officials of the
church (right) and government
and military (left), showing that
he is the leader of all three.
This mosaic is a reproduction
of one in Ravenna, Italy, that
was created in about 547 CE.
The tiny tiles of the original are
made of glass, stone, ceramics,
gold, silver and mother of pearl.

All of this meant the number of
people living in Europe was falling fast.

There were about 27.5 million in 500 CE. By 650 CE, there were just 18 million. There weren't enough people to farm the fields, so forests grew up and covered them. There are very few records of new science, art or writing from this time. Some kings and the people close to them were doing fine. But apart from them, life for people in Europe between 350 and 750 CE was nasty, brutish and short.

In the north of France, the Carolingians (also known as the Franks) went about attacking their neighbours. By 800 CE, they had conquered and united the central part of Europe. This new empire included what are now Germany, Austria, the Czech Republic, Slovenia, Switzerland, the Netherlands and parts of Poland, Belgium, France and Italy. The Franks also pushed the Lombards out of Rome.

At that time the Pope was the leader of all Christians. Pope Leo III in Rome had been worried that the Lombards weren't strong enough to protect his holy city. So he was very happy when the Franks arrived. He crowned their leader, Charlemagne, Holy Roman Emperor on 25 December 800 CE. The idea was that Charlemagne was the heir to the glory of the old western Roman Empire. There were other kings in the lands across Europe, but they were all supposed to unite under Charlemagne.

Charlemagne kicked off a new era of learning. Ancient books were copied. Schools were opened. Music was written. When Charlemagne died, there were wars for his crown. But things settled down again in 962 CE, when Otto I became Holy Roman Emperor.

Even the weather perked up. Cold, harsh winters gave way to what historians call the Medieval Warm Period. Between 950 and 1250 CE temperatures were even milder than they are today. Grapes grew as far north as Britain. Ice sheets melted, opening up routes across the northern seas.

A milder climate made for better crops. Better crops made for more tax money for kings. Richer kings started making a new kind of deal with their people. It went like this. Come and join my army for a fixed number of days a year. In return, I will grant you land so you can grow food and make a living. This bargain is known as feudalism, and the people who farmed the land were called *peasants*.

B etter weather helped northern European people expand into new lands. Enter the Vikings, people from what are now Denmark, Norway and Sweden. From as early as the 790s CE, the

This is a portrait of Charlemagne painted in 1825. He is seen holding a model of the Palatine Chapel, in Aachen, Germany, which is all that remains of a giant palace he had built for himself.

Vikings were excellent traders with brilliant shipbuilding and sailing skills. Starting in 793 they invaded large parts of England, Scotland and Ireland.

By 839 they had sailed deep along rivers into the heart of Europe and settled in what are now Ukraine, Belarus and Russia. They called themselves the Rus, a word that is thought to come from an old Norse term, *rods*, meaning 'men who row'. The name Russia comes from these early Viking settlers.

Going the other way, the Vikings discovered a sea passage from Norway to Iceland and settled there in 874 CE. In a little over a hundred years, melting sea ice allowed them to get to Greenland. According to a series of Viking stories, known as the sagas, Erik the Red named the place Greenland because he wanted to make it sound like a great place to live.

Rope for raising the sail

Steering oar

Actually it was mostly covered in glaciers, and there was very little green about it.

In about 1006 the Vikings reached the coast of what is now Canada. There Erik the Red's son Leif Eriksson built a small town in what is now the Canadian province of Newfoundland. This settlement, established nearly 500 years before Christopher Columbus's famous voyage in 1492, marks the first attempt by Europeans to make their homes in the Americas. But it failed. No one is quite sure why.

Some people think it had to do with an everyday part of the Scandinavian diet – milk. A Saga tells how local people attacked the Viking settlers just one day after buying milk from them. That's weird, right? One day, you're trading happily. The next day, one of you attacks the other.

Erik the Red, nicknamed for his fiery red hair, attracted about 2,000–3,000 people to his new colony in Greenland.

Longships were the secret of the Vikings' success. These fast vessels allowed the Vikings to attack enemies quickly and nimbly. The thin shape was ideal for travelling on rivers as well as across the seas.

Powerful square sail

Oars for up to 50 men

Dragon head to terrify enemies

Norman horses fall on sticks or stones set by the English to trip them

English soldiers defend a hill

SIMVL:ANGLI ET FRANC:INPRELIO:

Dead soldiers and horses

The Bayeux Tapestry is a 70-metre-long embroidered timeline, woven by hand in about the 1070s. It tells the story of William of Normandy's invasion of England. The scene above shows part of the Battle of Hastings in 1066.

Nowadays lots of people don't digest cow's milk well. In fact, more than eighty per cent of the native people of North America don't. The people the Vikings met didn't have cows, so they would never have tasted cow's milk before. Maybe the milk made them feel sick, and they thought the newcomers had poisoned them. Could that be why they attacked?

The Vikings never did permanently settle in North America, but for hundreds of years they continued to visit and cut down trees for wood to bring back to Greenland and Iceland.

It's interesting that lots of people in history are known by names that other people gave them. The word Viking means 'pirate', so you can bet they didn't call themselves that. And they in turned called the people they met in Canada *skraelings*, which meant 'wretches', or 'poor miserable people'. That wasn't a very nice name either.

Bishop Odo waves a club to encourage Norman soldiers

William of Normandy lifts his helmet visor to show his troops that he's alive after a fall from a horse

One of the biggest Viking settlements in Europe was around Rouen, in western France. Here they became known as Normans, which means 'people from the north'. (I bet they liked that better than Vikings.) The Normans' most famous ruler, William of Normandy, invaded England, winning the Battle of Hastings in 1066.

Like the Roman Empire before it, feudalism thrived on conquest. A king could give newly captured lands to knights and nobles, who in return provided arms and soldiers for further conquest and war. As a way of trying to stamp his authority on England, William the Conqueror, as William of Normandy became known, ordered a survey of his adopted home. The result was the Domesday Book of 1086, which lists the lands and belongings of more than 265,000 people. It includes farmers, blacksmiths, potters, shepherds, slaves and everyone else, too. It's an amazing snapshot of medieval life.

Big data like this allowed William to let loose his tax collectors so they could extract as much money as possible from these newly conquered people. Domesday means 'Doomsday', but William didn't call it that. The people did. That's because the book changed tax from something that the lord might or might not remember to collect into something that was as sure as death.

Warmer weather brought more food. By 1000 CE, the European population had recovered to more than 37 million. By 1340, it was at 74 million. Such big increases in wealth and people made leaders even more eager to find new lands to conquer and call their own.

William the Conqueror stamped his authority on England by building a series of massive and intimidating stone castles such as the Tower of London.

All this time – as we've been paying attention to Europe – the Islamic world was having troubles of its own. The first Islamic empire broke into parts and fought one another. By about 1030, a new Muslim empire called the Great Seljuk Empire was rising. Based in Persia, it ruled land from central Asia all the way to what is now Turkey. It was at war with the Byzantine Empire, and it was winning. The Seljuks even captured the Byzantine emperor himself at the Battle of Manzikert in 1071. Then they went on to take over much of what is now Turkey. Europeans were getting nervous.

Christianity had split in half in 1054 along similar lines as the Roman Empire had much earlier. Western European Christians became Roman Catholics. Byzantine Christians became Orthodox Christians. Even so, in 1095, Pope Urban II, head of the Roman Catholic Church, called for a single European army to come to the Byzantines' aid.

Christian crusaders carried shields depicting the cross of Christ.

Jerusalem had been captured by Muslim forces more than 400 years before, not long after the death of Muhammad. Jerusalem was, and still is, holy to Jews, Christians and Muslims, and they have fought over it for centuries. Pope Urban thought it would be a good idea for a new Christian army to retake the holy city while they were supporting the Byzantine Empire.

The Pope's call worked. Europe's Christian rulers united and set out to push back the Seljuks. This was the start of a series of wars called the Crusades. Knights in armour set out on horseback to fight people they thought of as infidels (or unbelievers). They were fighting in the name of God. Of course the people they were attacking were fighting in the name of that exact same God. They just called him Allah.

When Pope Urban II said that any Christian who lost his life fighting the Muslims would be rewarded by God with eternal bliss in heaven, people took notice. The response was overwhelming. The effects of these bitter struggles rumble on even today.

This First Crusade was surprisingly successful for the powers of Europe. They captured Jerusalem. In those days it was usual for conquering armies to do more than take over territory. They would kill the people whose territory they'd taken (sometimes this even happens today). When the crusaders captured Jerusalem, they massacred the Jews and Muslims who lived there. They didn't kill the Orthodox Christians of Jerusalem, but they accused them of helping the Muslims, and forced them to leave the city.

A new Roman Catholic Kingdom of Jerusalem was created, which lasted about eighty years. Because the Europeans had

This drawing from the 1200s shows an imaginary fight on horseback between Richard I of England (left) and Saladin, Sultan of Egypt and Syria (right).

removed almost the whole population of the city, they spent much of that time trying to persuade Christians to settle there.

Then in 1187 Saladin, the sultan of Egypt and Syria, recaptured the holy city, returning it to Muslim hands. The loss of Jerusalem gave European leaders a reason to unite again. In 1189 an alliance of European kings including Richard I of England, Philip II of France and Frederick Barbarossa of the Holy Roman Empire, all supported by Pope Gregory VIII, marched to take back the Holy Land once again.

This would never happen nowadays. Rulers don't go to war themselves. They send their armies and keep in touch from a distance. But in the Middle Ages, kings and queens rode off to war. Often they rode right at the front of the army.

This crusade was not a success. Frederick drowned while crossing a river. Philip fell ill and returned to France. Richard made peace with Saladin after realising that his forces would never be strong enough to retake Jerusalem.

Richard was then captured on his way home by Leopold V, Duke of Austria. Leopold handed him over as a prisoner to the new Holy

> ## To all free men of our kingdom we have also granted, for us and our heirs for ever, all the liberties written out below, to have and to keep for them and their heirs, of us and our heirs...

King John of England,
Magna Carta

Roman Emperor, Henry IV. A huge ransom was paid for the return of the English king, who hurried home.

In 1204 another crusade set out for Jerusalem but never even got close. Instead they turned their attention to the rich city of Constantinople, which was inhabited by fellow Christians. On 12 April, these supposed soldiers of Christ broke in and did what they would have done to an enemy city. They stole treasures, destroyed property and attacked women. If they had done this exact same thing in Baghdad or Jerusalem, it would have been counted as honourable. But Constantinople was a Christian city. What happened was described at the time as one of the most shameful moments in all Christian history.

European Christians were suffering, but the Middle Ages were a great time for lots of other cultures. We've already seen how Islamic people in Spain and throughout the Middle East were thriving, with new inventions and brisk trade that transformed many people's fortunes. And the southern Africa Kingdom of Zimbabwe, with its towering capital at Great Zimbabwe, had an extensive trading network stretching from their circular stone city all the way to China. Shards of Chinese pottery as well as coins and glass beads from the Middle East suggest that the Zimbabweans were thriving until about 1450, when famine and climate change led their trading hub into decline.

Meanwhile Europe was still tearing itself apart with revolt and unrest. King John of England was so unpopular that on 15 June 1215 he was forced to meet with a group of noblemen in a field near Windsor, by the River Thames. They demanded he agree to a charter that would limit his power. No longer would he be able to do anything he wanted because he believed his power came from God. Instead he would have to obey a list of sixty-three rules. The list was known as Magna Carta.

These rules included not taking people's money to pay for his wars without asking them first. He was not allowed to throw people in prison without a fair trial. And he was also not allowed to take all the best fish for himself out of the River Thames. The Pope declared Magna Carta illegal soon after. But for some historians, this moment marks the beginning of a new age in which the rule of law began to take control from moody kings and upstart warlords.

King John of England agreed to the rules in Magna Carta by stamping it with his Great Seal. He didn't stick to his promises, though, making him one of the most unpopular kings in English history.

But that process took a long time. And there are some parts of the world where the rule of law is still not a reality today. In the Middle Ages, nobles and knights just got more and more powerful while ordinary people became poorer and poorer.

Then, things took a turn for the worse. By 1315 a series of three wet, cold summers had brought most of Europe north of the Alps and the Pyrenees to its knees. Crops would not grow. There was no food to feed the animals. And salt was almost impossible to find. In that time and place, salt had to be made by evaporating salty water. And when it's raining or very humid, water doesn't evaporate well. The only way to preserve meat was with salt, so a shortage of salt was a disaster. No one but the richest landlords could afford to eat. Even the English king, Edward II, was unable to find enough bread to feed his court while touring the country that summer.

Survival meant killing farm animals and eating seeds saved for next year's crops. Terrible things followed. All over Europe, children were abandoned and left to find food for themselves. The German fairy story of Hansel and Gretel is thought to date from this time. Some elderly people even starved themselves to death on purpose for the sake of the rest of their families. Disease spread quickly through the poorly fed, weakened people. In 1276 the length of life for the average European was thirty-five years. By 1325 it had fallen to not much more than twenty. Then what happened the last time Europe was miserable and divided happened again. The plague was back.

Rats are usually blamed for spreading the appalling Black Death that struck Europe between 1347 and 1351. But humans were just as much to blame. As we saw before, this awful disease is caused by bacteria that live inside tiny insects called fleas. The fleas mostly prefer to live on small, furry creatures like rats. But if a human comes along, they'll hop right on. And, of course, anyone, human or animal, with an infected flea on them carries the bacteria anywhere they go.

This terrible plague was the same disease that had caused so many deaths in the 500s. This time it probably started in China in the 1330s and spread from there along the Silk Road.

In this painting from the 1300s, plague victims are blessed by a priest. Without the benefit of modern medicine, prayer was their only hope.

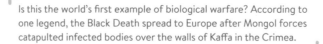

Is this the world's first example of biological warfare? According to one legend, the Black Death spread to Europe after Mongol forces catapulted infected bodies over the walls of Kaffa in the Crimea.

There is a legend of how it spread to Europe. As the story goes, in 1346 the Mongol ruler Jani Beg and his troops had the trading port of Kaffa on the north coast of the Black Sea surrounded. They were trying to force the city to surrender by keeping anyone from going in or out. This is called a siege. But so many of his troops got sick and died from the plague that he knew he would have to abandon his plans.

In a desperate last stand, Beg's few surviving troops loaded the bodies of their many dead fellows on to catapults, and hurled them over Kaffa's walls. At the time, a group of traders from Genoa in Italy were in Kaffa. Once they understood what was happening, they got on a ship back to Italy. But they had unintentionally brought some infected fleas with them. Most of the Genoese died on the ship, but the few who reached home passed on the killer disease.

Over the next three years, more than 40 million Europeans died. That was more than half the continent's population. Between 1348 and 1375 the average European lived to be just over seventeen years old, the lowest ever.

Feudalism eventually broke down because there simply weren't enough peasants left on the land to become soldiers. English kings like Henry V were forced to pay soldiers money or even to hire their own permanent armies. To get the money to do that meant more taxes on the people. But the people had the upper hand this time. Because there were so few of them, they could demand more power, freedom and fair pay in return for their labour.

See how interconnected the world has now become? Plague came to Europe on fleas from China. Ancient wisdom was preserved on paper and brought from Baghdad to Islamic Spain. Chinese pottery was being used in southern Africa. But what came next – from Asia to the rest of the world – was to change everything utterly, and for ever.

Gunpowder had been known in Europe since at least 1267. That's when a recipe for it appeared in a book called *Opus Majus*. But even though Roger Bacon, an Englishman, had written the book, no European army tried out cannons until 1346.

No one quite knows how the secrets of gunpower spread across Europe. The first use might have been in 1342 at the siege of the Spanish city of Algeciras. There, Muslims defending the city fired primitive firearms that shot pieces of iron over the city walls to drive off attacking Christian forces. The siege lasted almost two years.

English forces used Europe's first cannon against their arch-enemies, the French, at the Battle of Crécy in 1346. They didn't work very well, but over time the technology improved, transforming warfare.

> ## THE BESIEGED DID GREAT HARM AMONG THE CHRISTIANS WITH IRON BULLETS THEY SHOT.
>
> Juan de Marianas,
> historian

But in the end the Muslims surrendered. Gunpowder hadn't been enough to hold the city.

Four years later, a gunpowder cannon was rolled out by the English against their arch-enemies, the French, at the Battle of Crécy. Though the English won, the cannons didn't work so well. In fact, it was probably safer to be in front of one of those cannons than to be operating it.

But within a hundred years, guns were an army's first-choice weapons. Cannon fire could sometimes reduce a stone castle to rubble in just minutes. Handguns turned unskilled peasant fighters into lethal soldiers who could kill at a distance.

A Hungarian cannon engineer named Urban may have been the world's first arms dealer. It was 1452, and he had designed a huge cannon. Looking for someone to pay him to make it, he went to the Byzantine emperor, Constantine XI. Constantine turned him down. So Urban went to Constantine's enemy, Sultan Mehmed II, leader of the Ottoman Empire. Mehmed said yes. So Urban's giant gun ended up on the Ottoman side of an incredibly important battle.

And when I say giant, I really mean it. Each cannon was eight metres long, made of copper and tin. Some said it took fifty oxen to pull one and a crew of 700 men to fire it.

Nearly 750 years had passed since the last time Muslim forces had tried to take the city of Constantinople, capital of the Byzantine Empire and guardian of rich trade routes. In the meantime, the

Islamic world had gone through a lot of changes. New empires had replaced the older caliphates. One of them, based in Turkey, was the Ottoman Empire, Urban's new employer.

By the spring of 1453, a giant force of 80,000 Ottoman soldiers had gathered just outside the massive walls of Constantinople. Urban's cannons slowly rolled across the plains to just outside the city. Giant balls of stone and marble pounded Constantinople's walls. They landed with such force that it was said they smashed two metres into the ground. On 28 May 1453, the Ottomans broke through the city walls, and troops flooded inside.

When news of the fall of Constantinople reached Europe, it stunned the Christian world. With Constantinople went the remaining territory of the Byzantine Empire. That included the silver mines of Serbia and Greece, which were very important to Europe's economy.

Sultan Mehmed II did business with a Hungarian arms-dealer, helping him secure victory over the Byzantines in 1453.

And some people living in the former Byzantine empire were converting to Islam, which scared Christians.

Ottoman Sultan Selim I closed in even more. He invaded Egypt, cutting off historic trading links between Europe and east Asia. His successor, Suleiman the Magnificent, invaded Hungary in 1521. After winning the Battle of Mohacs five years later, Muslim armies massed outside the walls of Vienna, in what is now Austria.

It was only the harshest of winters that saved Vienna from falling, forcing Suleiman to call his troops home. He tried again in 1532 but again was stopped by bad weather. Very cold winters were getting more common by then, a trend that continued for hundreds of years.

But if the cold weather provided temporary relief for the people of Vienna, it proved fatal to the adventurous Vikings of Greenland. Plummeting temperatures were just too cold to handle. The sea ice closed in, and nobody could get to or from the frozen land. The people there disappeared completely. They must have starved or frozen to death.

Christian Europe was now surrounded. To the north lay ice, to the west an ocean that seemed too vast to navigate. The east and south were firmly in the hands of enemy Muslim traders and rulers. It's fair to say that Christian Europe was badly in need of a miracle.

Muslim attackers face off Christian defenders at the Siege of Constantinople in 1453.

Chapter 12

GOING GLOBAL

1415–1621
European explorers race
to conquer a 'New World'

Timeline

1443
The Portuguese
find a sea route to
African gold.

1488
Portuguese explorer
Bartolomeu Dias is the
first European to see the
southern tip of Africa.

1492
Ferdinand and Isabella
defeat the last Muslim
stronghold in Spain.

1492–1503
Christopher Columbus
completes four voyages
between Spain and the
Americas.

N

1494
Spain and Portugal
divide the world up
between them.

1517
Martin Luther
protests against the
Church, sparking
the Protestant
Reformation.

1522
Spain conquers the
Aztec Empire.

1620
English Protestants found
Plymouth Colony.

She was an eighteen-year-old princess and the heir to a throne. He was a prince, one year younger, and first in line to be king in another land. They met and a week later they were married. Her family was furious.

Sound familiar? No, this isn't the trailer from a Hollywood movie. Nor is it the blurb from a Shakespeare play. It's the true story of two monarchs who lived in what is now Spain – Isabella of Castile and Ferdinand of Aragon. And this story is not about love and romance. It's about power and politics.

When Isabella's brother, King Henry, died, a war broke out over who should lead the country of Castile: Isabella or her niece Joanna. But Isabella was ready for a fight. She had chosen to marry Ferdinand, a man whose father had a big army. She won the war with help from Aragon and became Queen of Castile in 1474, aged twenty-three. Five years later, Ferdinand's father died. So he became King of Aragon. Isabella and Ferdinand's marriage made them immensely powerful, ensured peace between Castile and Aragon, and eventually led to the modern country of Spain.

And what did Isabella and Ferdinand do with all their power? First of all, in 1492, they completed the Christian conquest of Spain by driving their Muslim enemies out of the southern state of Granada. Then they forced all the Jews and Muslims who had been peacefully practising their religions in the area to convert to Christianity or leave. Their plan was to make their countries 100 per

By combining their two countries, Ferdinand and Isabella became some of the most powerful monarchs in Europe.

cent Roman Catholic. The Pope called them The Catholic Monarchs. They also wanted to challenge the rising power of Portugal, their rival to the west.

Portugal had a huge head start. That's because over fifty years before, they had a prince who was a treasure hunter. In 1415, when Henry was twenty-one, he helped the Portuguese navy capture a north African town called Ceuta. Pirates based there had been kidnapping Portuguese villagers to sell into slavery in Africa. Henry's father, King John I of Portugal, wanted that to stop. Henry wanted to catch the pirates, too, but he also had his eyes on Ceuta for another reason – gold.

Muslim traders came into the town's market, their camels laden with treasure. They had travelled for forty days across the vast Sahara to the fantastically rich Songhai Empire, which controlled most

Islamic merchants traditionally used camels to transport salt, slaves and gold across the Sahara.

of West Africa. On the way to Songhai, the camel caravan carried blocks of salt mined in the desert. The Songhai had huge gold mines, but they didn't have enough salt to preserve their meat. So they were happy to trade their gold for the precious salt.

Gold might have been plentiful in Songhai but it was expensive in Ceuta. That's because its price included not just the cost of the salt that was used to pay for it but also the expense of carrying the gold hundreds of miles across the Sahara and big profits for the Muslim merchants. If only, thought Henry, a way could be found to get to that gold without having to cross the desert or pay those merchants!

Henry's plan was to reach the source of the gold by sea – sailing south along the west African coastline. He sent out expedition after expedition of intrepid sailors. When they came back, he had his map-makers update their charts so that they could be used for future expeditions.

Henry's first challenge was to navigate past Cape Bojador, just south of modern-day Morocco. This was the most southerly point

Portuguese explorers sailed in caravels – small, easy-to-manoeuvre sailing ships. Their triangular sails were used for sailing into the wind.

Europeans had reached. Because of its fearsome currents and strong winds, it was known as the place where sea monsters dwelt. Some thought it was the end of the Earth.

You have to hand it to Henry. He had perseverence. He sent out fifteen expeditions over ten years. Finally, in 1434, one of Henry's captains, Gil Eanes, found that by sailing far out to sea, he could catch winds that would push his boats further down the coast. Ten years later Portuguese sailors reached the Bay of Arguin, on the coast of what is now Mauritania. There they built a fort.

Now Henry was able to buy gold south of the desert and cut out the Muslim middlemen. But he had also found he could get super-rich another way – by buying and selling human beings as slaves. At first, the Portuguese kidnapped African sailors. But it didn't take long for the Africans to start fighting back and winning. So the Portuguese then bought people who had already been captured by African slave traders. Things went so well for the Portuguese (but not for the people they were buying and selling) that in 1452, Portugal celebrated by making its first ever gold coins.

Prince Henry died in 1460, but his successes inspired a generation of new explorers. If gold and people to enslave could be found just down the coast of west Africa, what other riches lay out there in the unknown world?

Cruzado coins were made by the Portuguese out of gold transported by sea from south of the Sahara.

Ｎew expeditions produced astonishing results. In May 1488, Portuguese explorer Bartolomeu Dias was the first European to see the southern tip of Africa. Maybe this was a new sea route to the spice-rich lands of east Asia? King John II of Portugal named Africa's southern tip the Cape of Good Hope.

Exciting progress like this possibly explains why John II rejected the advances of an ambitious sailor named Christopher Columbus. Columbus had sailed the whole coast of Europe and traded along the west African coast. So he relished the excitement of the unknown.

Columbus was gripped by a big idea. Like all educated Europeans of his day, he knew the world was round. He had also read a lot of books, including stories of the riches of the Mongol emperor Kublai Khan written by a famous traveller called Marco Polo. Polo's book *Il Milione* told of his travels through Asia between 1271 and 1295 and was one of the bestsellers of its day.

Columbus decided that Indonesia, China and Japan (the area the Europeans called the Indies) were actually closer to Europe if you went west across the ocean than if you went east across the land. If that were true, whoever found a westward sea route to the Indies would become very rich indeed. The country that paid for the trip would, too.

Columbus went to King John II of Portugal twice to ask for the money to fund his exploration. But the king was having none of it. Perhaps he knew Columbus was making a big mistake thinking it was so quick to reach China by sailing west. After all, he already had a lot of explorers and mapmakers hard at work. Columbus's request for funding was also rejected by Genoa, Venice and England. So, thought Columbus, why not try Portugal's chief rivals – Ferdinand and Isabella?

Christopher Columbus is the English version of Columbus's Latin name, Christophorus Columbus. He was called Cristòffa Cónbo in Ligurian (the language of Genoa, where he was probably born), Cristoforo Colombo in Italian, and Cristóbal Colón in Spanish.

Marco Polo (shown here leaving Venice, in what is now Italy, in 1271) was from a trading and exploring family. The Polos travelled all over Asia at a time when few Europeans knew anything about places far away. Marco Polo's bestselling book about his travels inspired many other explorers.

By January 1492, Granada had surrendered to the Catholic Monarchs, and more than 750 years of Muslim rule in Europe was over. Now that Ferdinand and Isabella were set on driving out the Muslims and Jews, they couldn't demand gold from them any more. And because of a deal made at the end of a war with Portugal, they couldn't get gold directly from Africa either. Therefore they needed to find a new source for the precious metal. They also wanted to stop Portuguese merchants grabbing the whole unknown world for themselves. And so they placed a bet on Columbus.

Columbus is often described as the discoverer of North and South America. But of course he wasn't. Many diverse cultures and civilisations were already living in the Americas when he got there. He just stumbled into their world. And the first Europeans in the New World had been the Vikings, though they hadn't stayed long. Columbus himself never stopped believing he had reached Asia, even after pretty much everyone else knew that he hadn't.

But Columbus's voyages were important for three reasons. First, he finished solving the puzzle of the Atlantic winds, a process started by Portuguese explorers of west Africa. Now any Europeans could follow his route west. Second, he began an epic rivalry between Spain and Portugal that got almost the entire globe mapped. Third, the colony he founded on the Caribbean island of Hispaniola (now Haiti and the Dominican Republic) became

> " ALL THESE ISLANDS ARE DENSELY POPULATED WITH THE BEST PEOPLE UNDER THE SUN; THEY HAVE NEITHER ILL-WILL NOR TREACHERY. "

Christopher Columbus, explorer and coloniser

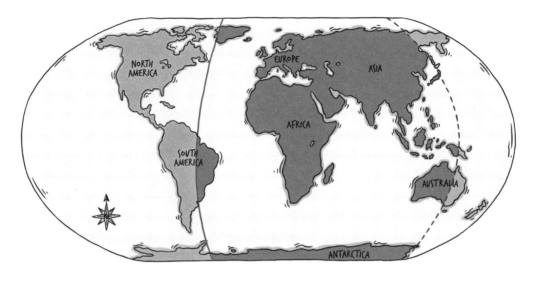

Treaty of Tordesillas (1494)

- - - Treaty of Zaragoza (1529)

Spanish territories

Portuguese territories

In 1494 Spain and Portugal ignored hundreds of independent civilisations around the world and divided the right to rule newly 'discovered' places along a line drawn down the middle of the Atlantic Ocean. In 1529 they agreed to another line along the Pacific coast of Asia. Together, these two treaties gave Africa and Asia to Portugal and most of the Americas to Spain.

the springboard for Spanish explorers and colonists preparing to conquer the rest of the Americas. Columbus had opened the floodgates. The Americas would never be the same again.

In 1494 Spain and Portugal signed a pact called the Treaty of Tordesillas. Incredible as it sounds today, this agreement divided the entire world into just two parts along a line drawn down the middle of the Atlantic Ocean. Everything 'discovered' to the east would belong to Portugal, everything to the west to Spain. Portugal got all of Africa. Clearly the people who already lived there didn't get a say. And when it came to the Americas,

Europeans established sugar cane plantations in the Caribbean and South America. The gruelling work was done by enslaved people brought over from West Africa.

that meant that Portugal got the area that would be Brazil, which sticks out further east than the rest. Spain got everywhere else. Of course, nobody asked the people who already lived in Africa, Asia or the Americas what they thought of this plan.

Most Europeans of the period were just fine with all of this. They believed that they were bringing Christianity and a future in heaven to the whole world. The idea was that if you were a Christian, you could go to heaven. If you were not a Christian, you would go to hell. So by converting native people to Christianity they were doing them a big favour, even if it meant the loss of everything the new converts cared about and a life of slavery. Looked at from centuries later, this whole idea seems appalling, but that really is what a lot of Europeans thought at the time.

Portuguese sailor Vasco da Gama was the first European to sail east around the Cape of Good Hope, arriving in India on 14 May 1498. The Portuguese settled along the coast of the Persian Gulf, India and Indonesia. They reached Japan about fifty years later. Meanwhile, Pedro Álvares Cabral, also from Portugal, sailed west, arriving in what is now Brazil in April 1500.

By the 1530s, the African slave trade was booming. Europeans were buying people in Africa and transporting them across the ocean to Brazil and the Caribbean, where most of the local people Europeans had tried to enslave had either died or escaped. There the Africans were forced to work harder than anyone should ever have to. One of the most notorious jobs was farming sugar cane and processing it into sugar. This work was so dangerous that most slaves died in less than five years if they didn't manage to escape first. The sugar they made was then shipped across the ocean and sold in Europe for high prices. The sugar growers were making so much money that they could afford to buy more people to work to death. Thanks to this ugly business, European nations got richer and richer.

And then there was gold. This shiny yellow metal was so valuable that the hope of finding it made Europeans willing to face any kind of danger. Spanish cousins Hernán Cortés and Francisco Pizarro were after gold when they set out on separate expeditions. Each of them was responsible for the destruction of a huge, powerful empire. Cortés brought down the Aztecs, Pizarro the Inca. They, and other Spaniards like them, were known as conquistadors – or conquerors. Quite how they made these conquests counts as one of the most extraordinary stories in all history.

Hernán Cortés was able to communicate with native people through Gerónimo de Aguilar, a Spanish sailor, and Malintzin, a Nahua woman who had been sold into slavery and given to Cortés as a gift.

When Cortés arrived off the coast of Mexico in the spring of 1519, he had just eleven ships, 110 sailors and 530 soldiers. But he then chanced upon a Spanish sailor who had been shipwrecked on a previous expedition. Gerónimo de Aguilar had been captured by the Aztecs and had lived among them as a slave for eight years. During that time, he had learned their language and customs.

Then a group of local Maya people gave Cortés twenty enslaved people as a gift. One of them, a woman named Malintzin, spoke both of the main local languages. Now with two translators, Cortés found he could make himself understood by just about anyone he might meet on his hunt for gold.

Cortés made a military alliance with two local peoples, the Totonac and Tlaxcalans. This wasn't so hard when he explained he wanted to defeat the Aztecs. The Aztecs demanded that the surrounding communities pay them taxes. So of course those communities were happy for a chance to conquer them.

The last Aztec emperor was Moctezuma II. During his reign the Aztec Empire reached its peak. But all was lost soon after his death in 1520.

Now Cortés and his small band of warriors had the allies they needed to advance to Tenochtitlán, the glorious capital of the Aztec Empire. You know, the one built in the middle of a lake.

The Aztec king was called Moctezuma II. After welcoming Cortés and his army as guests, the ruler soon found himself a prisoner in his own palace. Cortés demanded an enormous ransom in gold

as the price of the king's freedom. As more and more treasure was given over to the Spanish, the Aztec people got angrier and angrier at Cortés, his warriors, and the huge ransom demand.

This drawing of the 1521 final Siege of Tenochitlán is from a visual history by artists in or near Aztec territory, who created it only about thirty years after the fall of the Empire.

But within a few days Moctezuma lay dead. No one quite knows how he died. Did Cortés or one of his men kill him? Or perhaps a disgruntled Aztec official did the dastardly deed? Anyway, by the beginning of July 1520, furious Aztec citizens forced the Spanish to flee the city.

When the Spanish returned a few months later, they came with a huge new army, mostly made up of people sick of being under the thumb of the Aztecs. But worse killers than any army were the diseases the Europeans carried with them. They didn't know why the smallpox that they were used to in Europe was killing whole villages in the Americas. And the Americans didn't know why either. It seemed like a horrible supernatural plague.

We now understand what was happening. Like the bubonic plague that struck medieval Europe, smallpox is a highly infectious disease. Unlike bubonic plague, though, smallpox in Europe was what's called endemic. That means it was always around. It killed some people, but others survived. Over time, lots of people had already been exposed to the disease, so they were immune.

In the Americas, it was different. The smallpox virus had never been there before, so nobody had ever had it. It ripped through the native people of both North and South America. About forty

Expeditions by European explorers

ARCTIC OCEAN

Greenland

Siberia

England

Russia

JACQUES CARTIER 1534-41

JOHN CABOT 1497-98

North America

Portugal Spain

ATLANTIC OCEAN

HERNÁN CORTÉS 1519

CHRISTOPHER COLUMBUS 1492

Arabia

India

CHRISTOPHER COLUMBUS 1492-94

BARTOLOMEU DIAS 1487-88

PACIFIC OCEAN

Africa

INDIAN OCEAN

FRANCISCO PIZARRO 1531

South America

VASCO DA GAMA 1497-98

Cape of Good Hope

per cent of the Aztec population died within a year of their first contact with the Spanish. Weakened by these deaths and besieged by Cortés's army, Tenochtitlán fell into Spanish hands. More than 240,000 Aztecs died in the final eighty-day siege, some in the fighting and some from smallpox.

The way was now clear for a Spanish conquest of the whole region. The country was renamed New Spain, and a governor was appointed as overlord in 1524. When news of the discovery of Aztec silver mines began to filter back to Spain, more European adventurers set sail, hoping to get rich quick in the New World.

In 1529, Cortés's second cousin, Francisco Pizarro, received royal Spanish approval for a conquest of the Inca in South America. Pizarro's tactics were inspired by those of his cousin Cortés. On 16 November 1532, he arranged for some of his men to meet the Inca emperor, Atahualpa, in the central square of a hilltop town called Cajamarca.

Atahualpa approached the town square in a ceremonial procession with a large group of followers. Accounts of what happened next, written by the Spanish, claim that the emperor was ordered to abandon his native religion and accept the word of Jesus Christ. When Atahualpa refused, Pizarro's men charged on horseback from all sides of the square and his men opened fire.

Once it became clear that there was money to be made in the exploration and conquest of far-away civilisations, the countries of Europe rushed out to grab their share of the treasure. This map shows the routes of some of the explorers.

The surprise attack created mass panic. Huge numbers of Inca were killed in the confusion. From there the story is very similar to Moctezuma's. The emperor was captured and imprisoned in a small room.

A 'ransom room' was piled high with treasure to try and make the Spanish take money instead of executing Atahualpa, but the Spanish took the money and executed him anyway.

Not long after, huge ships, called galleons, were arriving in Spanish ports filled to the brim with Inca gold and Aztec silver.

Other European nations were also on the move. As early as 1497 merchants in Bristol, England, had paid John Cabot to explore the coast of North America. Jacques Cartier, a French navigator, sailed to what is now Canada on a series of expeditions for the French king, Francis I. In 1522, Portuguese explorer Ferdinand Magellan's expedition became the first ever to travel all the way around the world.

So far, most explorers were trying to get rich quick. But in northern Europe, a massive shift in the way people thought about themselves and their God was about to change that. It is called the Protestant Reformation.

You see, while rulers and merchants were making fortunes as usual, everyday people were no better off than before. And the Church wasn't helping. Imagine going to church on a Sunday morning only to be told by the priest that you are so sinful that what awaits you in the next life

Martin Luther fastened his list of ninety-five protests on the doors of Wittenburg Cathedral in 1517.

is eternal damnation in the fires of hell. Understandably, you'd feel terrified.

"Luckily," says the priest, "there is a solution. Confess your sins to me and they will be forgiven by God!" Sometimes you would have to do a good deed to achieve forgiveness.

But sometimes there was a catch. If your priest was corrupt he would demand money in exchange for forgiveness. As a result, priests and the Church became fabulously rich, while ordinary people continued to struggle to put food on their tables.

There was plenty of grumbling about the problem of corrupt priests, but the big moment came when a German monk called Martin Luther decided that selling forgiveness was completely wrong. In fact he went one step further. Luther argued that the only way to be forgiven for your sins was to have complete faith in Jesus Christ.

After German goldsmith Johannes Gutenburg invented the moveable-type printing press, books became much cheaper to buy. The most popular was a Latin translation of the Bible.

In 1517, Luther nailed a list of ninety-five complaints, known as the Ninety-five Theses, against the Catholic Church on to the door of a cathedral in Wittenburg, Germany. He also encouraged everyone to read the Bible instead of just letting priests tell them what it said. Of course not everyone could read. But an easy-to-use printing press had been invented by Johannes Gutenberg in 1450, so the Bible in Latin and later in other languages was available to anyone who could read it. And there's nowhere in the Bible where it says you have to pay money to priests to have your sins forgiven. You can see why many people felt abused and angry.

Luther's protest gave its name to a new form of Christianity, called Protestantism, which grew throughout Europe in the years that followed.

It wasn't just ordinary people who welcomed Luther's message. Rulers keen to break free of the Catholic Church also leaped on to the protesters' bandwagon, not necessarily for religious reasons. When the Pope refused to allow Henry VIII of England to divorce his Spanish wife, Henry declared that he, not the Pope, was head of the Church of England.

Protestantism spread elsewhere, too. Bitter enemies of Catholic Spain, such as Holland, Denmark and Sweden, became Protestant. Others, like France and Britain, went back and forth between the old and new faiths. In these countries, whatever religion you followed, you were in danger if the other side was in power. Neither

The Pilgrims left England in autumn 1620, arriving on the north-east coast of North America. Enough of them survived to establish a new permanent settlement.

Catholics nor Protestants were safe for long. And Protestantism itself splintered into many branches, or denominations, which frequently fought one another.

What would you have done if you had been alive then? Would you have chosen a side and joined in the fighting? Or would you have tried to mind your own business, hoping that everyone would just leave you alone? Both seem rather risky.

Of course, there was one other option. Escape.

Some people who got fed up with all the wars and arguments and danger did exactly that. In the autumn of 1620 a group of just over 100 English people set off with their families on a dangerous one-way voyage on board one of the most famous ships in history. It was called the *Mayflower*. There was already a thriving British colony in North America called Virginia, where a permanent settlement had started in 1607. And there was another British colony on the island of Bermuda, officially founded in 1612. The *Mayflower* wasn't heading to either of those places, though. Its passengers were off to start a brand new colony in an area the British called New England.

The leaders of the expedition were a group of about thirty-five protestants known as Puritans or Separatists. They were looking for a place where they could practise their religion and preserve their English culture. The rest of the voyagers were servants or farmers hoping to find a better life than they would have had back home. They settled in a town they called Plymouth, in what is now Massachusetts, United States. This motley crew was later known as the Pilgrim Fathers.

After being kidnapped into slavery, escaping and returning home, Tisquantum found his whole tribe dead. When the Pilgrims moved into his old village, he became an important adviser to their leaders and an ambassador between them and the local peoples of the area. Here, an artist of the 1900s imagines a scene where Tisquantum teaches some Pilgrims how to grow corn.

The Plymouth colonists had some very good luck. Early on, they found corn in Native American graves and storage areas. They stole it so they could have seeds to plant. They found an area of cleared land ready to build and plant on. They thought God had left it there for them, so they began building houses. There was no time to waste, because winter was closing in.

The settlers found out later that Plymouth was on the site of a Patuxet village that had been abandoned because the local people had died in a disease outbreak. The English called the disease 'Indian fever'. But it was probably smallpox brought over by European explorers.

Soon after the Pilgrim Fathers arrived, visitors began to appear. First came an Abenaki man named Samoset, who spoke a little English.

Then came a local Patuxet man named Tisquantum. He had lived in England and was fluent in the language. He offered to help the new settlers get to know the local people and learn to live off the land. What a miracle it must have seemed to the settlers to have Native Americans walk out of the woods speaking their language.

Even with all this good luck, they had arrived too late in the year to grow enough food, and it was a horrible winter. More than half of the original group died either of starvation or disease. But by September 1621, those who survived had a good harvest and a peaceful relationship with their neighbours. The settlers celebrated with their new neighbours, the Wampanoag. The US holiday of Thanksgiving was created to commemorate that moment.

The peace didn't last. It couldn't. With tens of thousands of British colonists flooding into Massachusetts alone, things were getting crowded. The Europeans continued to believe that anything they found was theirs to take. But, as you can imagine, the Native Americans, whose ancestors had been in the Americas for over 10,000 years, didn't like that idea one little bit.

> ALL GREAT, AND HONOURABLE ACTIONS, ARE ACCOMPANIED WITH GREAT DIFFICULTIES; AND MUST BE, BOTH ENTERPRISED, AND OVERCOME WITH ANSWERABLE COURAGES.

William Bradford, governor of Plymouth Colony

Chapter 13

REVOLUTIONS ALL AROUND

1543–1905
Science, freedom and robots

1789
French revolutionaries
storm the Bastille.

1543
Copernicus publishes
his theory that the
Sun is in the centre
of the universe.

1803
The Louisiana
Territory is purchased
by the United States
from the French.

1776
The United States
declares independence
from Britain.

1815
Napoleon is
defeated by
the British.

1869
The US Transcontinental Railroad is completed.

1829
George Stephenson's *Rocket* wins the Rainhill trials.

1876
Bell invents the telephone. Benz invents the petrol car.

1882
Electric power stations are opened in New York and London.

1905
Albert Einstein discovers that E=mc².

Jacques de Vaucanson was a French inventor who made clockwork robots. His constructions included a flute player who could play twelve different tunes and a waiter who could serve drinks at a party. His most famous robot was the Digesting Duck. It could flap its wings, eat food – and even poop out of the other end! De Vaucanson was part of a long history of people imagining and building lifelike machines. The Chinese built a clock with gong-ringing mannequins as early as 1088. Ismail Al-Jazari, a Muslim inventor who lived from 1136 to 1206, constructed several automatons, including one where automated musicians floated on a lake. In 1292 Count Robert II of Artois, in what is now northern France, had a garden full of robots, including waving monkeys.

In the 1730s, when de Vaucanson made his automatons, robot-making was a sign of the times in Europe. That's because these lifelike machines seemed to show clearly that nature could be copied and controlled by brilliant human minds.

The Digesting Duck – a clockwork creature that could eat, flap its wings and even poop out of its mechanical backside!

Though Muslim scholars had believed in the importance of reason and observation in understanding the world for hundreds of years, Europeans were now in the midst of their own revolution in thinking. Called the Enlightenment, this set of ideas offered individuals hope for power over their own lives as well as over nature.

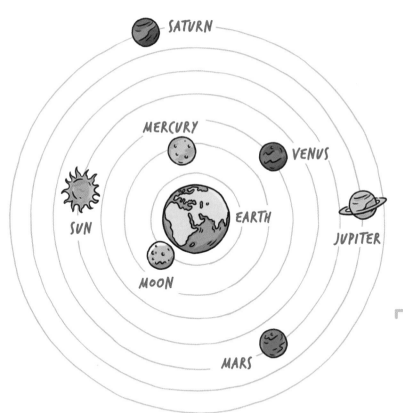

SATURN

MERCURY

VENUS

SUN

EARTH

JUPITER

MOON

MARS

This is the way people thought the universe was organised until Nicolaus Copernicus suggested the Sun and not the Earth was at its centre.

As we have just seen, the Protestant Reformation had already made people question the right of the pope and priests to tell them what to do. That was one of the first steps.

Another early step had been a radical book published in 1543 by Polish astronomer Nicolaus Copernicus. At the time, Europeans believed that the Earth was at the centre of the universe, with the Sun, the planets and all the stars moving around it.

Copernicus had looked at the way the planets moved in the sky and realised the observations only made sense if the Earth and the planets were all moving around the Sun. Copernicus's ideas were later proved correct by Italian astronomer Galileo Galilei. Here was another triumph of independent thinking over traditional beliefs.

Two great Enlightenment thinkers used reason and observation to develop other new ideas. French scientist and philosopher René

Descartes said the universe and its laws of nature were like a giant clockwork machine. Only humans had minds, he said, which made us special. According to Descartes, if we could figure out how the machine of nature worked, we could make it work for us.

You may have heard of Isaac Newton. He was a big observer and experimenter. Sometimes he was even reckless with his own body. Once he stared at the Sun to see what would happen to his eyes. He went blind for four days and was lucky to get his sight back afterwards. (Do not try this!)

Newton is most famous for wondering what makes an apple fall from a tree. Some people might say, well, apples are supposed to fall from trees. That's just what apples do. Applying the philosophy of Descartes, Newton wanted to explain a falling apple using the laws of nature. He said that an invisible force – gravity – was responsible. And that the size of this force was related to the size of an object.

An apple has gravity. The planet Earth has gravity. In fact, every object has gravity. But since the Earth is so much larger than the apple, it has much more gravitational force. That's why the apple is drawn to the Earth

Sir Isaac Newton was a genius at connecting things in his mind. It is said he was inspired to think of the idea of the universal force of gravity after seeing an apple fall from a tree.

The Moon

and not the other way round. Newton then looked up at the night sky, wondering why the Moon circles the Earth without pinging off into outer space or hitting the Earth like an apple. He figured out that because the Moon is smaller than the Earth, it must be drawn towards it by the Earth's larger gravitational force. But he also realised that there must be another force at work. That factor is speed. The Moon is moving so fast that when it falls, it misses the Earth entirely and travels in a circle around it. This delicate balance between speed and gravity is called an orbit. You see – discover the laws of nature, and the secrets of the universe are revealed.

Other Enlightenment philosophers said that individuals should have the freedom to make their own choices. Different people have different ideas about freedom. Remember the native people of Mexico who allied with the Spanish to defeat the Aztecs? They did it to be freed from having to pay taxes they thought were unfair. That same idea of freedom now sparked a brand new kind of revolution in North America.

In the mid 1700s, there was a terrible Seven Years War between a group of countries led by Britain and another group led by France. Some people think of the Seven Years War as the real first world war because it was fought all over the world, including in Europe, West Africa, India and North America, where it was called the French and Indian War. In more than a hundred years since the Virginia and

Plymouth colonies were founded, most of the East Coast of North America had filled up with British colonies. Because Britain had protected them against France during the war, it seemed only fair that the colonists should help pay the costs. So Britain raised their taxes.

The extra taxes made some colonists furious. They complained that they should not be taxed because they didn't get to vote in British elections. That's why, on 16 December 1773, a group of Massachusetts colonists protested against the new taxes, especially the one on tea. They dressed up as Native Americans, stole on to a British merchant ship in Boston Harbor, and ruined the cargo of tea by throwing it into the water.

North American colonists were furious at having to pay taxes to the British government. Some of them protested by dressing up as Native Americans and throwing chests of tea into Boston Harbor. This is one depiction of the events, drawn in the 1840s.

Following this famous event, known as the Boston Tea Party, thirteen of the

eighteen British colonies in North America teamed up to declare freedom from Britain. They formed a new nation called the United States of America. The rest chose to stay with Great Britain, and later became part of another new country, Canada.

In the Declaration of Independence, a document that stated the reason for the revolution, the thirteen colonies said that 'the Laws of Nature and Nature's God' entitled them to be independent. Then they went on to list all the ways they felt the British had mistreated them.

The war raged from 1775 to 1783. In the end, the United States won, becoming the first European colonies ever to secure their independence. They set up a government that tried to ensure the power of individuals by writing a Constitution giving each person a voice in government. The Bill of Rights, a set of ten amendments to the Constitution, protected the rights of individual citizens against the power of the government. Back then, only white men who owned property counted as citizens though.

> "WE HOLD THESE TRUTHS TO BE SELF-EVIDENT, THAT ALL MEN ARE CREATED EQUAL, THAT THEY ARE ENDOWED BY THEIR CREATOR WITH CERTAIN UNALIENABLE RIGHTS, THAT AMONG THESE ARE LIFE, LIBERTY AND THE PURSUIT OF HAPPINESS."
>
> Thomas Jefferson, United States Declaration of Independence

When the United States won its freedom from Britain, people all over the world sat up and took notice. If colonies could win their independence, maybe there was hope for other downtrodden people. French people were disgusted at how much money their king and his nobles spent feasting in enormous palaces while ordinary people starved.

French ideas of freedom were to do with fairness, equality and getting fed. Leaders of the ordinary people negotiated to get equal voting power for everyone. But they couldn't move fast enough. Popular anger spilled out like lava from an erupting volcano, directed at kings and nobles who stole the country's riches for themselves. Angry Parisians stormed a prison called the Bastille on the night of 14 July 1789 to take weapons and gunpowder and free some of the prisoners. This was the beginning of the French Revolution.

Before it was over, revolutionaries had used a new form of execution called the guillotine to chop off the heads of rich nobles, including King Louis XVI and his Austrian wife Marie Antoinette. Some non-humans were destroyed as well – including De Vaucanson's Digesting Duck, which he had given to Louis XVI as a gift.

The American Revolution inspired other colonies, too. By 1800 the French colony of Saint-Domingue, on the Caribbean island of Hispaniola, which Columbus had settled, was home to 450,000 enslaved Africans who produced almost half of the world's sugar. After a

Effective and deadly, the guillotine was used during the French Revolution to remove nobles and royalty who the revolutionaries saw as greedy and corrupt.

thirteen-year struggle they freed themselves of French rule in 1804. Their new country, Haiti, was the second liberated colony in the world after the United States and the first independent black-ruled republic in modern history.

Similar freedom movements followed in central and South America. On 20 July 1810, the people of Colombia (then called New Granada) declared their independence. Over the next few years, a series of Spanish and Portuguese colonies followed.

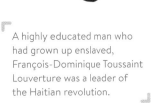

Newton's laws predict that when it comes to the physical world, for every action there is an equal and opposite reaction. Sometimes in history it is the same. In 1799, shortly after the French people had successfully overthrown their corrupt king, a new ruler seized absolute power. His name was Napoleon Bonaparte.

A highly educated man who had grown up enslaved, François-Dominique Toussaint Louverture was a leader of the Haitian revolution.

Napoleon's plan was to conquer Europe to make himself an empire. Wars cost money, and Napoleon cared more about his new European Empire than about American colonies. That's why in 1803, in the midst of losing the long battle to hold on to Haiti, Napoleon sold the French colony of New France to the United States for $15 million. The enormous parcel of land included what would become all or part of the US states of Arkansas, Missouri, Iowa, Oklahoma, Kansas, Nebraska, Minnesota, North Dakota, South

Though mostly remembered for trying to take over the world, Napoleon also made important changes in French government. He set up a system of public education and introduced the Napoleonic Codes, which guaranteed several civil rights, including freedom of religion.

Dakota, New Mexico, Texas, Montana, Wyoming, Colorado and Louisiana, as well as parts of the Canadian provinces of Alberta and Saskatchewan.

Britain successfully fought off invasion by Napoleon, but these Napoleonic wars on top of the loss of its American colonies left it desperate for money. So it used the Roman Empire strategy of expanding abroad once more.

In the 1780s, British sea captain James Cook explored the South Pacific. His expeditions led to the establishment of a British prison colony in Australia. It became routine for British courts to sentence criminals and people who couldn't pay their bills to be transported there.

Meanwhile British forces were out capturing colonies elsewhere. By the mid 1820s, large parts of India and Burma (now Myanmar) were under British control and providing vital supplies to the ever-growing British Empire. Saltpetre, one of the ingredients for gunpowder, came from India. Precious hardwoods for making ships came from Burma.

In Britain, thoughts about freedom were being focused in some people's minds on the idea of banning slavery. William Wilberforce was a tireless campaigner whose efforts eventually resulted in the

British parliament voting in 1807 to outlaw slave trading. In 1833 Britain went further, declaring slavery completely illegal throughout its empire.

W hen a barber from Bolton, England, called Richard Arkwright, invented the world's first water-powered cotton mill, it set off another type of revolution. This one is known as the Industrial Revolution. Arkwright's mill opened in 1771 in the village of Cromford in Derbyshire. It spun thin, strong threads which were then fed into a mechanical loom and woven into cloth. Never before had so few people been able to make so much fabric.

New machines changed lives for workers. A carpenter, for example, has to be skilled in many ways to make a fine piece of furniture. And he or she has to take the time to find the right tools for different stages of the job in hand. But a factory assembly-line worker waits for the arrival of the next partially made object as it passes down the line, ready to do a single task again and again and again.

Richard Arkwright's water-powered spinning frame transformed the manufacture of cotton and pioneered an Industrial Revolution.

Eli Whitney's cotton gin was a mechanical solution to the problem of removing seeds from cotton fibre.

The idea of mass production really took off in the United States. In 1801 an inventor named Eli Whitney demonstrated how he could assemble ten separate guns from a heap of interchangeable parts. Congress was so impressed that they awarded him a contract to produce 10,000 guns called muskets. Although it is now thought Whitney may have faked his presentation just to win business, the idea really did work. By the time of Whitney's death in 1825, American weapons factories were using the method to churn out thousands of guns each year.

Whitney is also famous for inventing a machine that could remove seeds from cotton fibre – an extremely time-consuming job when done by hand. His mechanical cotton gin ('gin' is short for 'engine') helped transform the economy of the southern United States. It made cotton farmers rich, greatly expanding the demand for enslaved people to farm cotton.

New machines were all very well, but there was still a problem. Until about 1825, factories and vehicles of all kinds still relied on getting power from animals, water or the wind. Without a breeze, sailing ships can get stuck at sea for days. Water-powered looms work just fine in places with flowing water. But in times of drought, they stand idle. If humans wanted to continue their experiments with freedom, they needed another breakthrough.

Which is exactly what happened when Richard Trevithick turned up the pressure on his *Puffing Devil* steam engine in Cornwall, England, in 1801. Here was a machine that didn't rely on the Earth's natural forces at all. No horses, no humans, no wind, no river or stream. All it needed were the plentiful, portable raw materials of the Earth itself – water in a tank and some wood or coal to make a fire. The heat turned the water to steam. The steam pushed through pipes to drive wheels. Here was the world's first fully independent source of mobile power.

Within thirty years, high pressure steam was connecting pieces of the world together. In 1829, a competiton was held at Rainhill, in Lancashire, England, to find a steam locomotive that could pull a wagon along a new fifty-six-kilometre-long railway line being built to connect the cotton-growing city of Manchester with the trading port of Liverpool. Inventor George Stephenson's *Rocket* won the

George Stephenson's *Rocket* was the most advanced locomotive of its day, bringing together the latest innovations.

Tall smokestack

Boiler

Firebox

day. The line opened to great fanfare on 15 September 1830. Britain went railway crazy. New companies were set up and people invested money in building railways, sometimes making fortunes, sometimes losing everything. By 1914 the landscape had been transformed by rail networks covering more than 35,000 kilometres and run by 120 competing companies.

Before the arrival of the railways, different parts of Britain had their own local time. For example, Bristol was eleven minutes behind London, because the Sun rises eleven minutes later there. But railway timetables could not work unless all clocks ran on the same standard time. So people started setting their clocks to the same time across the country. Eventually the rest of the world joined in, and the time zones we know today were established.

Railway mania also erupted across North America. One of the first American-built steam locomotives was the *Best Friend of Charleston*, which entered service in the same year as Stephenson's *Rocket*. Unfortunately, it was also the first locomotive to suffer a boiler explosion, tragically killing its fireman in June 1831.

On 10 May 1869, American engineers completed the Transcontinental Railway, connecting the east coast of the United States to California in the west. Now the United States was united in a new mechanical way. Canada followed with its own Canadian Pacific Railway, from Ontario in the East to British Columbia in the West. So by 1885, North America had two transcontinental railways.

Steam power also allowed ships to sail without being troubled by windless seas. The SS *Great Britain*, built by railwayman Isambard Kingdom Brunel, was launched in 1845. At almost 100 metres long, she was the first iron steamship to cross the Atlantic, taking just fourteen days.

But while Europe and North America were busy with their Industrial Revolution, much of the Far East, including China, Japan and Korea, retreated into hiding. From about 1600 to 1860 Japan tried to cut itself off from the outside world completely. The same is true for Korea, which was so successful at keeping itself out of the way of European influence that it became known as the Hermit Kingdom.

China also had little interest in expansion. Almost 100 years before Columbus reached the Americas, a Chinese Muslim admiral called Zheng He had taken a fleet of hundreds of huge ships and

On his voyages, Zheng He collected treasures of all kinds to bring back to the royal court in Nanjing, China. From his trip to Somalia in eastern Africa, he brought back giraffes, leopards, lions and zebras, which he called 'celestial horses'.

tens of thousands of sailors and passengers overseas to explore faraway lands. On at least one of his seven epic voyages in the early 1400s, he reached the east coast of Africa. But he wasn't like European conquistadors, waging war and enslaving people. Rather, he wanted to tell everyone about the glorious Chinese emperor, who, thanks to God in heaven, was supreme ruler of the world. In return, he collected exotic gifts from foreign rulers. His expeditions also led to extensive Chinese trade routes throughout Asia and Chinese colonies in South-east Asia.

But by 1520, China had abandoned its giant fleet and the idea of overseas exploration. Instead, invasions by Mongols from the north forced it to put all its energy into connecting and upgrading the Great Wall of China, turning it into one spectacular 8,850-kilometre barrier.

This extraordinary line of defence worked well for a while. Then China entered into a period of civil war leading to the end of the Ming dynasty, which had ruled since the time of the Mongols. By 1662 the Qing dynasty had taken charge. Like Japan and Korea, the Qing had little interest in dealing with Europeans. But starting about 1850 Western powers were snooping off the shores of Japan and sniffing up the rivers of China in their new steam-powered warships.

> "
> OUR CELESTIAL EMPIRE POSSESSES ALL THINGS IN PROLIFIC ABUNDANCE ... THERE WAS THEREFORE NO NEED TO IMPORT THE MANUFACTURES OF OUTSIDE BARBARIANS IN EXCHANGE FOR OUR OWN PRODUCE.
> "
>
> Qianlong, Emperor of China

Qianlong Emperor

Thousands of years ago ancient Greeks discovered that if they rubbed cloth against a mineral called amber it would produce a series of mysterious shocks or sparks. The word 'electricity' is actually based on the Greek word *elektron*, meaning 'amber'.

In the 1820s, English scientist Michael Faraday gave a series of famous demonstrations at a science club called the Royal Institution in London, England. Faraday showed how it was possible to move an object using an invisible force, called electromagnetism, that is created by passing electricity through a wire. This was the world's first electric motor. Then, in 1831, he showed how to generate electricity by waving a wire through a magnetic field. This is the principle used to produce electricity in a power station.

Once American inventor Thomas Edison perfected his design for cheap, mass-produced light bulbs, it became possible to create the world's first electrical power grid. In 1882 a steam-powered generating station linked fifty-nine customers in New York, United States, with electric power for the first time.

Electricity also gave rise to the first telegraph system. Then, in 1837 inventor Samuel Morse showed that it was possible to send messages using his Morse code across a distance of nearly sixty-five kilometres from Washington, DC, to Baltimore, Maryland. Within twenty years the whole of North America was

Thomas Edison never gave up. It took him and his team of engineers more than five years to work out how to make a light bulb work without it exploding when connected to an electric current.

connected by wires. By the 1860s cables were even being laid under the seas, allowing instant communication between North America and Europe. The first cable ran from Ireland to Newfoundland, Canada.

So when Scottish-born Canadian-American inventor Alexander Graham Bell came up with a way of sending voice signals over electrical wires, he got very excited indeed. On 10 March 1876, Bell spoke the first ever words over a telephone line to his assistant Thomas Watson, who was in the next room.

It's possible Alexander Graham Bell was not the first person to invent a telephone. Others were working on the idea at the same time. But he was the first to register the invention with the United States patent office so got the rights to make and sell phones. In this picture from the *Detroit News*, an unknown man demonstrates Bell's telephone.

In 1888, Bertha Benz, wife of inventor Karl Benz, publicised her husband's experimental car – the first to run on petrol – by driving it more than 100 km to visit her mother. She took her teenage sons along so they could push the car to get it started. When the car broke down on the way, she fixed it herself. This was the very first time anyone had driven a car for more than a few metres.

Machines were now changing every walk of life. But if you had to choose one that made the biggest difference of all, my guess is that many people might vote for the motor car. Everywhere but in big cities, it's hard to imagine living in the world today without the freedom of going anywhere you like, whenever you like, in a car.

Surprisingly, in 1900 almost all the cars in New York were electric. Edison's new power transmission system led to a surge in interest for creating cars that could be charged up at home. But by 1915 electric cars were in steep decline, thanks to our next revolutionary invention.

German scientists Nikolaus Otto, Gottlieb Daimler and Wilhelm Maybach developed a series of petrol engines beginning in 1876. A few years later German mechanic Karl Benz used one of them to build the world's first petrol car. Here was a far lighter, faster mobile machine than those powered by either electricity or steam.

Of course motor cars rely on plentiful supplies of petrol, which comes from petroleum, often called crude oil, found deep in the Earth. The first modern oil wells were dug in the late 1850s to provide a source of fuel for lamps. Now, with the invention of petrol cars, demand for oil increased very quickly.

On 10 January 1901, prospectors at Spindletop in the US state of Texas struck oil that gushed out uncontrollably at a rate of 100,000 barrels a day. And it kept on gushing for the next nine days until someone could work out how to stop the flow. Local farmers were furious that their crops were drowning in oil, but a new age of exploration had truly begun.

The first spectacular oil geyser at Spindletop was just the beginning. In all over 75 million barrels of oil were pumped out of the area before it went dry in 1936.

Bicycle-shop owners Orville and
Wilbur Wright invented the first
heavier-than-air powered aeroplane.

Henry Ford applied mass production techniques to cars. His
factories built more than 16 million Ford Model Ts between 1908
and 1927. New roads were built by goverments keen to support
people's passion to travel wherever and whenever they chose.

In 1903 two brothers who owned a bicycle shop had the brilliant
idea of seeing if they could fly by putting a pair of wings on a
bicycle and then mounting a small petrol engine on the back. On
17 December, Orville and Wilbur Wright successfully flew the first
controlled, powered flights near Kitty Hawk, North Carolina, in the
United States. Their flights lasted only between twelve and fifty-
nine seconds, but they proved that it was possible to build a petrol-
powered flying machine that could carry human beings.

Within fifteen years the idea had been developed into
sophisticated aeroplanes. World War I (1914–1918) picked up the
pace, with nations on both sides of the conflict using aircraft to spy
on enemy forces and drop bombs. Mass production techniques were
quickly applied to making aircraft. During World War II (1939–1945),
almost 800,000 planes were built.

magine finding a source of power that would last for ever. This final frontier was approached in 1905 in a series of scientific papers written by German physicist Albert Einstein. Newton's theories of motion and gravity seemed fine for large objects, he said, but they don't work so well when you zoom right in to look at what's happening at the level of atoms.

Einstein worked out that atoms themselves are held together by an almost unimaginably strong force, which, if it could be unlocked, might provide a massive source of untapped power. The famous equation that shows this relationship is $E=mc^2$, where E = energy, m = mass (stuff), and c = the speed of light.

Einstein worked out that there was enough trapped energy in a single grain of sand to boil a kettle 10 million times. The starting gun had now been fired on a nuclear race, as rival scientists and engineers tried to find ways of splitting atoms and releasing limitless quantities of energy.

Giant advances in science and engineering were now shaping and reshaping the world, bringing us within touching distance of how we live today. But there's one more step on our journey before we can get there. Sadly, it is not an easy one to take, as we are about to see.

Albert Einstein worked out that the universe is not what it seems. In this picture, he is writing an equation to calculate how crowded (or empty) the Milky Way is.

Chapter 14

WORLD AT WAR

1845–1945
When everyone started fighting everyone else

1851
Gold is discovered
in Australia.

1850–64
As many as 20 million
people die in the Taiping
Rebellion in China.

1914
As much as ninety per cent
of the African continent
is colonised by European
countries.

1914
World War I breaks out after the assassination of Archduke Franz Ferdinand of Austria.

1917
Vladimir Lenin seizes control of Russia during the Russian Revolution.

1939
Germany invades Poland, triggering the start of World War II.

1945
World War II comes to an end.

We have travelled through many periods of history and seen a lot of war. But the time between 1845 and 1945 seems to me to have been the most brutal. For reasons that I find hard to work out, appalling violence and fighting between humans erupted in almost every part of the world.

No one really knows why it happened. Maybe it was because the number of people in the world was increasing quickly thanks to advances in farming and technology. In 1804 the world's population passed 1 billion. By 1950 it had more than doubled to 2.5 billion. Perhaps having so many more people increased the chance of clashes between countries and cultures. Or maybe having such a connected world made some people feel jealous or deprived and others greedy.

Europeans spent the beginning of this 100-year period busily trying to take over the whole world. Most of the Americas were now claimed. But Europeans saw the chance to gain more control over South Asia, the Middle East and Africa. They had been buying goods and people in Africa for hundreds of years. Now they started moving there and setting up colonies. Africa is a strikingly diverse continent, with as many as 3,000 ethnic groups speaking 900 to 1,500 languages. When Europeans began carving it up, they paid no attention to ethnic boundaries or the needs or ways of life of the local people.

North Africa was the first to feel the effects of European settlement. In 1834 French troops invaded Algeria. There they

One of several wars going on in 1845 was the first Anglo-Sikh War. This conflict was fought between the British East India Company and Sikh Empire in what is now Pakistan and northern India. The East India Company was founded to trade with India and China but also colonised and controlled large parts of India.

built roads for transporting goods and materials to Europe. By 1848 more than 100,000 French people had settled in the territory. They farmed the land and exported cotton.

The Scramble for Africa, as it became known, kicked off in 1881. At that time about ten per cent of Africa was controlled by European countries. Twenty years later, European control had increased to more than ninety per cent. The people of colonised Africa were forced to raise crops such as coffee, cacao, rubber, cotton and sugar for export. Others had to mine precious minerals such as copper, diamonds and gold. While treasure flowed out of Africa, European countries grew richer.

Gold was discovered in Australia in 1851, and Europeans rushed to get rich quick. In just twenty years, Australia's population rose from 437,000 to 1.7 million. European settlers did very well. But the Australian people who had been there before the Europeans didn't. Europeans stole their land and brought them European diseases. By 1900, the Aboriginal Australian population was less than a third of what it had been when the first British settlers landed on their shores.

By about 1840, people in Europe had grown very fond of buying Chinese tea, silk and porcelain. But there was a problem. The Chinese didn't really want to buy anything made in Europe. That meant European traders had to pay in silver for goods from China, but nobody in China was paying in silver for goods from Europe. This caused a silver shortage for European countries.

The Scramble for Africa

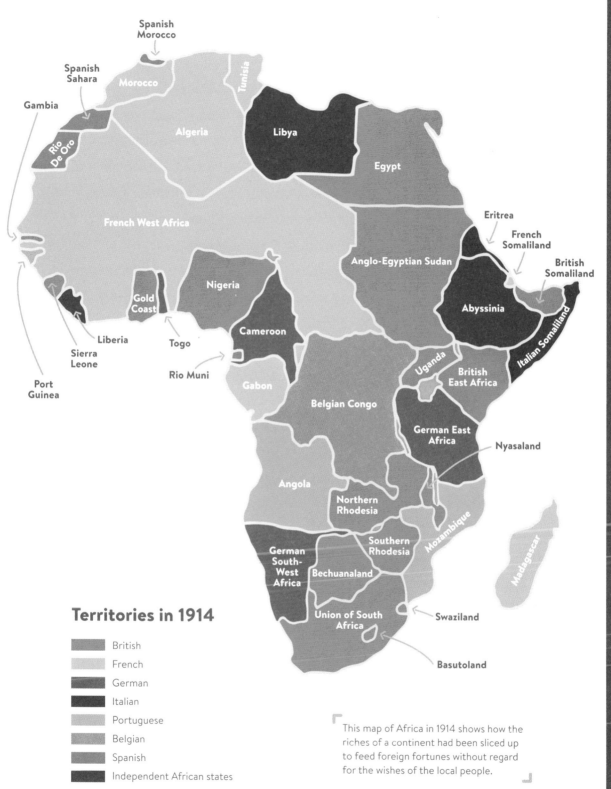

Spanish Morocco

Spanish Sahara

Gambia

Morocco

Tunisia

Algeria

Libya

Egypt

Rio De Oro

French West Africa

Anglo-Egyptian Sudan

Eritrea

French Somaliland

British Somaliland

Nigeria

Gold Coast

Cameroon

Abyssinia

Italian Somaliland

Liberia

Togo

Rio Muni

Gabon

Uganda

British East Africa

Sierra Leone

Port Guinea

Belgian Congo

German East Africa

Nyasaland

Angola

Northern Rhodesia

German South-West Africa

Bechuanaland

Southern Rhodesia

Mozambique

Madagascar

Union of South Africa

Swaziland

Basutoland

Territories in 1914

- British
- French
- German
- Italian
- Portuguese
- Belgian
- Spanish
- Independent African states

This map of Africa in 1914 shows how the riches of a continent had been sliced up to feed foreign fortunes without regard for the wishes of the local people.

British traders eventually came up with something Chinese people would pay silver for – the drug opium. Opium is very addictive. Nowadays heroin is made from it. The drug was illegal in China, so the British sold it to drug dealers, who smuggled it into the country. The silver they got in return made it easier for Europeans to buy more Chinese silk, tea and porcelain.

The Chinese government tried to stop the flow of the drug, but the British went to war to keep bringing it in. These wars are called the Opium Wars. British traders really didn't care that the Chinese people were suffering. They didn't care that they were breaking Chinese law. All they cared about was getting their silver.

As the Chinese people's addiction to opium grew stronger, the Chinese government grew weaker. Finally the people's unhappiness boiled over. In 1850 a man named Hong Xiuquan raised a giant army to challenge the Qing government. He claimed to be the long-lost brother of Jesus Christ. Hong and his huge band of followers set up a rival kingdom in southern China, with its capital at Nanjing. They called their country the Heavenly Kingdom of Great Peace. And they replaced the teachings of Confucius with Hong's own translation of the Christian Bible.

A gigantic civil war usually called the Taiping Rebellion broke out between these two rival parts of China. No one was safe. The war lasted fourteen years, from 1850 to 1864. It is not clear exactly how many people died. Estimates range from 20 million to 70 million. It was the most deadly civil war in the history of the world.

Opium poppy

The Taiping Rebellion happened in one of the oldest countries in the world. But at the same time something similar was taking place on the other side of the world in one of the newest countries, the United States of America. The US was also bitterly divided. By then, the northern states had mostly outlawed slavery. Those against slavery – called abolitionists – said if all men are created equal as the Declaration of Independence said, then surely nobody should be enslaved, regardless of the colour of their skin.

> **FOUR SCORE AND SEVEN YEARS AGO OUR FATHERS BROUGHT FORTH, ON THIS CONTINENT, A NEW NATION, CONCEIVED IN LIBERTY, AND DEDICATED TO THE PROPOSITION THAT ALL MEN ARE CREATED EQUAL.**
>
> Abraham Lincoln, Gettysburg address

Southern slave owners strongly disagreed. Enslaved people were so valuable that they couldn't imagine life without them. Enslaved workers grew cotton, tobacco, sugar cane and other crops. They did skilled jobs such as carpentry. And they also worked in their owners' houses, cooking, cleaning and caring for children.

For a while the country survived by agreeing to disagree. Each state decided for itself whether to allow slavery. But when new

Ellen and William Craft escaped slavery in Georgia in 1848. Ellen, who had light skin, disguised herself as a man and posed as a rich white planter. With her husband, William, pretending to be her servant, she bought train tickets, and the two of them rode to freedom in the North.

This 1865 poster, based on an illustration by Thomas Nast, commemorates US President Abraham Lincoln (in the lower circle) shortly after he had been shot and killed by an angry southerner. It celebrates Lincoln's Emancipation Proclamation, in which he declared all enslaved people in the states that had broken away from the Union to be free. Nast envisions life for a future African American family gathered around their modern woodstove (centre). To the left are the evils of slavery, including being beaten and being sold. On the right, happy future African American children attend school and free workers collect wages.

states were joining the United States, fights broke out over whether they would allow or ban slavery.

Then Abraham Lincoln, who had spoken out against slavery, became president in 1861. Eleven southern states decided enough was enough. They declared themselves no longer part of the United States and formed their own country, called the Confederate States of America. Between April 1861 and the spring of 1865 more than 600,000 people died in a brutal civil war. The northern states eventually won, forcing the breakaway states back into the union. Four million people were released from slavery. New amendments were adopted into the US Constitution that outlawed slavery and gave African American men the right to vote. However, white women couldn't vote, so neither could African American women. And there was still a long road ahead to true equality.

I am sorry to say that our 100 years of terrible warfare are only just warming up. Back in Europe things were spinning out of control. The creation of two new countries made things a lot more competitive. The Italian city-states merged to become the modern country of Italy in 1861. Ten years later, German Chancellor Otto von Bismarck united twenty-five German states into a single mighty nation. This new Germany was headed by Emperor Wilhelm I. He was very aware that Germany had been left out as other European nations had built up mighty empires. So Germany took over parts of Africa, including present-day Namibia, Rwanda, Ghana and Tanzania. All of this made France and Britain very nervous.

Gradually, two rival alliances emerged. Britain, France and Russia were on one side. On the other were Germany, Italy and Austria-Hungary, an empire made up of what are now Austria, Hungary, Czech Republic, Slovakia, Slovenia, Croatia, Bosnia and Herzegovina, and parts of Poland, Serbia, Ukraine and Romania.

France was keen to win back lands lost to Germany in 1870. Italy and France were arguing over colonies in Africa.

This political cartoon shows Otto von Bismark sweeping up smaller German states into a new super-nation.

Russia was battling with Austria-Hungary for control of lands near the Black Sea. And Britain was terrified of Germany's craving to build a rival empire. By 1914 Europe was like a box of fireworks just waiting for someone to strike a match.

That match was struck by Serbian student Gavrilo Princip in Sarajevo, Bosnia. It was 28 June 1914. Princip was angry because he thought Bosnia should be free from the Austro-Hungarian Empire. So he shot and killed Archduke Franz Ferdinand, heir to the throne of Austria-Hungary, as he rode by in his car.

Because Princip was Serbian, Austria-Hungary blamed the Serbian government for the assassination and invaded Serbia in revenge. But then everything got completely out of hand. Serbia's allies – Britain, France and Russia – lined up on one side. Austria-Hungary's ally – Germany – lined up on the other. One assassination had turned into a war that involved almost all of Europe. At times it was so confusing that many of the soldiers didn't even know why they were fighting or whom they were killing.

Archduke Franz Ferdinand of Austria-Hungary and his wife, Sophie, Duchess of Hohenberg, were attacked twice on 28 June 1914. The first time, a grenade missed and exploded under the car behind them. The second time, Gavrilo Princip shot them both from about a metre and a half away. They died within an hour.

Soldiers in World War I had to fight in dreadful conditions, often living in trenches filled with mud and in constant fear of attack.

This war, later named World War I, was fought mostly in Europe between 1914 and 1918. The United States entered the war on the side of the British and their allies in 1917. Before it was all over, about 20 million people were dead, either in the fighting itself or of a horrible flu that broke out during the war.

Russia hasn't featured much in our story so far, but now it comes centre stage. From prehistoric times, this vast country has always been home to a wide range of ethnic groups. Then, as we saw earlier, the Viking Rus settled in Russia around 840 CE, and a wave of settlement by the Mongols followed.

From 1547, Russia was ruled by kings and queens known as tsars and tsarinas. Like most rulers, they had their good sides and their bad sides. The first tsar was Ivan the Terrible, who created a huge empire. Peter the Great, who ruled from 1682 to 1725, modernised the country by supporting science and technology and starting Russia's first newspaper. Catherine the Great, who ruled from 1762 to 1796, was planning to free Russia's serfs, who, like slaves, were the property of nobles. But in the end she needed the nobles on her side so changed her mind and took away the few rights the serfs had instead.

In 1917, three years after the outbreak of World War I, Russia collapsed into chaos. The war had weakened the country, and the people blamed Tsar Nicholas II. Food shortages made people miserable, hungry and cross. And nobody trusted Grigori Rasputin, a royal adviser who called himself a holy man.

Women in the city of Petrograd revolted over the shortage of bread in February 1917. Across the country others joined the protest. In March, Tsar Nicholas was forced to resign the throne. After a power struggle, Vladimir Lenin and Leon Trotsky seized control of the government, in what is known as the Russian Revolution. In May the following year the Tsar and his family were executed.

Lenin and Trotsky were eager to try out an experimental form of government called communism. The basic idea had been developed by a German philosopher named Karl Marx who proposed that the world would be a better place if governments were run by the workers. He also believed that workers should own the companies they work for.

Civil war now broke out between two sides – Lenin's communist army (Reds) and those who didn't like the idea of communism (Whites). Britain, France, the United States and Japan supported the Whites. In June 1923 Lenin's Red Army won the war. They changed the name of Russia to the Union of Soviet Socialist Republics (USSR), or Soviet Union.

Revolutionary posters like this one inspired people to throw off the chains of the Tsar and support Lenin's Russian Revolution, which he promised would result in better lives for workers.

But what started off as a great idea got hijacked by someone who cared only about под Ленинским знаменем Коминтерна — вперед!

Дени

ДА ЗДРАВСТВУЕТ ПЕРВОЕ МА

power. Joseph Stalin ruled with an iron fist from 1924 to 1953. Terrible things happened. Anyone who disobeyed Stalin was either executed or sent to labour camps, known as gulags, in bitterly cold Siberia. During his reign, Stalin is believed to have caused the deaths of over 20 million of his own people.

Some people thought World War I had been so awful that Europeans would never want to go to war again. It was even called 'The War to End All Wars'. But sadly, that's not how it turned out. In fact, its end sowed the seeds of an even more devastating conflict.

The Treaty of Versailles, the peace agreement that ended the war, blamed Germany. As punishment, the German people had to give up all their weapons and pay 96,000 tonnes of gold, which would be worth £1.8 trillion today. Even though they were allowed to pay over many years, the punishment left them very poor and very angry.

One man who took part in World War I felt deeply let down. His name was Adolf Hitler. In his view, Germany's leaders had dragged the country into a war and then lost it. Hitler wanted to go back to the ideas of ancient Sparta. He would make sure that Germany had only the strongest people. This, he said in his book *Mein Kampf*, would make Germany great again.

After Adolf Hitler came to power in 1933 he set about making sure everyone in Germany obeyed him. His dreams of conquering Europe were shattered by the Nazi defeat in 1945.

The downtrodden people of Germany liked what they heard. So on 30 January 1933 Hitler was voted in as head of the German government, a position known as Chancellor.

Almost immediately Hitler's real plans became clear. He believed his country needed more space for its growing population. He also decided that the best way to improve the German economy was to give people jobs building weapons. Tanks and aeroplanes could scare Germany's neighbours into giving it more land. And if that failed, they could be used to take the land by force.

Hitler used emergency powers to make himself a dictator. He then banned all political parties except his Nazi party. That way he could control everything. Finally, he introduced a secret police force. Its members spread through the country to make sure anyone saying anything against Hitler was spotted and punished.

In 1938 Hitler's armies rolled eastwards into Czechoslovakia, a country that is now the Czech Republic and Slovakia. (Austria-Hungary had broken up after World War I.) Britain, France and Russia were still hoping that they could persuade Hitler to stop without actually having to go to war. But the next year Hitler

The Panzer IV was the workhorse of the German tank force during World War II. More than 8,000 were built between 1939 and 1945.

invaded Poland, and Europe collapsed into a second dreadful conflict that lasted until 1945. Hitler's forces advanced rapidly through Europe, invading Belgium then France. Nobody could stop them. By May 1941 it looked like Hitler's dream of European conquest might come true.

This was Europe's darkest hour. Between 1941 and 1945, Hitler's Nazis ran a group of prisons known as concentration camps. In some, prisoners were worked to death. In others, they were executed. In all about 11 million innocent people were killed. The victims included about 6 million Jews and 5 million other people the Nazis thought were inferior. There were Roma (also known as Gypsies), gay and transgender people, people with disabilities, political opponents and others. This atrocious crime is known as the Holocaust.

The United States formally entered World War II after Japanese forces bombed its Pacific fleet in Pearl Harbor, Hawaii. This shows the USS *Arizona* shortly before it sank. In all, 18 ships were destroyed and 2,403 Americans died in the attack.

W orld War II wasn't just fought in Europe the way World War I had been. It truly included most of the world. That's because in the 1930s, Japan had started to do what European countries had been doing for 400 years – build a mighty empire.

In 1931, even before Hitler came to power, Japan invaded the north-eastern Chinese province of Manchuria. A few years later it launched a full-scale invasion of China with 350,000 soldiers. They used aeroplanes to bomb cities all over the country.

Japan and Germany both wanted to defeat the Soviet Union, and each wanted to dominate its part of the world. So Japan signed the Tripartite Pact with Germany and Italy in 1940. That also made it officially an enemy of Britain, France and the United States.

China fought back against Japan, and Britain and the United States helped them by preventing the Japanese from getting the fuel they needed. Without oil, Japan could not power its army, navy or airforce. No oil, no victory.

That's why Japan launched a surprise attack on Pearl Harbor, Hawaii, on 7 December 1941. It hoped that the United States cared more about helping its friends in Europe than about saving China from Japan and would just let Japan have its oil.

But Japan was wrong. Attacking Pearl Harbor proved a terrible mistake. The United States had been helping Britain with weapons. But now US president Franklin D. Roosevelt had the reason he needed to convince his country they had to fight. The United States entered the war in 1941, both in Europe and in Asia.

The fighting was brutal. It ended in Europe first. On 30 April 1945, Hitler's army was surrounded on all sides by British, American and Soviet forces. He knew he was about to lose the war, so Hitler shot himself in his underground hideout near the German capital of Berlin. Without its leader, Germany surrendered.

But that wasn't the end of the war. Remember $E=mc^2$? In 1933 Albert Einstein had been touring America. As a Jew, he was so worried about the rise of Hitler that he decided to stay in the US instead of returning to Germany. When war broke out, Einstein and another scientist, Leo Szilard, wrote a letter to President Roosevelt. They warned what might happen if Nazi Germany found a way to unlock all that energy trapped inside atoms. They feared that a new generation of superbombs would surely help the Germans win.

Once the United States entered the war, the government started a top-secret project. Its goal? To make sure the United States, with support from Britain and Canada, developed nuclear bombs before Nazi Germany did.

The programme, known as the Manhattan Project, succeeded in unlocking the power of the atom before Germany did. But in the end Germany wasn't the target. On 6 August 1945 the people of two Japanese cities, Hiroshima and Nagasaki, were the first to feel the power of this terrible force. Only one bomb was dropped on

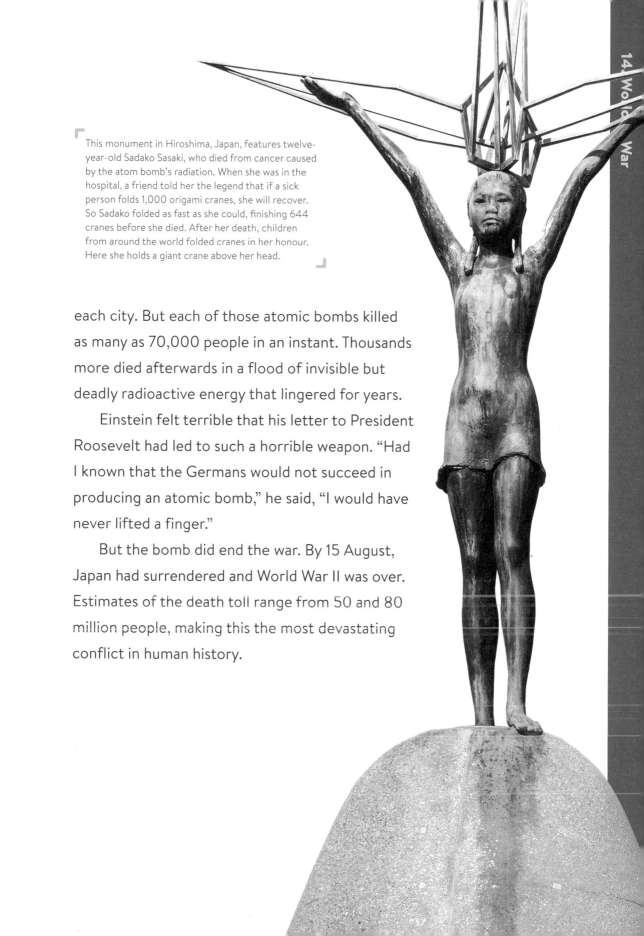

This monument in Hiroshima, Japan, features twelve-year-old Sadako Sasaki, who died from cancer caused by the atom bomb's radiation. When she was in the hospital, a friend told her the legend that if a sick person folds 1,000 origami cranes, she will recover. So Sadako folded as fast as she could, finishing 644 cranes before she died. After her death, children from around the world folded cranes in her honour. Here she holds a giant crane above her head.

each city. But each of those atomic bombs killed as many as 70,000 people in an instant. Thousands more died afterwards in a flood of invisible but deadly radioactive energy that lingered for years.

Einstein felt terrible that his letter to President Roosevelt had led to such a horrible weapon. "Had I known that the Germans would not succeed in producing an atomic bomb," he said, "I would have never lifted a finger."

But the bomb did end the war. By 15 August, Japan had surrendered and World War II was over. Estimates of the death toll range from 50 and 80 million people, making this the most devastating conflict in human history.

Chapter 15

To BE CONTINUED...

1945–Present
The shaping of the world we know
and what might come next

Timeline

○ **1945**
World population
reaches 2.5 billion.

○ **1945**
The United Nations is
established to prevent
another world war.

○ **1947**
India gains its independence
from Britain.

○ **1947**
The Cold War
begins.

○ **1948**
The United Nations
adopts the Universal
Declaration of
Human Rights.

1969
Neil Armstrong becomes the first person to step on the Moon.

1981
IBM launches the world's first personal computer.

1989
The Berlin Wall comes down.

2001
11 September terrorist attacks.

2018
The world's population reaches 7.6 billion.

Are you feeling a little dizzy? I certainly am. We've been whizzing at tremendous speed through history and around the world to the last one-hundredth of a second before midnight on our twenty-four-hour clock. And even though we are almost at the end of a book about history, there are some stories that will have to stay unfinished.

Take plastic. In 1855, the British inventor Alexander Parkes made the very first type of plastic. He called it Parkesine after himself. It was great for waterproofing coats. Variations on his recipe, which included cooking a mixture of chemicals and natural fibres, were developed in Britain and the United States.

Nowadays most of the plastic we use comes from petroleum, the same oil that fuels our cars. And since just after World War II, plastic has become a huge part of our lives. Plastic is in our toys. Plastic fibres (called synthetics) are in our clothes. We carry things in bags made of plastic. We use plastic furniture. We wrap food in plastic to keep it fresh. We make artificial legs and arms and heart valves from it. We even make cars and planes out of it. Plastic vehicles are lighter than metal ones so use less fuel and cause less pollution.

But like all stories, it's not that simple. It took a while for anyone to see the problem with all the plastic, but there is one. Because plastic is so cheap to buy, we throw a lot of it away. And the big snag is we don't know of any fungi or microbes that can break down plastic. That means almost all of the plastic that has ever been made still exists today.

Tupperware, plastic containers that give people an inexpensive and convenient way to store food, have been on sale since 1948.

Tupperware Home Parties

An albatross hunting for squid has caught a plastic shopping bag instead.

A lot of waste plastic ends up either buried in the ground or, worse, floating in the seas. Here it can do huge damage to fish and seabirds who can't help eating tiny plastic particles or getting caught in floating plastic rubbish. When that happens they can get sick or even die. And ocean currents gather floating plastic into areas called gyres. The biggest is called the Great Pacific Garbage Patch. It's hard to measure its size, but experts say it's at least as big as the US state of Texas, or three times the size of France.

How does this story end? We don't know. Some plastic is recycled and made into new plastic. Some is burned to create energy. And some scientists think microbes might be evolving to be able to break it down. But so far, none of these solutions is nearly enough. What on earth can we do with all of this plastic?

D id you know that babies are being born around the world right now at the rate of more than four a second? That's about 353,000 babies every day! And did you know that only about 151,000 people are dying each day? So that means on average the world's population increases by more than 200,000 people each day. That is why the Earth is now home to 7.6 billion people, three times as many as in 1945.

The big reason we have so many more people is science. New drugs, vaccines, operations, tools and life-support machines can prevent and cure disease, helping people live longer. We have new

chemicals and technologies to grow more food in less space. Cars and planes are safer, and so are factories. So fewer people die in accidents. Many countries have systems to make sure citizens have enough to eat and a place to live even if they can't provide those things for themselves. The average person in the world now lives to the age of seventy-one – that's forty years longer than in 1900.

The Great Pacific Garbage Patch was first written about in 1988, but most people learned about it after a sailor called Charles Moore found it in 1997 on the way home after completing the Transpacific Yacht Race. He was astonished to find this gigantic area of plastic waste drifting in the sea.

   Remember that giant meteorite that killed off the non-flying dinosaurs 65 million years ago? It triggered a mass extinction, the death of many life forms all at once. Today many scientists think we are in the middle of another mass extinction. This time the meteorite has come in the form of humans and the towns and cities, roads and factories we build.

Some inventions that are good for people are not so good for other living things. Giant dams provide electricity for humans. But they also destroy homes for animals such as otters and beavers. Artificial fertilisers pollute streams. Plus our building destroys animal habitats and gets in the way of migrations. And then there's all that plastic.

In 2018, a team of scientists figured out a way to estimate the weight of all living things on Earth. It turns out humans are only a tiny part, about one of every 10,000 kilograms of Earth's life. But we have had a huge impact on the whole. Since we started farming, eighty-three per cent of the wild mammals on land have gone extinct, along with half of the plants.

Forests take in carbon dioxide and give off oxygen. But humans cut down trees for paper and hardwood and to make space for farming. This has led to the destruction of precious

The Amazon rainforest is 5.5 million square kilometres, an eighth of the size of North and South America together. Most of it is in the country of Brazil, which struggles to balance the needs of its people to make a living and the needs of all living things for a stable climate. This photograph shows an area being cut down in northern Brazil.

rainforests, such as the Amazon in Brazil. And that's a problem – for us and for much of the rest of life on Earth, too.

In 1896 Swedish climate scientist Svante Arrhenius was the first to suggest a link between the amount of carbon dioxide (CO_2) in the air and global warming. Lots of extra CO_2 is being pumped into the air by pollution from power stations, cars and aircraft, which burn coal, gas and oil. Meanwhile, less CO_2 is being removed from the air because of our shrinking forests. That's why levels of CO_2 have almost doubled since 1832. And all that CO_2 has made the world warmer than it has been at any point in the last 100,000 years.

A warmer world makes the ice caps and glaciers melt. As this happens, sea levels rise. Remember when we talked about the time before there was an ice cap at the North Pole and the sea was forty-two football players deeper than it is now? Well, if we stay on our current path, we'll have that deeper ocean back. That means London, New York, Montreal, Tokyo, Shanghai and most other low-lying communities will be under water. The warming climate will also change habitats. Some animals will be able to migrate and adapt. Others will go extinct.

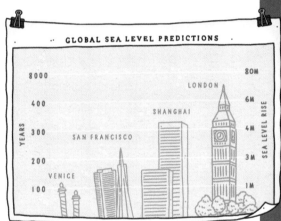

If global warming continues, sea water will eventually cover the Earth's biggest cities. This chart shows one projection of how many years and how much sea level rise it will take for these four to be affected.

No one really knows how long it might be before all the ice melts – anything from 500 years to 5 million years, perhaps. What happens next? That story isn't over either.

Another unfinished story is the age-old tale of war and peace. After World War II, people hoped we were entering a time of peace. In October 1945 a group of countries got together to form a new international organisation. They called it the United Nations (UN). The idea was to unite the world and prevent another world war. The UN helps out countries suffering from famine or war. It also tries to get the whole world to agree to obey a set of international laws. Not everyone always sticks to the rules, but having them in place makes a difference.

Following the founding of the UN, the world-war-exhausted countries of Europe began to loosen their grip on their colonies.

Mahatma Gandhi had spent thirty years organising non-violent protests against British rule in India. In 1947 he finally saw his dream of Indian independence realised. A string of other British colonies also gained their independence, including Sri Lanka (1948), Sudan (1956), Malaysia (1957), Kenya (1963), Zambia (1964), Zimbabwe (1980) and Australia (1986). France, Italy, Germany and the United States also gave up control of most of their overseas possessions.

Great stuff, right? But it didn't mean everyone was getting along. The most powerful countries in the world had split into two camps. One group included the western European countries, Japan, the United States and Canada. They practised capitalism, a system where individuals own companies and can get rich from their profits. Capitalists believe

United Nations flag

this is the best way to give everyone an equal chance to do well in life.

The second group embraced communism, Karl Marx's idea of the government owning all businesses. They believed that way profits can go to benefit all the people, not just those who are lucky or smart enough to start a successful company or get a high-paying job. As we saw, the Soviet Union was communist before World War II. China became communist after a civil war that took place right after.

Capitalists and communists each wanted other countries to join them in their way of life. And neither of these groups wanted the other to grow too powerful. So, led by the United States and the Soviet Union, the two groups built thousands and thousands of nuclear bombs. They put them in missiles that could be shot up into space and across oceans, and pointed them at one another. It hadn't taken long for World War II friends to become enemies and for World War II enemies to become friends.

This time is known as the Cold War. It was called 'cold' because it never heated up into fighting with nuclear weapons. But the threat of nuclear war made people feel so chilled to the bone it scared them into not attacking first. This idea became known as MAD

> ## " THE WEAK CAN NEVER FORGIVE. FORGIVENESS IS THE ATTRIBUTE OF THE STRONG. "
>
> Mahatma Gandhi, independence activist and civil rights leader

After Germany lost WWII, it was divided in half. East Germany was communist and West Germany was capitalist. The German capital, Berlin, was divided, too, even though it was located inside East Germany. East Germany built a wall – known as the Berlin Wall (above) – in August 1961 to keep people from moving between the two parts of the city. The wall was torn down in 1989, and the two Germanies reunited the next year.

– Mutually Assured Destruction. Some people believe MAD has been good for keeping the peace, because each group knows that if they start a nuclear war, the other side will fire back, and everyone will die.

And maybe it did keep a sort of peace. But more than sixty smaller shooting wars – including the Korean War and the Vietnam War – were fought during the Cold War. In most of them, the communists and capitalists supported opposite sides. They equipped their allies with conventional weapons (not nuclear ones), military training, and sometimes even soldiers. So even the Cold War was pretty hot sometimes.

The Cold War was also responsible for what's called the Space Race. In 1957 the Soviet Union launched the world's first ever satellite, *Sputnik*, which could orbit the Earth in space. The Americans found the idea of their enemies spying from space too much to stomach. From that moment, the US committed itself to putting a person on the Moon by the end of the 1960s. And they did it! Neil Armstrong was the first, followed by eleven others.

> " THAT'S ONE SMALL STEP FOR A MAN, ONE GIANT LEAP FOR MANKIND. "
>
> Neil Armstrong, astronaut

Today all kinds of new spacecraft are being developed in the United States, Europe, China and Russia. One rocket, called *Falcon Heavy*, is being built by a private company called SpaceX. The company's owner, Elon Musk, hopes *Falcon Heavy* will soon take people to Mars and back again. Its rockets are fully reusable. They come back to Earth and land upright on the launchpad.

The Cold War officially ended in 1991 when the Soviet Union broke apart into its fifteen republics. Russia and China embraced some parts of capitalism. And in 2007 when a new community of twenty-eight nations known as the European Union was formed, nine of the former Soviet republics were part of that group.

Neil Armstrong was the first person ever to set foot on the Moon. Twelve astronauts walked on the Moon between 1969 and 1972. No one has been back since.

By now the world was breathing a sigh of relief as prospects for World War III seemed to fade away. But still none of this stopped dozens of smaller wars from happening all over the place.

This period also saw the rise of another kind of war. This one doesn't need a big army. The goal is to make your enemy scared and bring attention to your cause. It's called terrorism.

Remember how World War I was started by someone who wanted freedom for his country? Well, the biggest mass murder in Canadian history had the same motivation. It was the bombing of an aeroplane in 1985. Air India Flight 182 was on its way from Canada to India, carrying a suitcase with a bomb in it. When the bomb exploded, the plane broke into pieces and crashed into the sea, killing everyone on board.

The bombers were members of an Indian-Canadian group. They wanted an independent country for Sikhs, one of India's religious

minorities. They were furious at the Indian government for killing over 1,000 Sikhs in a raid on a temple where rebels were hiding. The 329 people on Flight 182 – most of them Indian Canadians – were innocent victims. They were killed in revenge and to draw attention to the terrorists' cause.

Terrorists can be anyone. The Oklahoma City bombing in 1995 killed 168 people. The bombers were white Americans angry at the US government for attacking a religious cult whose members refused to let them in to search for illegal weapons. The 11 September 2001 attacks, which destroyed the Twin Towers of the World Trade Center in New York City and killed about 3,000 people in New York, Washington DC, and Pennsylvania, were the work of a militant Islamist group known as al-Qaeda. They were angry because they believed that the United States was unfair to Muslim countries and overgenerous to the mostly Jewish country of Israel.

Not all terrorism involves killing. There are other ways to frighten people. In Nigeria, a terrorist organisation called Boko Haram has kidnapped teen girls from their schools. The message? Girls shouldn't go to school. This group believes that girls should marry very young instead of being educated, so they're trying to scare families into keeping their daughters at home.

Terrorists almost always attack ordinary people going about their ordinary business. To mourn those innocent victims, people across the world create public shrines with flowers and messages and hold candlelight vigils like this one, held in London, in response to the 2014 attack on a school in Peshawar, Pakistan.

Terrorist attacks and local wars don't look as if they're going to stop anytime soon. But at least for now we seem to have moved away from giant wars that kill millions of people. That's one thing to be grateful for.

Peace is not just about countries and causes, though. It's also about individuals and how we treat one another every day. On 10 December 1948, three years after the founding of the United Nations, its members adopted a Declaration of Human Rights that includes 30 articles, each a right that should be protected. Among many other things, it says all forms of slavery must be banned. It says people should be allowed to move freely around the world. It says everyone should be able to practise whatever religion they choose or no religion at all. It says governments are responsible for their people having enough food to eat and access to healthcare.

These rules are not legally binding. Few countries in the world guarantee their citizens all of them. But the Declaration has been very important because many countries have used it as a basis for their own laws.

In the United States, activists of the civil rights movement of the 1950s and 1960s risked their lives to change the treatment of African Americans in the South. Since soon after the American Civil War, laws across the South had kept African Americans separated from white people. Trains and buses had special sections reserved for whites only. White kids and African American kids went to separate schools, and I bet you can guess which ones got the new books and the indoor toilets. And unfair voting rules kept African Americans from voting even

When Rosa Parks took an illegal seat on her bus in 1955, she knew what would happen. She had already been thrown off that bus before, and by the same driver. She also knew jails were dangerous places for African American women. But she and other activists had agreed that this was the right time to stand firm. (By the way, there were no cameras on the bus. This picture was staged later.)

though the US Constitution said it was their right.

One activist leader was Rosa Parks. In 1955 she refused to give up her seat on a bus for a white man. This sparked a protest, called the Montgomery Bus Boycott, where thousands of African Americans refused to ride their city's buses for over a year, until a judge ruled that buses had to allow anyone to sit anywhere, regardless of the colour of their skin.

> **I HAVE A DREAM THAT MY FOUR LITTLE CHILDREN WILL ONE DAY LIVE IN A NATION WHERE THEY WILL NOT BE JUDGED BY THE COLOUR OF THEIR SKIN, BUT BY THE CONTENT OF THEIR CHARACTER.**
>
> Martin Luther King Jr., minister and activist

One of the other leaders of that boycott was Martin Luther King Jr., who became the most recognised figure of the civil rights movement. Little by little, the combination of well-organised non-violent protests and judges willing to overrule southern laws shifted public opinion in the country.

In 1964, the US Congress passed a series of new laws called the Civil Rights Acts. These laws protected equality for African Americans. Now, more than fifty years later, conditions for African Americans are much better but still not fully equal. Racial prejudice has not gone away, and a new movement known as Black Lives Matter has picked up the struggle for equal treatment of African Americans.

After a white man, George Zimmerman, was found innocent of murder when he shot unarmed African American teen Trayvon Martin in 2012, three activists – Alicia Garza, Patrisse Cullors and Opal Tometi – created the Black Lives Matter movement to draw attention to the violence and abuse African Americans suffer at the hands of the police and others in the United States.

While the US civil rights movement was at its height, protests broke out in South Africa, a majority black country that at the time was ruled by white people. The government made laws separating people based on the colour of their skin and preventing black people from having any power. That system was called apartheid. In 1962 one of the anti-apartheid movement's leaders, Nelson Mandela, was jailed for life. He was eventually freed after serving twenty-seven years in prison. In an extraordinary turn of the tables, Mandela was elected president of South Africa in the country's first free election after apartheid ended, in 1994.

As president, Nelson Mandela set an example to people of all backgrounds by creating a Truth and Reconciliation Commission. Hundreds of people, including government officials, told the truth to the public about their part in the horrible system of apartheid. Mandela's vision was based on forgiveness. He did not seek revenge for what had happened in the past, but looked forward to a peaceful future.

Nelson Mandela

It's not just skin colour differences that lead to unfair treatment. Women have struggled for equality since well before World War II. It wasn't until 1893 that any country in the world gave women the right to vote. New Zealand was first, followed by Australia, Finland, Norway, Denmark and Iceland. Then, in 1918, many of the European countries that had been involved in World War I

Malala Yousafzai launched a worldwide campaign to help girls have the right to a good education in all countries. The schoolgirl, who was shot for her views in Pakistan when she was just 12 years old, was awarded the Nobel Peace Prize in 2014.

followed, including Russia, the United Kingdom and Germany. In 1920, so did the United States. The last country to give women equal voting rights with men was Saudi Arabia, in 2015.

But getting gender equality in other areas of life – such as women and men being paid the same amount for the same job – has been much more difficult. Even worse, there are countries where girls still don't have the right to an education or to chose whom to marry. And women own less than twenty per cent of the world's land.

The good news is that the struggle goes on, and more and more powerless groups are successfully fighting for their rights. People with disabilities have fought in many countries for changes that give them equal access to education and jobs. And gay and lesbian people have recently gained the right in some places to live and work openly without fear of discrimination and to legally marry the person they love. All of these struggles for equality continue, with history being written every day.

One of the tools that has helped some modern equality movements is the computer. IBM introduced the first personal computers in 1981. Since then, computers, mobile phones and the Internet have utterly transformed the world. It's hard to imagine life without them. We now use computers and smartphones for gaming, reading, shopping, making friends and taking pictures. We use them for sending messages, writing, doing research and watching movies. We use them to find people with similar interests and concerns. And we use them to share news and videos of the things that make us laugh and things that make us cry. That way others will see what is going on, and people can work together to make the world a better place.

Advances in computer science have also given us robots that go way beyond what anyone imagined in the days of the Digesting Duck. Robots have been working in factories for a long time. And they do jobs that require going places people can't, like inside the human body. And with artificial intelligence in them, they can call the doctor's office to make your appointment and will soon be detecting cancer and even identifying criminals. Future robots with artificial intelligence might be so lifelike that we won't be able to tell if we're speaking with a robot or a person.

Robots will come in handy when we set out to colonise space. Even before humans visited the Moon, people longed to travel to other worlds themselves. It's been a long wait, but new generations of rockets will at least offer a taste.

Steve Jobs co-founded Apple, a US computer company, in 1976. He launched the iPhone, the world's leading smartphone, in June 2007.

· 333 ·

It's even possible that in the next fifty years, we'll be building cities on the Moon and Mars. Maybe then ordinary people will be able to visit.

With so much changing so fast, it is hard to imagine what the world might be like in fifty years or 500 years, let alone 5,000 or 50,000 or 5 million years. Maybe humans will come up with great inventions that will solve the problems of the world today. For example, think about what might happen if and when scientists manage to generate energy the way the Sun does, in a process called nuclear fusion? A world fuelled by fusion would have unlimited supplies of cheap energy that creates no pollution. Maybe we could slow down or stop global warming.

With the human population growing fast, how can we possibly feed everyone without destroying even more animal habitats? Maybe artificial food is the answer. Scientists have already developed ways to grow meat in a laboratory using stem cells. This means one day we may be able to eat meat without raising or killing any animals.

An incredible array of robots is working for humans now. *Curiosity* (below) is one of rovers searching the surface of Mars for signs of past or present life. The newest artificial hands (right) can be controlled with our brains just as real hands are. Honda's Asimo robot (far right) can walk, climb stairs and interact with people.

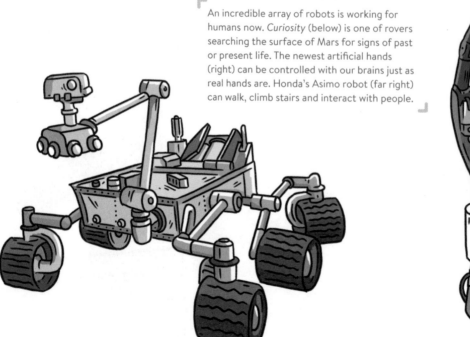

Science on its own cannot create a peaceful, thriving world, though. To do that we need to make wise choices about how to live and how to treat one another and our world. One thing we can do to help us make good decisions is to think big about the past. Our long journey through time might help us identify danger signals to watch out for and natural and human strengths to assist us.

Our first danger signal is absolute power. History shows us that countries can be hijacked by people who crave power over others. These rulers can cause wars in their bid to gain even more power. Often the people of a country give these strong rulers a lot of power on purpose and don't realise how dangerous it can turn out to be, as the Germans did when they elected Adolf Hitler in 1933.

Also watch out for big differences between rich and poor. Throughout our story there have always been extremely wealthy people and really poor people. Think of Mansa Musa's gold or the treasures that King Tutankhamun took with him to the afterlife.

Then think of enslaved people across the globe, from ancient Greece to the American South. And remember the desperate European peasants living through the bubonic plague and the native peoples of the Americas, Africa and Australia, whose freedoms, livelihoods and lives were taken from them by invaders who cared only about wealth.

Sometimes the difference between rich and poor becomes too great for ordinary people to bear. Then anger can easily spill over into violence. Remember how that happened in the French and Haitian and Russian Revolutions? Right now, the world's richest eight people own more than fifty per cent of the entire wealth of the globe. Could this be a war waiting to happen?

But there is good news, too. Possibly the biggest lesson of history is one that makes the rest of them seem not so scary. Nature does not progress – it changes and adapts depending on the conditions. When eyesight evolved in trilobites during the Cambrian Period, other creatures had to adapt or die. Humans do something similar. We adapt to new situations. After all, that's how our species thrived in the ice ages, by moving around and changing our lifestyles as the giant glaciers came and went.

In fact, humans are super-adapters. We change our ways and invent all kinds of new machines in an effort to make the world easier to live in. And if there's one reason to have real hope for the future, it's that throughout all history, even when the future looked very grim, humans have adapted.

Now, at last, as we zoom out and look with wonder at the story of all Earth history, the clock is striking midnight. Whatever happens next, one thing is certain: the first one-thousandth of a second in a brand-new day is bound to be an exhilarating, incredible moment – far more amazing than anything you can make up.

When astronauts visited the Moon they saw the first ever Earthrise. Seeing pictures of the whole planet as a fragile blue jewel surrounded by the black void of space helped launch a new environmental age. What will become of our precious planet in future? It's up to us all.

Afterword

I wanted to include everything, I really did. But, of course, we all know that's impossible. The story is just too big. Instead, I have tried to provide an overview of all history – natural and human – and suggest how key moments and events link together.

But, oh the number of things that I had to leave out! I wanted to include a lot more of the different cultures of the world, including the Maori of New Zealand, the San people of the Kalahari Desert in southern Africa and the Sami of far northern Europe. I wanted to cover the migrations that have created our diverse modern world, from the Irish escaping from the potato famine in the 1850s to today's Syrians fleeing a brutal civil war.

I also wish we'd had room for many more bold movers and shakers, from diplomats such as T. E. Lawrence and Arundhati Ghose to leaders such as Mikhail Gorbachev, who dared to think differently. And when it comes to the incredible number of inventions that have changed the world, or the struggles for equality, or the heroes who saved humans, animals, buildings and whole ecosystems, or the artists, writers and musicians who enrich and inform our world, well – don't get me started!

So, I have an idea. I'd love to slice this story another way. How about *Absolutely Everything Else*? It will be a book that covers the same enormous span of time as this volume but explores it in an entirely different way. I'm not ready to share the details, but I do have a favour to ask. It would be wonderful to know what you'd like to see in the next book. I am especially interested in little-known people or events you think should be included – the forgotten heroes, heroines and villains of history and the small moments with outsized impacts on the planet, life and people. So please send me your ideas, and I will do my best to include them.

If you go to www.whatonearthbooks.com and follow the link, your message will come directly to me. I am waiting to hear from you!

Christopher Lloyd

A gift from France to the United States in 1886, the Statue of Liberty, which stands in New York Harbour, was originally intended to celebrate the end of slavery but came to symbolise the welcome the United States has offered to immigrants, particularly during the late 1800s and early 1900s.

References

Author's note on the research

I began my working life as a journalist, and that background – plus the research I did for my previous history books for adults and children – gave me a good start researching this one. In fact, as I began work on this book, I intended to make it a young people's adaptation of my adult world history book *What on Earth Happened*, first published in 2008.

But as I started reviewing what on Earth *had* happened since I wrote the adult book, I saw how much the world – even its history – had been shifting and changing around me during the previous ten years. There were exciting discoveries in physics, biology, palaeontology and archaeology, and of course current events, that changed the stories I wanted to tell. But it wasn't just about finding new things to add. Modern perspectives about the past, present and future have shifted too, and in some really interesting ways. Much of the material I had highlighted in 2008 just wasn't quite right for 2018.

So, with the help of my editors, I dived back in. I read recent books, scientific papers and articles in newspapers and magazines, selecting new stories and adding new perspectives to old ones. And I wrestled with the best way to talk about the uncertainty that attends all of our efforts to understand the world. Hopefully all this is done in a way that is accessible, interesting, accurate and balanced for young readers – and adults, too. So, in the end, *Absolutely Everything* isn't the young readers' edition I originally planned. It's an entirely new book in its own right. That's how research works. You might start down one path, but what you find leads you off in new directions you couldn't have anticipated. And that's why it's so much fun. The one thing in life that I find more exciting than anything else is seeing what's around the next corner. Thank goodness for corners.

The full list of sources for this book is too long to include here, though for a taste, please take a look at the quote sources below.

Quote sources

p.14 Parsons, Aaron. 11 October 2016. 'After our universe's cosmic dawn, what happened to all its original hydrogen?' *The Conversation* (theconversation.com); **p.17** Wolpert, Stuart. 28 January 2017. 'Moon was produced by a head-on collision between Earth and a forming planet' *UCLA Newsroom* (newsroom.ucla.edu); **p.24** Walcott, Charles D. 1916. 'Evidences of Primitive Life' *Annual Report of the Board of Regents of the Smithsonian Institution 1915*: 246 (Government Printing Office, Washington, DC); **p.38** Pogue, David. 23 October 2008. 'An Interview with E.O. Wilson, the Father of the Encyclopedia of Life' *The New York Times* (nytimes.com); **p.42** Tudge, Colin. 2006. *The Variety of Life*: 571 (Oxford University Press, Oxford, UK); **p.44** Preston, Richard. 3 December 2012. 'Flight of the Dragonflies' *New Yorker* (newyorker.com); **p.47** Sander, P. Martin. 17 August 2012. 'Reproduction in Early Amniotes' *Science* Vol. 337, Issue 6096: 806 (AAAS, Washington, DC); **p.56** Horner, Jack interviewed by Stahl, Lesley. 12 November 2009. 'Scientists Dino Findings Making Waves' *60 Minutes* (cbsnews.com); **p.64** Rohrseitz, Kristin and Tautz, Jürgen. 1999. 'Honey bee dance communication: waggle run direction coded in antennal contact?' *Journal of Comparative Physiology A* 184: 463 (Springer-Verlag, Berlin and Heidelberg, Germany); **p.70** Smith et al. 26 November 2010. 'The Evolution of Maximum Body Size of Terrestrial Mammals' *Science* Vol. 330, Issue 6008: 1218 (AAAS, Washington, DC); **p.79** Wilford, John N. 11 August 2010. 'Lucy's Kin Carved Up a Meaty Meal, Scientists Say' *New York Times* (nytimes.com); **p.82** Cam, Deniz. 30 December, 2017. 'How Cooking Made Us Smarter: A Q&A With Suzana Herculano-Houzel' *BrainWorld* (brainworldmagazine.com); **p.98** Huxley, Thomas H. 1894. 'Biogenesis and Abiogenesis' *Collected Essays* Vol. VIII: 244 (Macmillan, London); **p.110** Layard, Austen. 1853. *Discoveries among the ruins of Nineveh and Babylon: with travels in Armenia, Kurdistan, and the desert*: 204 (G. P Putnam & Co., New York); **p.112** Kramer, Samuel N. 1963.

The Sumerians: Their History, Culture and Character: 4 (University of Chicago Press, Chicago, USA); **p.122** Carter, Howard. *Howard Carter's Diary and Journal 1922*: 5 November 1922. Transcript retrieved from Griffith Institute (griffith.ox.ac.uk); **p.128** Hughes, Bettany. 26 January 2014. 'How women's wisdom was lost'. *The Guardian* (theguardian.com); **p.139** Lam, Wengcheong. Winter 2014. 'Everything Old is New Again' *Journal of Anthropological Research* vol. 70, no. 4: 511 (University of Chicago Press, Chicago, USA); **p.141** Eno, Robert (translator). *Confucian Analects* 15.24 (Indiana University, Bloomington, IL, USA. (indiana.edu); **p.143** Muller, F.M. (trans.). 1990. *Hymns of the Atharva-Veda* VI 142: 141. (Atlantic Publishers & Distributors, New Delhi, India); **p.158** Herodotus. 1920. *The Histories* 1.74.2. Trans. Godley, A. D. (Harvard University Press, Cambridge, MA, USA); **p.165** Pritchard, J. B. (ed.). 1969. *Ancient Near Eastern Texts Relating to the Old Testament*: 316. (Princeton University Press, Princeton, NJ, USA); **p.170** Vergano, Dan. 25 February 2014. 'Gladiator School Discovery Reveals Hard Lives of Ancient Warriors' in *National Geographic* (nationalgeographic.com); **p.172** New Testament. John 13:34, King James version; **p.184** Recinos, Adrián. 1950. *Popol Vuh: The Sacred Book of the Ancient Quiché Maya*: 83. Trans. Goetz, D and Sylvanus G. M (University of Oklahoma Press, Norman, OK, USA); **p.193** Bey, Lee. 17 August 2016. 'Lost cities #8: mystery of Cahokia – why did North America's largest city vanish?' *The Guardian* (theguardian.com); **p.202** The Koran 16:97 (*The Study Quran: A New Translation and Commentary* 2015 edition); **p.216** Fitzgerald, C. P. 1954. *China: A Short Cultural History*: 382 (The Cresset Library, London); **p.221** Walsh, Bryan. 10 March 2014. 'How Climate Change Drove the Rise of Genghis Khan' *Time* (time.com); **p.238** Davies, G. R. C. 28 July 2014. 'English Translation of Magna Carta' *British Library* (bl.uk); **p.244** Cross, Robin. 7 June 2012. *50 Events You Really Need to Know: History of War*: 60 (Quercus, London, UK); **p.256** Zamora, Margarita. 1993. *Reading Columbus*. Berkeley: University of California Press: 192 (ark.cdlib.org); **p.269** Bradford, William. 1912. *History of Plymouth Plantation 1620–1647* Vol. I: 60 (Houghton Mifflin Company, Boston, MA, USA); **p.277** Jefferson, Thomas et al. 4 July 1776. 'Declaration of Independence: A Transcription'. Transcript retrieved from National Archives (archives.gov); **p.286** Backhouse, E. and Bland, J. O. P. 1914. *Annals & Memoirs of the Court of Peking*: 326 (Houghton Mifflin Company, Boston and New York); **p.288** Bell, Alexander Graham. 'March 10th 1876' from Lab Notebook: 40. Transcript retrieved from Library of Congress (lcweb2.loc.gov); **p.301** Lincoln, Abraham. 19 November 1863. 'The Gettysburg Address'. Transcript retrieved from Cornell University (library.cornell.edu); **p.313** Rosen, Rebecca J. 23 November 2011. "'I've Created a Monster!' On the Regrets of Inventors". *The Atlantic* (theatlantic.com); **p.323** Gandhi, Mahatma. 1969. *All Men Are Brothers*: 171 (United Nations Educational, Scientific and Cultural Organization, Paris); **p.325** Armstrong, Neil. 21 July 1969. Transcript ed. Jones, E. M. and Glover, K. Retrieved from NASA (hq.nasa.gov); **p.329** King, Martin Luther, Jr. 28 August 1963. Transcript retrieved from the Avalon Project, Yale Law School (avalon.law.edu)

Further reading

If you fancy exploring world history in different ways, then here's a selection of books that I think do a good job pulling all the pieces together.

Published for young people

Bryson, Bill. 2009. *A Really Short History of Nearly Everything.* (Delacorte: New York)

Deary, Terry and Brown, Martin. *Horrible Histories* series. Scholastic (New York and London)

Lloyd, Christopher. *The Big History Timeline Wallbook: Unfold the History of the Universe – From the Big Bang to the Present Day.* (What on Earth Books: Tonbridge, UK)

2013. *History Year by Year.* (DK: London and New York)

2015. *When on Earth?: History as You've Never Seen It Before* (DK: London and New York)

2016. *Everything You Need to Ace World History.* (Workman: New York)

Published for adults but accessible to young adults

Bryson, Bill. 2003. *A Short History of Nearly Everything.* (Broadway Books: New York)

Gaarder, Jostein (tr. Moller, Paulette). 1994. *Sophie's World: A Novel About the History of Philosophy* (Farrar, Straus and Giroux: New York)

Gombrich, E. H. (tr. Mustill, Caroline) 2005. *A Little History of the World.* (Yale University Press: New Haven, CT, USA)

MacGregor, Neil. 1996. *A History of the World in 100 Objects.* (Viking: New York)

O'Brien, Patrick, ed. 2010. *Atlas of World History*, 2nd edition. (Oxford University Press: New York)

Image credits

Glossary

Aboriginal Australians
The native peoples of Australia, who arrived on the continent around 40,000 years ago.

Algae
Organisms that use photosynthesis to make energy and are the ancestors of plants.

Amphibians
Group of animals that live partly in the water and partly on land. Examples include frogs and toads.

Anthropologist
Studies how humans live together and behave in societies now and in the past.

Apartheid
System used in South Africa from 1948 until 1994 that separated people by skin colour.

Archaeologist
Studies physical remains left behind by humans, including tools and ancient ruins.

Arthropods
Animals with hard external exoskeletons and no backbones, like beetles and crabs.

Astronomer
Studies space objects and phenomena, such as stars and gamma rays.

Assyriologist
Studies the history of the ancient Assyrian Empire and surrounding region.

Astronaut
Travels into space.

Astrophysicist
Studies the forces, matter and energy that make up the universe, from collapsing stars to speeding comets.

Atom
A combination of neutrons, protons and electrons that is the smallest unit of a particular substance.

Automaton
A machine built to repeatedly perform the same task.

Biologist
Investigates the mechanisms and varieties of life, including its origins.

Buddhism
Religion based around the teachings of Siddhartha Gautama, often known as the Buddha.

Capitalism
System where things like land and property are owned by individuals and companies, not the government, and people compete to make a profit.

Catholicism
Christian religious group with a single leader, the Pope.

Christianity
Religion founded on the teachings of Jesus of Nazareth.

Civil rights leader
Leads others in the effort to improve equality in society.

Civil war
Conflict in which different groups within a single society fight against each other.

Climate change
Process in which environmental conditions on Earth change over time.

Colony (biology)
Group of individual organisms of a single species living together and supporting each other.

Colony (history, politics)
Settlement established by a group, usually a nation, in foreign territory.

Communism
System in which productive enterprises, such as factories, are owned by everyone and wealth is shared.

Confucianism
System of influential teachings developed by the ancient Chinese thinker Confucius.

Conquistadors
Spanish explorers and soldiers who conquered the New World in the 1500s.

Constitution
Document outlining the basic laws and systems of government in a particular country.

Cosmochemist
Studies the chemical make-up of the universe through extra-terrestrial objects such as meteorites and asteroids.

Crusades
Series of Medieval religious wars fought by Christian Europeans, mostly against Muslims.

Cuneiform
One of the earliest writing systems, developed in the 3000s BCE.

Cyanobacteria
Tiny organisms, each only a single cell, that produce energy by photosynthesis.

Dendrochronologist
Studies the make-up of tree rings for information about Earth's atmosphere in the past.

Democracy
Political system where the people have power over their leaders, often choosing them by majority vote.

Dictator
A ruler who governs with total power and without the approval of the people.

DNA
A chemical in the nucleus of cells that carries the instructions for how a living thing develops and functions.

Domestication
Process of breeding species to be more useful to humans than in their wild form.

Dreamtime
According to Aboriginal belief, a legendary period in the past when heroes created the universe.

Dynasty
A series of rulers or leaders from a single family.

E=mc^2
Equation in physics which shows that matter can be converted into huge amounts of energy.

Egyptologist
Studies Ancient Egypt, including searching for and exploring ruins.

Electricity
The movement of electrons, particles which carry electrical charge. Used by humans to power machines.

Entolomogist
Studies insects, the most diverse and numerous group of animals on the planet.

Eukaryotes
Organisms with cells containing a nucleus and other structures that create things the body needs.

Explorer
Travels into the unknown to explore new lands, before reporting back with their findings.

Extinction
The end of a species, when all individuals have died out.

Fertile Crescent
Area in the Middle East and Egypt where farming developed around 10,000 years ago.

Feudalism
Medieval system in which people swear oaths of military service in return for land.

Fish
Group of animals with backbones which live in water. Examples include sharks and goldfish.

Five Pillars of Islam
The five fundamental requirements of Sunni Islam.

Fossil
Preserved remains or traces of a living organism from a long time ago.

Fungi
Group of organisms that feed on living or once-living things and reproduce using spores.

Galleon
Large wooden ship developed in the 1400s and 1500s, mainly used in war.

Glacier
Mass of compacted snow and ice which exists year-round and spreads out over time.

Globalisation
System which links people across the globe through trade and industry.

Global warming
The steady increase of average world temperature over time, today caused in part by pollution.

Golden Age
A period in history when major advances in technology, art or other areas are made.

Gravity
Fundamental force of the universe. All objects have gravity, pulling other objects towards them.

Gyre
System of ocean currents which circle a central point and can cover thousands of miles.

Hajj
Pilgrimage to the Muslim holy city of Mecca, a religious requirement for every Muslim.

Hieroglyphs
Writing system which uses pictures to represent sounds or entire words.

Hinduism
Religion based around gods, religious texts and cultural traditions, which originated in India.

Historian
Studies history in all its forms, from the beginnings of civilisation to the present day.

Holocaust
Mass killing of 11 million people, including 6 million Jews, by the Nazis during World War II.

Human rights
Belief that humans have fundamental rights to certain things, such as freedom of religion and the right to an education.

Indigenous
People or organisms native to a particular region, often used when discussing the arrival of another group.

Industrial Revolution
Period of rapid industrial development. In particular the Industrial Revolution of Europe in the 1700s and 1800s.

Insects
Arthropods with six legs, three body-parts and usually wings as well, such as beetles.

Inventor
Designs machines and other gadgets to solve problems and improve lives.

Islam
Religion based on the visions and teachings of the Prophet Muhammad.

Judaism
A religion based on the Hebrew Bible and the first to develop monotheism.

Mammals
Group of animals with backbones which produce milk and mostly give birth to live young.

Mesoamerica
Region in Mexico and Central America where ancient civilisations developed.

Mesopotamia
Lush region in the Middle East where powerful ancient empires developed.

Migration
The movement of large groups of people or animals from one place to another.

Monotheism
Belief in only one god.

Mummy
Dead body of a human or animal that has been preserved either accidentally or on purpose.

Musket
A long gun that was used, particularly in war, before rifles were invented.

Muslim
A follower of Islam.

Nazism
German political movement beginning in the 1920s and led by Adolf Hitler.

Necropolis
A large cemetery, especially an ancient one. Means "city of the dead" in Ancient Greek.

Neurons
Cells which form the nervous systems of most animals and transmit information signals around the body.

Neuroscientist
Studies the nervous system, in particular the brain.

New World
North and South America, continents unknown to Europeans, Africans and Asians until the 1400s.

Nomad
Moves around regularly rather than settling in a single place permanently.

Nuclear (physics)
Relating to the nucleus at the centre of atoms.

Olympians
The twelve principal deities in the Ancient Greek religion, believed to live on Mount Olympus.

Orthodox Christianity
Christian religious group today found primarily in Russia, Eastern Europe and Greece.

Palaeontologist
Examines the remains of ancient organisms, from dinosaurs to giant fungi, to learn about prehistoric Earth.

Pangaea
Supercontinent made up of all Earth's continents pushed together, it existed 250–150 million years ago.

Pantheon
The particular gods and goddesses worshipped in a religion.

Philosophy
The study of fundamental questions about human experience and the way we think about the world.

Physicist
Studies the science of matter, energy and the forces that relate them.

Plate tectonics
Movement of the giant tectonic plates making up Earth's crust.

Pollen
Reproductive cells produced by flowers and some other plants, and essential to the development of seeds.

Primates
Group of large-brained mammals which includes monkeys and apes, including humans.

Protestant
A Christian who rejects the authority of the Pope and believes faith is key to religious practice.

Reincarnation
Belief that dead souls return to Earth in new bodies or even as different animals.

Reptiles
Group of egg-laying animals with skin covered in scales. Includes lizards and snakes.

Revolutionary (n.)
A person who revolts against a political system as part of a movement to bring change.

Robot
A machine that resembles a human or other living creature.

Sauropods
Group of long-necked, plant-eating dinosaurs. Included the largest dinosaurs.

Science writer
Investigates scientific stories and discoveries and reveals their findings to the world.

Silk Road
Network of trade routes reaching from China to western Europe and based around silk trading.

Smallpox
Highly infectious disease which causes spots to erupt across the skin and can cause death.

Telegraph
Early electrical communication system used to quickly send codes which can be translated into messages.

Terrorism
Strategy which relies upon fear to achieve a particular goal, usually through violence.

Theropods
Group of two-legged dinosaurs, most of which ate meat and had feathers.

Trilobites
Extinct water-dwelling arthropods with three body segments. Once widespread throughout the oceans.

United Nations
International organisation established in 1945 after World War II to promote peace and dialogue between nations and human rights across the globe.

Vascular plant
Plant with a system of tubes inside it for transporting water and nutrients.

Vikings
Nordic European people who explored and conquered distant countries, beginning in the 800s CE.

Index

A

abacus, the 211, 212
aeroplanes 291
Africa 78, 96, 97, 168, 210–11, 227, 238, 254, 255, 258, 259, 297–9, 303, 330–31
    see also Egypt
Aguilar, Gerónimo de 259, 260
Alexander the Great 165, 166–9
Algeria 297–8
Allah 201–2
alphabets 161–2
al-Qaeda 327
Americas, the 95–6, 178–97, 256, 258, 262–4, 267–9, 275–7, 278–80
    see also United States
ammonites 29, 67
amphibians 40, 41, 45–6, 47
ants 63, 64–5
apartheid 331
apes 70, 71, 78–9, 83
Archimedes 168
Aristotle 166, 207, 208
Arkwright, Richard 281
Armstrong, Neil 325
arthropods 39
artificial intelligence 333
artificial selection 101
Ashoka, Maurya King 147–8
Assyrians 109, 111
asteroids 18, 67–9
astronomy 116, 191, 214, 273, 274
Atahualpa, Inca Emperor 263–4
Athens 154–5, 156–7, 165
atomic bombs 312–3
atomic energy 293
atoms 14, 293
Attila the Hun 175
Australia 29, 91, 96, 280, 298, 331–2
Australian Aboriginals 195–6, 298
Austria 228, 247, 303, 304, 309
automatons 272
Aztecs, the 184, 188–9, 259–63

B

Babylon/Babylonians 109, 112, 164, 197
Baghdad 207, 208, 210, 211, 212, 238, 243
ball games 183
battles 147, 165, 233, 235, 243–4, 247
bats 66
Bayeux Tapestry 232–3
bees 60, 61, 63–4
Bell, Alexander Graham 288
Bermuda 267
bibles 162–3, 164, 172, 265
Big Bang 12, 13, 14
birds 56, 57, 58, 59, 67
Bismarck, Otto von 303
Black Death 240–42
Black Lives Matter movement 330
Boko Haram 327
Book of the Dead 121
Boston Tea Party 276
Brahmagupta 212
brains, human 79–81, 82–3, 213
Brazil 70, 258, 320–21
Britain 280–81, 303, 304, 306, 309, 312, 332
    Industrial Revolution 281–2
    Magna Carta 238–9
    Norman conquest 233–4
Brunel, Isambard Kingdom 284–5
Buddha/Buddhism 142–3, 144–8, 205, 215
Byzantine Empire 175, 226–7, 235, 244–5, 247

C

Cabot, John 262, 264
Cabral, Pedro Álvares 258
Cahokia/Cahokians 192–3
Cai Lun 204–5
Calusa, the 194
Cambrian Period 24–30
Canaan 161–2, 163, 164
Canada 23, 24–5, 195, 231, 232, 264, 277, 284, 288, 312, 326
capitalism 322–3, 325
carbon dioxide 49, 320, 321
Carboniferous Period 26, 43, 47
Carolingians 228–9
cars 289–90, 291
Cartier, Jacques 262, 264

Catherine the Great 305
cave drawings 86, 87
Charlemagne 228–9
chess 132
China 132–51, 204, 214, 216–9, 221, 222–3, 238, 241, 285–6, 298, 300, 311, 323, 325
    see also paper; silk
chocolate 179–80
Christians/Christianity 172–5, 203, 235–7, 243–7, 258, 266
    see also Crusades
Cleopatra 108, 122–3
climate 22, 45, 49, 74–7, 95, 186, 219–21, 229, 234, 240, 247, 321
Cold War, the 323–5
Colombia 279
Colosseum, Rome 170, 171
Columbus, Christopher 231, 254–7, 262, 278
communism 306, 323
compass, the 132, 218–9
computers 332–3
Confucius 140–42, 205, 300
conquistadors 259–64
Constantine I, Emperor 175
Constantine XI, Emperor 244
Constantinople 135, 174, 175, 227, 238, 244–7
Cook, Captain James 280
Copernicus, Nicolaus 273
coral reefs 27, 29
Córdoba, Spain 208–10
corn 178–9, 185, 196, 197, 268
Cortés, Hernán 188, 259, 260–61, 263
Cretaceous Period 26, 55, 60
Crusades 235–8
cyanobacteria 18–19
cycads 42
Cyrus the Great, of Persia 164–5

D

Darius I, of Persia 165
Declaration of Human Rights 328
Declaration of Independence (US) 277, 301
democracy 155, 156, 157

Descartes, René 273–4
Devonian Period 26, 27, 29, 30
Diamond Sutra 215
Dias, Bartolomeu 254, 262
Digesting Duck (robot) 272, 278
Dimetrodon 47, 65
dinosaurs 52–9, 65, 67
Diocletian, Emperor 174, 175
DNA 20, 60–61, 62, 71, 90, 91
dogs 100
Domesday Book 233–4
dragonflies 43, 44
Dreamtime, the 195–6

E

Earth, the 15–17, 18, 20–21, 26, 31,
    62, 69
eclipses 158–9
Edison, Thomas 287, 289
education 204, 205, 207
Egypt 113–23, 128, 163, 167, 197,
    203
Einstein, Albert 293, 312–13
electricity 287–8, 289, 320
engines 282, 283, 289, 291
Enlightenment, the 272, 273–4, 275
Eocene Period 26, 69–70
Eratosthenes 168
Erik the Red 230–31
eukaryotes 20
Euphrates River 109, 111
European Union 325
evolution 19–20, 26
Exodus 163
extinctions, mass 31, 47, 49, 52, 65,
    93, 95–8, 319, 320
eyes 25, 66, 213–4

F

Faraday, Michael 287
farming 100–2, 125, 132–3, 139, 154,
    178–9, 185, 193, 196, 208–9, 240,
    320
Ferdinand of Aragon 250–51, 255–6
Fertile Crescent 99, 101, 169
feudalism 229, 233, 242
Fibonacci 211, 212
fire, controlled 81–2
fish 30, 39, 59
Ford, Henry 291
fossils 23–5, 27, 29
    ants' and termite nests 64, 65

dinosaur 53, 54, 56–9
    human 83
    human footprints 84, 99
    plant 34, 36
    primate 70, 71
France 228–9, 233, 272, 277–8, 279,
    280, 297–9, 303, 304, 306, 309,
    310
    French Revolution 277–8, 337
Francis I, of France 264
fungi 20, 34, 35, 36, 37–8, 41

G

galaxies 12, 15
Galilei, Galileo 214, 273
Gama, Vasco da 258, 262
Gandhi, Mahatma 322–3
genes 60
Genghis Khan 221–23
geometry 168
Germanic tribes 175, 227
Germany 228, 303, 304, 305,
    308–10, 311, 312, 324, 332
Gilgamesh 111
glaciers 76–7, 95, 231, 321, 337
gladiators 169, 170
global warming 49, 96, 321, 334
gold 210, 251–2, 253, 256, 259–60,
    264, 298
gravity 14, 17, 274–5, 293
Great Pacific Garbage Patch 318–19
Great Wall of China 148–9, 286
Greece 154–61, 162, 165, 167, 197;
    gods and goddesses 158–9
Greenland 195, 230–31, 232, 247
Gregory VIII, Pope 237
griffinflies 43–5, 47
Guatemala 184, 186, 187
guillotine, the 278
gunpowder 132, 218, 243–4, 280
Gutenberg, Johannes 265

H

Hagar Qim, Malta 127
Haiti 256, 278–9, 337
al-Haytham, Ibn 213–14
Henry VIII, of England 266–7
Henry, Prince of Portugal
    251, 252–3
Hinduism 143–4, 145
Hitler, Adolf 308–10, 311, 312, 335
Hohokam, the 193

Holocaust, the 310
Homer 156, 157–8
Homo erectus 80–81, 83, 84, 90
Homo floresiensis 84, 85
Homo habilis 79–80, 81
Homo heidelbergensis 84, 85, 90
Homo neanderthalensis 84–7, 90,
    91, 92
Homo sapiens 84, 85, 87, 90, 91–2
Hong Xiuquan 300
horses 70
humans 52, 62–3, 71, 77, 96–8, 337
Hundred Schools of Thought 140,
    142, 149
Huns 175, 227
hunter gatherers 92–5
hydrogen 14
hypotheses 44

I

Ibn Sina 213, 214
Inca, the 191–2, 263–4
India 132, 133, 135, 139, 142, 145, 147,
    150, 206, 209, 212, 280, 322, 327
Indus Valley civilisation 123–4, 125,
    132, 133
Industrial Revolution 281–2
insects 39, 43–5, 61–2
    see also ants; bees; termites
Internet 333
Inuit, the 195
iron 137–9
Isabella of Castile 250–51, 255–6
Islam 202, 203
    see also Muslims
Israelites 162–3
    see also Jews
Italy 171, 175, 212, 227, 228, 242,
    255, 303, 311

J

Japan 148, 206, 258, 285, 286, 306,
    311, 312–3
al-Jazari, Ismail 272
Jefferson, Thomas 277
jellyfish 28, 29, 39
Jericho 102, 103
Jerusalem 163, 164–5, 171, 172, 173,
    235, 236–7, 238
Jesus 171–3, 201, 202
Jews 164–5, 172, 173, 236, 256, 310,
    327

Jobs, Steve 333
John, King of England 238–9
John II, of Portugal 254–6
Judaism 164, 172–3
Jurassic Period 26, 55
Jurchens 217
Justinian I, Emperor 226–7

K

Kaaba, Mecca 201
karma 143–4
al-Khwarizmi 211
al-Kindi 211
King, Martin Luther, Jr. 329, 330
Koran, the 202, 207
Korea 148, 206, 285, 324
Kublai Khan 223, 255

L

Legalism 149
Lenin, Vladimir 306
Leo III, Pope 228
Liangzhu civilisation 132
Lidar 187
Lincoln, Abraham 301, 302
Lombards 227, 228
Longshan civilisation 132
Louis XVI, of France 278
"Lucy" 78–80
Luther, Martin 264, 265–6

M

Magellan, Ferdinand 264
magma 21
Magna Carta 238–9
mammals 30, 52, 65–7, 69–71;
    extinction of 95–8
Mandela, Nelson 331
Marie Antoinette, queen 278
Marx, Karl 306, 323
Mary, Virgin 172, 201
mass production 281–2, 291
Maurya Empire 147–8
Maya, the 184–7, 194, 196, 211, 260
Mecca 201, 203
medicine 213, 318
Mehmed II, Sultan 244, 245
Merneptah Stele 162
metal 102, 132, 136, 137–9
    see gold; iron; silver
meteorites 49

meteors 68
Mexico 178, 179
    see also Aztecs; Maya; Olmecs
Mezquita, the 209
Michelangelo 212
Milky Way, the 12, 15, 20, 293
Minoan civilisation 128–9
Moctezuma II, Aztec ruler 260, 261
Mohenjo Daro 123
money 103, 123, 253
Mongolia/Mongols 219–23, 242,
    286, 305
monkeys 70–71
monotheism 164
Moon, the 17, 273, 275, 325, 333–4,
    337
Morse, Samuel 287
Moses 163, 202
Muhammad, prophet 201–3, 207
mummification 94, 118–20, 125
Musa, Mansa, king of Mali 210, 211
Musk, Elon 325
Muslims 201–3, 206–10, 235–6,
    243–7, 256, 285–6
    scholars 207–8, 213–14, 272

N

Napoleon Bonaparte 279–80
Nasca Lines 189–91
Natufians 99–100, 102, 161
Nazis 308, 309, 310, 312
Neanderthals 84–7, 90, 91, 92
nectar 61, 63
Newton, Sir Isaac 274–5, 293
New Zealand 331
Nicholas II, Tsar 306
Nile River 113, 114, 115, 163
Nineveh 110, 111
Normans 233
Norte Chico, Peru 125–6, 128
Nubians 115–17, 137
nuclear power/weapons 293, 323–4
numbers 111–12, 132, 181, 211–12

O

oceans 18–19, 20, 21, 22, 27–31
Odoacer 175
oil 290
olives 154, 160, 196
Olmecs 180–84
Olympic games 155, 159, 183
oracle bones 136–7

Ordovician Period 26, 27, 31
Otto I, holy Roman Emperor 229
Ottoman Empire 244–5, 247
Ötzi the Iceman 94–5
oxygen 19, 20, 39, 44, 320

P

Palaeozoic Era 25, 26, 27
Pangaea 45, 49
paper 132, 204–7, 211, 214, 217, 320
Parks, Rosa 328, 329
Patuxet, the 268–9
Pearl Harbor 310, 311
Permian Mass Extinction 31, 47, 49,
    52, 65
Persepolis 164, 165, 167
Persia 164–5, 166, 167, 203, 235
Peru see Inca, the; Norte Chico
Peter the Great, Tsar 305
pharaohs 108, 114, 115, 116, 117, 120,
    121, 122–3, 128, 163
Philip II, of Macedon 166
Phoenicians 161, 162, 168
photosynthesis 19, 34, 36, 39
Pilgrim Fathers 266, 267–9
Pizarro, Francisco 259, 262, 263
placoderms 30–31, 39
plague, bubonic 227, 240–42
plants 34, 35, 36, 41–3, 69, 320–21
    flowering 60–62
plastic 316–319
plate tectonics 20–2
Pleistocene Extinction 93, 95–8
polar bears 74, 195
pollen 61, 63
Polo, Marco 255
Popol Vuh, the 184–5
population 318–19, 334
    European 227–8, 234, 240, 242, 297
Portugal 251–7, 258, 259
pottery, Greek 155
primates 70–71
Princip, Gavrilo 304
printing 132, 214–17, 265
Prometheus 81
Protestantism 264–7, 273
pyramids 114, 117, 121, 125, 184, 187, 188

Q

Qianlong, Emperor 286
Qin Shi Huang 148–50, 204
quipu 126, 127, 191–2

R

railways 283–4
rain 31, 34
rainforests 320–21
Rashid-al-Din 221
Reformation, Protestant 264–7, 273
reincarnation 117, 144, 146
reptiles 46–7, 52, 59, 67, 96
respiration 20
rice 132–3, 209
Richard I, of England 237–8
robots 272, 333–5
Roman Catholic Church 235, 251,
    265–6
Romans 123, 168–75, 226, 235
Roosevelt, Franklin D. 311–13
Rosetta Stone 107
rubber 180–81
Russia/Soviet Union 222, 230,
    303–4, 305–8, 309, 312, 323, 325
    Revolution 306, 337

S

Sahara 113, 115, 209, 251–2
Saladin 236–7
sarcophagus 120, 122
Saudi Arabia 201, 332
sea scorpions 31, 39
sea squirts 29, 30
seeds 42, 62, 100–1
Selim I, Sultan 247
Seljuks 235
serfs 305
Seven Years War 275
sexual reproduction 60–61
ships 168, 219, 230, 231, 252, 264,
    267, 282, 284–5, 286
Siberian Traps 49
Siddhartha Gautama 142–3, 144–6
Sikhs 297, 326–7
silk 133–5, 196–7, 241, 298
Silurian Period 26, 27, 30
silver 245, 263, 264, 298, 300
slavery/slaves 154–7, 163, 169–70, 171,
    253, 258, 259, 280–81, 301–2, 303
smallpox 262–3, 268
Snowball Earth 22
Socrates 159
soil 38
Solon 156
Songhai Empire 251–2
Soviet Union see Russia

space travel 325, 333–4
Spain 227, 250–51, 257, 258
    conquistadors 259–64
    Muslims 208–10, 243–4, 250, 256
Sparta/Spartans 157, 160–61
Spartacus 169
sponges 27
Stalin, Joseph 308
stars 14, 15
steam power 283–5
Stephenson, George 283–4
Stonehenge 116, 126–7, 191
sugar plantations 258, 259, 278
Suleiman the Magnificent 247
Sumerians 108–12, 128
Sun, the 15, 16–17, 20, 127, 274
Szilard, Leo 312–13

T

Taiping Rebellion 300, 301
Taizu, Emperor 216
tanks, German 309
tectonic plates 21–2, 74
telephones 288
telescopes 214
Tenochtitlán 188–9, 260–3
termites 63, 65
terrorism 326–7
Thales of Miletus 158, 159
Theia 16, 17
Theodosius I, Emperor 175
Tiktaalik 40
Timbuktu, Mali 210, 211
Titus, Emperor 170
tools 79, 80, 85, 87, 93, 102, 103, 112
Tordesillas, Treaty of 257, 258
totem poles 194, 195
trade 103, 135, 238, 251–2, 298, 300
transpiration 41
trees 36, 38, 42, 62, 219–20
Trevithick, Richard 283
Triassic Period 26, 53, 54–5
trilobites 25, 42
Trojan war 156, 157–8
Trotsky, Leon 306
Tutankhamun, tomb of 121–2

U

United Nations 322, 328
United States 277, 279–80, 305, 306,
    311–12, 313, 322, 323, 327, 332
    African Americans 301–3, 328–30

civil rights 328–30
civil war 301–2
electricity 287–8
mass production 282
Native Americans 268–9
see also Americas, the
universe, the 12, 14
universities 132, 210, 211
Urban 244, 245
Urban II, Pope 235, 236

V

Vaucanson, Jacques de 272, 278
Vedas, the 143
Versailles, Treaty of 308
vertebrates 30
Vietnam 148, 206
Vietnam war 324
da Vinci, Leonardo 172, 212
Vikings 229–33, 247, 256, 305
Visigoths 227
volcanoes 16, 18, 22, 49

W

Walcott, Charles Doolittle 23–4
wheels 102, 112
Whitney, Eli 282
Wilberforce, William 280–81
William the Conqueror 233, 234
wings 43, 44–5, 57, 291
women 108, 122–3, 128, 160–61,
    303, 327, 331–2
World Trade Center (9/11) 327
World War I 291, 304–5, 308, 331
World War II 291, 309–13
Wright, Orville and Wilbur 291
writing 107–9, 120–21, 124, 129,
    136–7, 161–2, 168, 184
Wu, Han Emperor 204
Wu Zetian 204, 205

Y

Yangtze River, China 132
Yellow River, China 132, 133
Yousafzai, Malala 332

Z

zero 132, 181, 211, 212
Zhao Bing, Song Emperor 223
Zheng He 285–6

Acknowledgements

This book could not have happened without the super-human efforts of a great many people. I am especially grateful for the advice and support of Richard Atkinson, Natalie Bellos, John Gordon-Reid, Steve Carpenter and Mark Skipworth.

I'm also incredibly grateful to the team at What on Earth Books, all of whom have played a role in making this book happen.

Ali Glossop, project manager, has lived and breathed *Absolutely Everything* for months. Without her co-ordination and total professionalism, it could never have happened.

Assunção Sampayo, designer, has thrown herself into every detail of this book, making sure its pages pulsate with energy.

Andy Forshaw, art director, has been my wing-man, illustrator and greatest of friends for over ten years. None of this would have happened without you.

Nancy Feresten, publisher, has edited, mentored and chaperoned this story all the way from the Big Bang to the present day, transforming it from a pedestrian caterpillar into a soaring butterfly.

I am also hugely thankful to Justin Poulter for a fantastic cover and to Patrick Skipworth, Catherine Brereton, Brenda Stones, Michelle Harris, Felicity Page, Emily Krieger, Cynthia Wolf, Justine Taylor and Vicki Robinson for photo editing, fact checking, indexing, glossary writing, copyediting and proofreading. Without all of this support, the book would be a terrible mess. Of course, any remaining errors are mine alone.

Jen Hedley and Lucy Allen, marketing mavens, are hard at work right now making sure – with incredible creativity – that the book reaches its audience. And without an audience, there is no point to any book. So, thanks to you, too.

Thanks to the ever-dependable Helen Jones who oils our wheels, making everything run smoothly. I am so grateful!

And without Bob Worcester's huge enthusiasm and support for all we do at What on Earth Books, this book (and many more to come) would not, and could not, have happened. Thank you.

I am hugely indebted to my parents, Angus and Wanda Lloyd, who have given me constant support and shown unrelenting interest in all my endeavours over the years.

I dedicate this book to my fabulous girls. Were it not for Matilda getting bored at school all those years ago, she, her sister Verity, their lovely mother Virginia and I would never have spent five wonderful months together in a campervan travelling around Europe. And I would never have done all that open-air washing up, which ultimately led to the idea for this book!

And for our home educating adventure, my wife Virginia gets the credit. Not only has she been the most fabulous mother, but she is also the most supportive, loving wife anyone could wish for. I can't thank you enough.